THE SOVIET ARMED FORCES,
1918–1992

THE SOVIET ARMED FORCES, 1918–1992

A Research Guide
to Soviet Sources

Compiled by
John Erickson and
Ljubica Erickson

Research Guides in Military Studies, Number 8

Greenwood Press
Westport, Connecticut • London

Library of Congress Cataloging-in-Publication Data

Erickson, John.
    The Soviet Armed Forces, 1918–1992 : a research guide to Soviet
sources / compiled by John Erickson and Ljubica Erickson.
       p.   cm.—(Research guides in military studies, ISSN
0899–0166 ; no. 8)
    Includes bibliographical references and index.
    ISBN: 0–313–29071–7 (alk. paper)
    1. Soviet Union—Armed Forces—History. 2. Soviet Union—Politics
and government—Bibliography. I. Erickson, Ljubica. II. Title.
III. Series.
Z6725.R9E75
[UA770 1996]
016.355′009470904—dc20   95–41983

British Library Cataloguing in Publication Data is available.

Library of Congress Catalog Card Number: 95–41983
ISBN: 0–313–29071–7
ISSN: 0899–0166

First published in 1996

Greenwood Press, 88 Post Road West, Westport, CT 06881
An imprint of Greenwood Publishing Group, Inc.

Printed in the United States of America

The paper used in this book complies with the
Permanent Paper Standard issued by the National
Information Standards Organization (Z39.48–1984).

10 9 8 7 6 5 4 3 2 1

CONTENTS

PREFACE

The roots of this volume go deep, having had the best part of fifty years to implant themselves. Given such a passage of time it is not surprising therefore that they have had to be both resilient and tenacious, strong enough to withstand distractions and digressions, to sustain the protracted quest for books, the business of analysis, the assessment of utility and the appreciation of rarity. On a more pedestrian note, over time no small amount of luggage of readily replaceable clothing has been discarded in order to provide essential space for irreplaceable books.

The subliminal origins of this bibliography date back to the immediate aftermath of the Second World War, to the sights and sounds of a victorious Red Army, fresh from its triumphs over the *Wehrmacht*, its march from national liberation to foreign conquest completed. Here was a force obviously formidable yet mysterious, tanks and trucks in fungicidal green colouring, drab but dangerous. Throughout the Second World War we had been heavily exposed to and genuinely encouraged by the public, propagandistic praise heaped on the 'heroic Red Army', a theme encouraged and amplified by <u>Soviet War News</u>, the wartime newspaper published by the Press Department of the Soviet Embassy in London, the files of which still retain a certain interest, if only as ready access to Stalin's Orders of the Day.

Here was a military machine which could now be viewed at first hand, though not without certain difficulties. The Soviet Army, the immediate post-war successor to the Red Army, presented a mixture of the modern, even the ultra-modern co-existing with Party emblemata and stolid Russian signs and symbols. As the Iron Curtain clanked into position, my own area of vision, like that of so many others, became increasingly cramped, a circumstance which paradoxically served to intensify the search for more knowledge, not merely of Soviet small-arms, details of order of battle, or the whereabouts of a particular mechanised corps but of the background and the nature of this armed force. The literature on this subject seemed to be scant, the tide of propaganda had ebbed long ago, the only prospect appeared to be a protracted and possibly arduous search for source material.

The transition from army intelligence to university life and academic research proved that the cloak of secrecy surrounding Soviet military organisation was not as impenetrable as had been advertised. What was lost by observation in the field was more than compensated for by library resources and book shops. Once the iron grip of Stalin and 'Stalinist military science' had been relaxed, the tide of Soviet military publications began to flow more strongly. Until that reached full flood, which gradually it did, there was much to be learned from the captured German military documents. *Wehrmacht* wartime intelligence on the Red Army, information amassed in General Reinhard Gehlen's *Fremde Heere Ost* (Foreign Armies East) files proved to be a very important preliminary guide for further investigation and research. The records of the *Auswärtiges Amt* (German Foreign Ministry) proved to be yet another treasure trove. Many thousands of pages covered German military representation in the Soviet Union, bundles of secret files disclosing much, if not all, of the secret *Reichswehr*-Red Army collaboration during the 1920s and early 1930s.

These are 'secrets' which have recently been re-discovered, not least on the Russian side. A notable example was provided in July, 1990 with the publication in the English-language edition of the Moscow journal International Affairs (1990, No.7, pp. 95-113) of 'Soviet-German Military Co-operation, 1920-1933 Documents published for the first time' by S.A. Gorlov, followed by three further articles by S.A. Gorlov in association with S.V. Ermachenkov '*Voenno-uchebnye tsentry reikhsvera v Sovetskom Soiuze*' published in *Voenno-istoricheskii Zhurnal* 1993, Nos. 6-8. That swoop on the archives which resulted in *Fashistskii mech kovalsia v SSSR* by Iu. D'iakov and T. Bushueva, published in Moscow by Sovetskaia Rossiia in 1992, though interesting in parts, is perhaps best treated with a deliberate measure of circumspection.

The growing volume and the increased availability of Soviet military publications in the mid-1950s together with the insights provided by German military records greatly facilitated the writing of The Soviet High Command 1918-1941 first published in London by Macmillan in 1962, a publication which indirectly provided my 'passport' or 'entry ticket' to senior Soviet military circles in Moscow. This resulted in an opportunity to talk with the senior commanders of those soldiers I had seen years ago, to inspect and investigate aspects of the military-historical work being undertaken and to discuss it with the authors themselves, as well as being introduced to the labyrinthine world of Soviet military archives. Professor Samsonov, director of the publishing house NAUKA, provided many valuable insights into the background and the reputability (or otherwise) of a wide range of Soviet military publications.

Past, present and an unpredictable future have inevitably impinged on this bibliography. In compiling it two aspects became increasinly apparent. The first was that the professional academic study of the Soviet military in the western world has lasted barely fifty years, if, that is, D. Fedotoff White's The Growth of the Red Army published by Princeton University Press in 1944 is taken as the first substantial academic publication utilising a wide range of indigenous Soviet material. The second facet was that, as far as I could ascertain, throughout the period of the Cold War no bibliography of Soviet publications on the Soviet military establishment, beginning with its origins in 1918, was generally available, though no doubt they abounded in closed intelligence collections. It would be a dereliction of duty not to mention the two volumes by Michael Parrish, The U.S.S.R. in World War II: An Annotated Bibliography of Books Published in the Soviet Union, 1945-1975, Garland Publishing, 1981 or yet again Gerda Beitter *Die Rote Armee im 2. Weltkrieg. Eine Bibliographie ihrer Truppengeschichten im Zweiten Weltkrieg* published by Bernard & Graefe Verlag (Koblenz) in 1984. However, these volumes are expressly confined to the period of the Second World War even as they admirably fulfil their specific purpose.

The present bibliography is intended to cover a wider field, namely, the period from the birth of the Red Army and the origins of the Soviet military system to the demise of the Soviet Union and with it the disappearance of the Soviet Armed Forces, as they had come to be known. Several reasons recommend themselves for compiling a bibliography of this nature at this particular juncture. The first and most compelling is that which has already been mentioned: the demise of the Soviet Union and its military machine, which offers a fixed time frame, the years 1918-1992. The second consideration is that here is (or was) a 'non-renewable resource', giving this compilation something of a conservationist cast. A third and highly significant feature has been the increased availability of Soviet military publications which were hitherto classified, in particular, the disclosure of the 'Special collections' (*Spetskhran* collections) as well as individual and collective works either forgotten or deliberately withheld from sight.

Uncovering such a wealth of sources owes much to the work of Dr. Kent Lee and East View Publications in Minneapolis, Minnesota, where conceivably pride of place goes to the complete set of the Soviet General Staff's multi-volume classified series on the operational experience of World War II. This collection includes the 26 volumes of the *Sbornik materialov po izucheniiu opyta voiny*, 43 volumes of combat documents, 19 volumes of military history materials and 23 volumes of tactical examples. Key sections of the 'War Experience' volumes have also appeared in translation in issues of The Journal of Soviet (now Slavic) Military Studies edited by Colonel David M. Glantz. This citation of East View materials on Soviet records of World War II would not be complete without reference to the Soviet Naval Staff's chronology of Soviet naval operations.

It is incontestable that the study of Soviet military organisation and military affairs will be transformed by the opening of former Soviet archives, though many years will pass before the sheer volume can be mastered, either by Russian historians or those from abroad. The present volume is not one which is concerned primarily or even marginally with archives, but even at this early stage limited access to archives and archivists has made it possible to improve the assessment of the utility, scope and reliability of printed books, whether monographs, memoirs or documentary collections. A case in point was provided by a recent discussion in Moscow with Dr. L.V. Dvoinykh at *TsGASA* (now re-designated *RGVA*) with respect to the four-volume documentary publication *Direktivy komandovaniia frontov Krasnoi Armii (1917-1922)*. The integrity of the documents presented there cannot be doubted, though selection (or omission) had been subject to certain 'politically acceptable' criteria. Nevertheless, Volume IV (Part 7) provides a list of documents duly identified but not printed in the preceding three volumes.

Selectivity alone, however, does not mean that everything Soviet must be assigned to the category of what one bookseller wittily described as 'strictly land-fill material'. Selectivity has perforce been applied here, since this bibliography lays no claim to comprehensiveness. Even assuming that it could be managed, such an enterprise would demand multiple volumes and years of work to encompass not only former Soviet repositories but also the substantial holdings which have accrued over decades in western collections. The basic aim here has been to provide the essential minima to assist the investigation of the Soviet military establishment in its various aspects, whether institutions, doctrine, operational experience, technology, biography. We initially intended to include no more than 850 entries. This target had to be substantially revised in the light of increased accessibility to publications which had been hitherto closed or difficult to examine at first-hand, and because many more volumes recommended themselves.

This is no mere list of titles. Each volume entered here has had to 'earn its place', and be reviewed, examined and evaluated against a 'check-list' of five categories:

The **first** relates to the theme or subject-matter of the publication in question, which in most instances is self-explanatory.

The **second** concerns the author or authors and the provenance of the work.

The **third** involved the degree to which archive or documentary material was utilised.

The **fourth** reviewed the extent to which additional bibliographical information or bibliographical supplements were furnished with the particular volume or volumes.

The **fifth** revolved round a special indicator, *tirazh*, the print-run. This is an immportant guide to the significance and the function of the work in question (coupled with a particular readership address, for example, to 'generals, admirals and officers of the Soviet armed forces', to political workers, or to arms specialists and technical officers).

It is only in rare instances that inclusion has been warranted on the basis of a single distinguishing feature, in which event that happened to be predominantly authorship or some commanding singularity, even rarity. Otherwise most of the titles included here have satisfied a minimum of three and not infrequently four of the stipulated criteria. We have arranged each citation with an entry number, numbers which run consecutively throughout the whole book. We have furnished an author index keyed to the entry numbers, but we considered this inadequate in itself, not wholly serving the convenience of the reader, hence our choosing to present a subject index which is similarly keyed to entry numbers.

*

The problem of mass is formidable. At a rough guess there are probably some 20,000 volumes and more extant treating the 'Great Patriotic War of the Soviet Union 1941-1945' alone. To meet this challenge of sheer bulk wherever possible Soviet bibliographies have been included together with publications that themselves furnish substantial bibliographical information. In order to convey profiles of subject matter the method of entering books has not been in alphabetical order after the author's name but rather in chronological sequence of publication, with the aim of producing 'representative samples' within a given subject area. Wherever possible such 'samples' have been modelled on the lines of the holdings of a working military library such as that of the Institute of Military History in Moscow with its shelves of well-thumbed volumes.

The difficulty has been to determine what constitutes 'essential' material and to establish which publications are representative, reliable and durable. At the same time we had to consider the interests of potential users of this volume whose definition of 'essential' may vary from the most recondite specialist topic, such as underwater robotics, to details of daily life in a Soviet battalion or how to drive a Soviet tank, no mean feat given the unforgiving nature of that beast.

There are, of course, works which have attained classic status and without which no bibliography of Soviet military publication would be complete, a roll of honour which includes: Svechin, Tukhachevskii, Triandafillov, Frunze, possibly Sokolovskii's *Voennaia strategiia*. Below that august rank come publications now regarded as 'standard works', many of them dating back to the 1920s and published before the Stalinist stranglehold tightened. One example is the three-volume work <u>Grazhdanskaia voina 1918-1921</u> edited by A.S. Bubnov, S.S. Kamenev and R.P. Eideman (the entire editorial board perishing in Stalin's purges). The doctrinal writings of the 1930s, including the newly declassified writings of Tukhachevskii and the emergence of the unpublished text of his *Novye voprosy voiny. Chast' pervaia. Vooruzhennye sily i ikh ispol'zovanie* (1932) clearly require substantial recognition in their own right. There is also the reprint phenomenon, one example of which is the *Politizdat* publication of N.E. Kakurin's two-volume work, *Kak srazhalas' revoliutsiia*, first published in 1925-26, appearing now under the editorship of A.P. Nenarokov and with a print-run of no less than 100,000.

Soviet memoirs present their own singular problems and, bulk apart, are perhaps the most awkward items to handle. The *genre* automatically lends itself to doctoring and deceit, to self-justification and vainglory, characteristics by no means confined solely to Soviet memoir literature. The highly literate memoirs of the leading figures involved in the Bolshevik seizure of power and engaged in the Civil War which flourished in the 1920s are in a class of their own, but like much else were driven out of sight and almost out of mind under Stalin. The post-1945 memoirs of Soviet Marshals and lesser figures demand treatment of a different order.

On 26 May, 1992 *Krasnaia zvezda* published Colonel Andrei Zharikov's account of 'writing the Marshals' memoirs', his own recollection of acting as ghost writer, 'editorial assistant' (*referent po pechati*) specifically to the Marshals Biriuzov and Koniev. Marshals Vasilevskii, Malinovskii, Bagramian and M.V. Zakharov employed their own *referenty*, who in the fashion of Colonel Zharikov, had access to the archives and compiled research reports on wartime operations and command relationships. All of this, however, was filtered and fitted to the particular view of himself and his record entertained by the Marshal himself.

The 12-volume *Istoriia vtoroi mirovoi voiny 1939-1945*, the first volume of which appeared in 1973, utilised a considerable amount of material derived from the memoirs of senior Soviet commanders. To ensure that these publications conformed to 'the spirit of the times' the Main Political Administration set up a special group to monitor this type of publication, removing 'whole lumps' if the substance was deemed 'unsuitable.' Twenty-one years after Marshal K.K. Rokossovskii's memoirs first appeared, the deleted passages were finally published in *Voenno-istoricheskii Zhurnal*, 1989 No. 5.

The ten editions through which the memoirs of Marshal G.K. Zhukov have passed provide yet another example of the difficulty of establishing what or which is the essential, authentic Zhukov. Desperately eager to have his name included in these illustrious memoirs, Brezhnev 'gate-crashed' the first edition with a purely fictional incident added at his express prompting to the text. The circumstance of the Novorossiisk bridgehead in 1943 was included with Zhukov supposedly wishing 'to discuss the matter with L.I. Brezhnev, Chief of the Political Department of the 18th Army, but at that time, he was away on the "little land" (*malaia zemlia*) where heavy fighting was going on'. So a non-event was transformed into spurious history. Zhukov responded bitterly, commenting: '*Umnyi poimet*', 'The bright people will catch on'. Zhukov's own manuscript made no mention of the successful operations of A.A. Grechko's 56th Army. The reference to Brezhnev was subsequently replaced by a passage dealing with Novorossiisk, but that was finally removed from the 7th edition and any trace of 'fictional history' completely erased from Volume 3 (p. 25) of the 10th edition published in 1990. The 500 or so volumes of the series *Voennye memuary* which began publication in the late 1950s vary enormously in scope, reliability and value. Some of the more reputable derive not from the concoctions of the great and the famous but from lower down the scale, from officers exploiting their personal papers (*lichnyi arkhiv*), frequently supplemented by invaluable, even rare photographs. Given both the quantity and the diversity of this type of publication, all that could be ventured is a form of sampling covering types (and ranks) of author, date of publication and subject-matter.

After consultation with my co-author and chief compiler, coincidentally wife and *alter ego*, it was decided to attempt to make the materials of this bibliography more accessible to non-Russian speakers who have an interest in Russian and former Soviet military affairs by translating book-titles. The readership rubric has been added where it was supplied, for example, 'for generals, admirals and officers' which usually indicated an authoritative officially approved study, practical guides directed to 'sergeants, crews' or volumes directed to 'technical specialists'. By the same token we have not ignored any particular recommendation or observation recorded by authors or editors with respect to any noteworthy characteristics of archive sources, special collections or memoir material used in the publication.

In addition to presenting publications in chronological order to build up a 'profile' of publication, closer analysis of the *tirazh*, the print-run, can suggest a form of typology. Though quite common in the pre-1941 period, disclosure of the size of the print-run, clearly suspended for security reasons during and immediately after the war, re-appeared in the early 1960s. Mass publication explains itself. Throughout the publication cycle of the 6-volume history of the *Istoriia Velikoi Otechestvennoi voiny Sovetskogo Soiuza 1941-1945* the print-run increased from 150,000 for Volume One to 210,000 for Volume Six. The increased size of the print-run was accompanied by the enlargement of Khrushchev's own 'cult of personality', where in Volume Three Khrushchev as a mere member of the Military Soviet of a Front was mentioned 41 times, while the Supreme Commander-in-Chief himself, Stalin, received only half that number of citations throughout the text. The 'non-person' Zhukov, as yet under a cloud, was entirely excluded from Volume One, which also gave a somewhat distorted picture of the Soviet General Staff.

The print-run for formation (army/division) histories was usually in the order of 20000-25,000 copies. The wartime history of the 18th Army in which L.I. Brezhnev served proved to be a spectacular exception with 65,000 copies printed, replete with copious photographic evidence of Leonid Il'ich at the front. A stirring piece of Brezhnev's prose stood at the head of the second edition of *Poslednii shturm Berlinskaia operatsiia 1945 g.*, published in 1975 by *Voenizdat*. That study was first published in 1970 under the names of F.D. Vorob'ev, I.V. Parotkin and A.N. Shimanskii. It was a discreetly pruned version for open circulation of the classified study *Berlinskaia operatsiia 1945 goda* produced in 1950 and edited by Major-General N.A. Talenskii, a substantial General Staff volume to which both Vorob'ev and Parotkin had earlier contributed.

Publications with print-runs of 8,000 were probably intended mainly for military academies, those over 13,000 to 18,000 for military schools. The lowest end of the scale is represented by print-runs of 5,000 and less, dropping below 2,000 and in some instances reduced to a few hundred. Bibliographies appear to have been published in a range of 2000-3000 copies, presumably destined for library holdings. Technical studies and monographs understandably were produced on a limited scale, given the highly specialised readership, for example, the volume on the theory of rocket engines, *Teoriia raketnykh dvigatelei* edited by Academician Glushko running to 6,000 copies or L.I. Balabukh's *Stroitel'naia mekhanika raket* to 4,000. The volume on the design and testing of ballistic missiles published by *Voenizdat* in 1970 had a print-run of 6,400. Documentary publications based on archives rarely produced more than 6,500 copies, 4,000 being more representative. The 'protocols and resolutions' of *Tsentrobalt* published in 1963 were in an edition of only 1,400 copies. This has been no quest for rarity for its own sake but from the 'conservationist aspect' there is a reasonable case for looking very closely at editions with very limited print-runs.

Though this bibliography is concerned primarily with the Soviet armed forces and Soviet military organisation, the section on 'Imperial Antecedents' is designed to draw attention to the very wide scope and high level of scholarship demonstrated by Soviet research into the Imperial Russian Army and pre-1917 military organisation. There is also the problem of the continuity of institutions and procedures, even though the designations might have changed. 'Soviet' is perhaps in a number of instances something of a slight misnomer, for during the 1920s much of the research and writing was carried out by ex-Imperial officers, prominent among them General A.M. Zaionchkovskii while his son, Professor P.A. Zaionchkovskii and a major authority in his own right, was firmly implanted in the Soviet period. The latter is noted for such work as *Voennye reformy 1860-1870 godov v Rossii* or the massive multi-volume bibliography *Istoriia dorevoliutsionnoi Rossii v dnevnikakh i vospominaniiakh*. The volume *Voprosy voennoi istorii Rossii* edited by V.I. Shunkov and published in 1969 with the *tirazh* of 3,300 copies contains the bibliography of Professor Colonel L.G. Beskrovnyi's publications from 1931-1968, once again demonstrating the great sweep of this type of military research throughout the Soviet period.

During the Great Patriotic War much of that effort was harnessed in the cause of Russian patriotism, while in the post-war period it was possible to discern the premeditated exploitation, even manipulation of military history to comment on the contemporary scene. One example is Professor K.F. Shatsillo's discussion of the dangers induced by the pre-1914 *disproportsiia*, the imbalance in force structures brought about by misplaced lobbying. Military history was frequently utilised to illustrate or emphasise current problems or to convey a sense of continuity embracing the wide span of Russia's military achievements. With respect to the latter, Russian military tradition, Soviet research and publication produced a substantial and sustained volume of work, for which reason this has been included under 'Antecedents'. Though beyond the time-frame of Soviet publication, Major-General V.A. Zolotarev has continued this commitment and recently refurbished the image of the 18th century Russian army and its accomplished practitioners, among them Saltykov, Rumiantsev, Suvorov in *Apostoly armii rossiiskoi*, 412 pp., published by 'Aviar' in Moscow in 1993. President Yeltsin signalled his own awareness of the significance of continuity with the decree promoting the celebration of the 300th anniversary of the founding of the Russian navy, dating back to 20 October, 1696.

The final section, 'Breakthrough Books', though breaching the restriction of exclusive Russian-language publication, is intended to add a further perspective to this bibliography. These publications cover the period 1944-1994, the span of professional academic publication on Soviet military affairs. 'Breakthrough books' are defined as those which have either by dint of source material, exposition or insight radically influenced the perception and discussion of Soviet military affairs. None would deny the great influence which studies by Dr. Raymond L. Garthoff have exercised since the 1950s or what Colonel David M. Glantz has achieved with his operational studies of Soviet battlefield performance and the evolution of Soviet military thought. In brief, the function of all the books cited here is, in the words of one reviewer, to 'demythologise' the Soviet military. Paradoxically, studies of the Soviet military and Soviet military policies may well flourish anew and undergo a qualitative transformation since the demise of the Soviet Union itself, which facilitated more immediate access to archives and to key individuals. A striking illustration is furnished by Professor David Holloway's magisterial study, <u>Stalin And The Bomb</u> <u>The Soviet Union and Atomic Energy 1939-1956</u> published by Yale University Press in 1994, a uniquely important volume in uncovering the deepest of deep Soviet secrets.

Terminology can always present its own problems. The usage here relating to Soviet military organisation, weapons, military-educational systems, arms and services has been standardised following the style employed in US Department of the Army 100-2-1/3 <u>The Soviet Army</u> Washington, DC, dated July, 1984, in particular, 100-2-3 (Troops, Organisation, Equipment). We have used Ground Forces (capitalised), Motorised Rifle Troops, Tank Troops, Rocket Troops and Artillery, Air Defence Troops as accepted designations, Military Schools, Higher Military Schools and Military Academies as classifications within the Soviet military-educational system. The arrangement of post-1945 publications in 'Arms and Services' follows the order of preference employed by *50 let Vooruzhennykh Sil SSSR* (Moscow, Voenizdat, 1968), namely, Strategic Rocket Forces/SRF (*Raketnye voiska strategicheskogo naznacheniia*), Ground Forces (*Sukhoputnye voiska*), Air Defence Troops (*Voiska PVO strany*), Air Forces (*Voenno-vozdushnye sily*), Navy (*Voenno-morskoi flot*) and Rear Services (*Tyl vooruzhennykh sil*). Where illustrations are identified, this can signify technical drawing in the context of publications dealing with weapons, armour, artillery, aviation and technical illustration (tank gear-boxes, suspensions systems, turret lay-out). Publications dealing with tactics and tactical doctrine usually include an abundance of tactical diagrams, some black-and-white but not infrequently in colour (red/blue). Maps are one of the great bonuses of Soviet military publications, where no expense seems to have been spared, particularly with the 'map supplements' supplied with operational studies of Moscow (1941), Stalingrad (1942-1943), Kursk (1943) and Berlin (1945). Illustrations should also be taken to include photographs, which can be divided into those furnishing purely technical details and others derived from archives or special collections, a prime example of which is the collection of striking photographs, 'Album of the Red Army', *Raboche-Krestianskaia Krasnaia Armiia* published by IZOGIZ in Moscow in 1934, with extensive portraits of those commanders (collective and individual) who perished in the purges as well as rare photographs of Stalin. Most of the copies of this publication were reportedly destroyed.

*

In this volume it has been our intention to render a compact guide to a minimum number of those Soviet publications on the Soviet military system, including elements of its Imperial precursors, in a form which would accommodate both wider interests and those which belong more properly in the domain of the specialist. In both instances we have attempted wherever possible to facilitate access to further references by selecting those publications which themselves incorporate or utilise substantial bibliographical support.

We have tried to be discerning about accessibility. These volumes and many hundreds more, including a collection of technical publications which we have not included, are to hand in Edinburgh. An abundance of Soviet publications as well as those of Imperial Russia is available in the great libraries of the West, a wealth of information obtainable without setting foot on Russian soil: the Library of Congress and the great collections of the libraries of the universities of the United States of America. In Great Britain the British Library, Humanities and Social Sciences, successor to the British Museum Library, unquestionably the largest in the United Kingdom, maintains its Slavonic and East European collections, with systematic acquisition dating back to 1837. The mechanisms of international inter-library loan worked and still works admirably to meet a variety of needs, functioning even during the chill days of the Cold War, much to the credit of the professionalism of Soviet librarians who rarely failed to rise to the occasion. No doubt it will be supplemented and eventually supplanted by electronic communication and transfer.

This bibliography represents but a minute fragment of massive library holdings whether in the east or in the west. If after any fashion it encourages a general reader in his or her wider interests, informs a journalist, assists a researcher, meets a specialist requirement, promotes fresh interest, illuminates an obscure issue or incident, records what is estimable, confirms a supposition or clarifies a source, it will have gone some way to meet its very modest objectives.

J.E. and L.E.

Edinburgh
July, 1995

ACKNOWLEDGEMENTS

Over many years we have received advice and generous assistance from a wide circle of colleagues, associates and friends in east and west alike, but our immediate indebtedness is to the Leverhulme Trust of Great Britain whose research grant made it possible to travel to Moscow with the express purpose of consulting librarians and archivists as well as specialists in the field of Soviet military history and military publication. Our particular thanks go to Major-General V. A. Zolotarev, Director of the Institute of Military History, and to his officers, to Dr. L.V. Dvoinykh, Deputy Director of *RGVA*, Dr. L.A. Rogovaia, Department Chief in *RTsKhIDNI,* and Dr. V. Iu. Afiani, Deputy Director, *TsKhSD*. We would also wish to acknowledge that special personal help afforded to us by Dr. S. V. Kudryashov and Dr. V. M. Gobarev not only in chasing down specific books but also chasing along the streets of Moscow. Professor G.A. Kumanev and Professor O.A. Rzheshevskii of the Institute of General History spared no effort to identify key bibliographical studies which had hitherto been inaccessible to us. Professor A. N. Mertsalov and Professor L. A. Mertsalova made their distinctive contribution to the present work by sharing with us the range of their own extensive bibliographical research. It was also a privilege to be able to consult at length with Colonel A.G. Kavtaradze and to benefit from his encyclopaedic knowledge of both Imperial and Soviet Russian military organisations.

Even during the Cold War, when frosty days turned to icy weeks, the world of books seemed to enjoy a certain insulation from animosity and prejudice. In several respects this volume is a tribute to the late academician A. M. Samsonov for his patient instruction and counsel, and it is also an affirmation of gratitude to the late Lieutenant-General S. P. Platonov, Major-General E. A. Boltin, Colonel I. I. Rostunov, Colonel N. V. Eronin, Colonel D. M. Proektor, Colonel V. A. Anfilov, Colonel V. M. Kulish and Colonel L. Semeiko. It may be with the passage of years they are no longer mindful of us but we retain pleasing memories of long talks, amiable exchanges, engaging insights, purposeful advice. To this must be added the willing co-operation of librarians to whom also the Cold War divide meant little or nothing. In the context of expertise combined with friendship, which is a circumstance always to be cherished, we would wish to record our deep appreciation for seemingly inexhaustible help and encouragement to Mme. Kira Caiafa.

Life abounds in oddities and perhaps this is expressed nowhere more strikingly than in the world of bibliophiles. One bizarre but very welcome circumstance was being presented with a copy of _Vremennyi Polevoi Ustav RKKA PU-36_ acquired in a second-hand book shop for the enormous sum of one shilling and three pence (old British money, about six new pence or a few cents). Under what circumstances or for what reasons Marshal Tukhachevskii's brain-child turned up in an English used book store is a mystery offering no ready explanation. However, there was nothing occasional about the assistance in tracking down recently declassified former Soviet military publications rendered by Dr. Carl Van Dyke, whose expertise spans both the Tsarist and Soviet period.

If there are oddities and vagaries in collecting books, it seemed at times that these paled into insignificance compared with the quirkiness of the computer. Such imperfections as exist are our responsibility, though they would have been much magnified, not to say gross, if Ms. Crystal Webster from University of Edinburgh Computing Services and Mr. Mark Erickson from University of Sunderland had not each lent their invaluable technical assistance at critical junctures, thus averting further domestic tribulation while advancing the cause of camera-ready copy. By the same token, in the matter of the conception, formulation and assembling of this volume the responsibility for shortcomings, defects and deviations is ours alone, not to be charged in any wise against all those individuals and agencies who generously, willingly, unstintingly, often disinterestedly helped us over many years in a multiplicity of fashions.

PART ONE

ARCHIVE GUIDES

Russian State Military-Historical Archive *Rossiiskii gosudarstvennyi voenno-istoricheskii arkhiv (RGVIA)*

Established in 1925 as the **Military-Historical Archive of the RSFSR**, *Voenno-istoricheskii arkhiv RSFSR*, combining the **Military-Academic Archive**, *Voenno-uchebnyi arkhiv VUA*, with its origins dating back to 1797 and the "Map Depot Special to His Imperial Majesty", created as the *VUA* in 1867, subordinated to the Main Administration of the General Staff in 1906 and the "Lefortovo archive", dating from 1819 as the Moscow section of the Inspectorate of the Department of the Main Staff, plus archives of the Moscow Military District and military records of the First World War 1914-1918.
In April 1933 designated **Central Military-Historical Archive of the USSR**, *Tsentral'nyi voenno-istoricheskii arkhiv SSSR, TsVIA SSSR* and in 1941 changed to **Central State Military-Historical Archive**, *Tsentral'nyi gosudarstvennyi voenno-istoricheskii arkhiv SSSR (TsGVIA SSSR)*. Re-designated in 1991 Russian State Military-Historical Archive. **Tel: Moscow 261-20-70. 107005 Moscow, ul. 2-ia Baumanskaia 3.**

1. Avtokratov V.N. *et al.*, TsGVIA Putevoditel'. V trekh chastiakh. **Guide to the TsGVIA. In three parts**. Moscow, GAU TsGVIA, 1979. Covers the period 1700-1918. Volume I 1-277 pp. Sections 1-3: **1.** Record Groups Central military administration and military institutions of Russia. **2.** Local military-administrative organs of Russia. **3.** Military-historical documents and cartographic materials of the Higher Military-Academic Archive (VUA) Volume II: 279-574 pp. Sections 4-12: **4.** Record Groups Field Armies 1914-1918 and corps formed during military reforms 1860s. **5.** Field administration Supreme High Command, C-in-Cs Fronts and armies 1914-1918. **6.** Corps and division administrations 1831-1918. **7.** Brigades, regiments, independent units. **8.** Staffs of specialist troops, Cossacks, reserves, frontier troops. **9.** Rear Military-medical institutions. **10.** *Materiel*-technical services and medical supply. **11.** Military-educational institutions. **12.** Record group personal files (by name). Volume III: 575-725 pp. Appendixes. Conversion table for Record Groups covering Sections **1-12.** Deployment of armies to Fronts 1914-1918. List of documentary publications using

TsGVIA archives. Indexes, names, places, subjects. Detailed contents list. Tirazh all vols. 600.

Russian State Military Archive *Rossiiskii gosudarstvennyi voennyi arkhiv (RGVA)*

In 1925 the Red Army Archive *Arkhiv Krasnoi Armii (AKA)* was established as an independent institution subsequently designated the **Central Archive of the Red Army** *Tsentral'nyi arkhiv Krasnoi Armii (TsAKA)* on 7 April, 1933 and subordinated to the Central Archive Administration of the USSR. In April 1938 *TsAKA* was placed under the control of the *NKVD*. In March 1941 the archive was re-designated **The Central State Archive of the Red Army** *Tsentral'nyi gosudarstennyi arkhiv Krasnoi Armii (TsGAKA)*. The archive was evacuated from Moscow in 1941 and returned in 1944. On 13 August 1958 *TsAKA* became *Ts-GASA Tsentral'nyi gosudarstvennyi arkhiv Sovetskoi Armii* and in 1991 was designated the Russian State Military Archive, comprising 32.798 *fondy* (Record Groups), some 1,721.392 files. **Tel. 159.80.91; 125884 Moscow, ul. Admirala Makarova, No. 29**

2.   Arkhivy SSSR. Arkhiv Krasnoi Armii. Vypusk 1 **Archives of the USSR. Archive of the Red Army. Issue No. 1**, Moscow, Shtab RKKA (Red Army Staff) Voenno-istoricheskii otdel, 1933. 135 pp. A preliminary guide to Red Army archives, *TsAKA (Tsentral'nyi arkhiv Krasnoi Armii)*, the basic records dealing with the Red Army central administration, fronts, armies, divisions, with an explanation that the guide was as yet incomplete since not all the relevant documents had been properly sorted.

3.   Dvoinykh, L.V. Compiler-in-chief, Annotirovannyi perechen' fondov Tsentral' nogo gosudarstvennogo arkhiva Sovetskoi Armii **Annotated listing of the Record Groups of the Central State Archive of the Soviet Army**, Moscow, GAU, 1987. In five volumes. Declassified February, 1989. Volume I 389 pp. Central and Main Administrations of the Soviet Armed Forces, Fronts, Armies. Groups of forces: Front, army, division, brigade, local. Administration of arms: cavalry, artillery, auto-armoured, aviation. Republic, military district administrations, Rear Services, Supply. Volume II 344 pp. Administrations, corps: rifle, cavalry, mechanised and tank, aviation, PVO, special, independent. Divisions: rifle, cavalry, artillery, tank, motorised, aviation, Red Army international divisions. Volume III 459 pp. Brigade administrations: rifle, motor-rifle, reserve, international, cavalry, artillery, auto-armoured, mechanised and tank, aviation, airborne, PVO. Volume IV 388 pp. Brigade administrations, Military-educational establishments, personal files. Volume V 243 pp. Index: subject, places, names. Conversion table, Record Group listing by number, volume, page numbers. List of abbreviations. All vols.: Tirazh 50.

4.   Dvoinykh, L.V., Kariaeva, T.F., Stegantsev M.V., Ed., Tsentral'nyi gosudarstvennyi arkhiv Sovetskoi Armii. Putevoditel' v dvukh tomakh. **Central State archive of the Soviet Army. A guide in two volumes**. Minneapolis, East View Publications, 1991 and 1993. Volume I 420 pp. Seven sections **(1-7): 1.** Central administration (1917-1941), **2.** Administration of arms (artillery, armoured troops, engineers, signals, aviation), **3.** *Materiel*-technical support, **4.** Military-

education institutions, **5.** Republics, regions, **6.** Military districts, **7.** Front and army administrations: individual armies, 'special assignment' aviation armies. Volume II 531 pp. Six sections **(8-14)** continued from Volume I. **8.** Administration/staffs rifle corps and divisions, **9.** Cavalry corps and divisions, **10.** Arms: artillery, aviation, **11.** Special troops: frontier troops, territorial formations, transport, **12.** 'Fortified areas', *URs*, fortresses, **13.** Military Academies, institutes, schools, **14.** Administration/forces Far Eastern Republic. Appendixes. Distribution of divisions in armies (1918-1941), Territorial composition of military districts. Listing of documentary publications published by *TsGASA*, list of abbreviations. Index (by the Russian alphabet) of military administrations, institutions, Red Army major strategic forces and formations. Each volume contains extremely detailed summaries and analysis of the scope of the archive holdings for each subject.

Central Archive of the Unified Armed Forces, *Tsentral'nyi arkhiv Ob''edinennykh Vooruzhennykh Sil (TsAOVS)* formerly **Central Archive of the Ministry of Defence**, *Tsentral'nyi arkhiv Ministerstva Oborony (TsAMO)*. **Tel.: 095 137 90 05/546 56 04; 142100 Podol'sk, (Moskovskaia Oblast'), ul. Kirova 74.** Application through the Director, Historical-Archive and Military-Memorial Centre of the General Staff of the RF Armed Forces *Istoriko-arkhivnyi i voenno-memorial'nyi tsentr General'nogo shtaba VS Rossiiskoi Federatsii*. Responsible for *TsAOVS* and *RGA VMF*, Sankt Peterburg, **Tel.:296 53 48. 103160 Moscow, ul. Znamenka No. 19.**

Russian Centre for the Conservation and Study of Documents of Contemporary History, *Rossiiskii tsentr khraneniia i izucheniia dokumentov noveishei istorii (RTsKhIDNI)*, formerly **Central Party Archive** *Tsentral'nyi partiinyi arkhiv (TsPA)*. **Tel.:229 97 26; 103821 Moscow, ul. Pushkinskaia No. 15.**

5. Kozlov, V.P. Ed., Kratkii putevoditel' fondy i kollektsii sobrannye Tsentral'nym Partiinym Arkhivom **Short guide of the Record Groups and Collections gathered by the Central Party Archive**, Moscow, Blagovest, 1993. Holdings of State Defence Committee *GKO* directives, *Politburo* records wartime decisions, (*osobye papki*, special files for declassification), Defence Commissariat *NKO* files. Card index of *APRF* (Presidential Archive). Records of Central Staff Partisan Movement *TsShPD*, personal papers of P.K. Ponomarenko. *Agitprop* in wartime Red Army. Personal papers of Zhdanov, Stalin, Kalinin, Voroshilov (as a member of the *Politburo*). Wartime records of local Party organs at *obkom, kraikom* levels. Wartime living conditions 1941-1945. (Note: Protocols of the *GKO* planned for publication 1995 by the Institute of Military History, Moscow).

Russian State Archive of the Navy *Rossiiskii gosudarstvennyi arkhiv Voenno-Morskogo Flota (RGA VMF)*
Established in 1724 as the state archive of the Admiralteistvo-kollegiia, in 1827 designated the **Naval Ministry Archive**, whose holdings in 1918 were transferred to **Naval Section of the Unified State Archival Holdings** *EGAF*. In 1934

the **Naval Historical Archive** *Morskoi istoricheskii arkhiv* was established, which in 1937 became the **Central State Naval Archive** and in 1941 the **Central State Archive of the Soviet Navy** *Tsentral'nyi gosudarstvennyi arkhiv Voenno-Morskogo Flota SSSR (TsGA VMF SSSR)*. Re-designated 1991 Russian State Archive of the Navy. **Tel: 315-90-54; 191065 Sankt Peterburg, ul. Khalturina No. 36.**

6.   Nadvodskii, V.E. Tematicheskii putevoditel' (dokumental'nye materialy dorevoliutsionnogo flota Rossii). **Thematic guide (documentary materials of the pre-revolutionary Russian navy)**, Leningrad, TsGAVMF SSSR, 1966.   315 pp. Covers the development of the Russian Navy to 1917. Organised into four parts. **1.** Organisation, shipbuilding, naval artillery, mines and counter-measures, naval aviation, signals, manning, training, ports, hydrography, naval medicine. **2.** Wars from the Great Northern War to World War I and expeditions, circumnavigation **3.** Revolutionary movements in the navy **4.** Civil history. Appendixes and indexes. List of Record Groups, index of names, geographical names, ship names, publications based on naval archives, illustrations, abbreviations.

7.   Malevinskaia M.E., Efremova N.Iu., Spravochnik po fondam Sovetskogo Voenno-Morskogo Flota. **Handbook of Record Groups of the Soviet Navy**, Leningrad, TsGAVMF SSSR, 1991. 543 pp. Also East View Publications, Publisher's note (Kent D. Lee) and English-language preface. Covers the period 1918-1940. **Eleven parts. 1.** Revolutionary-democratic institutions (including Provisional Government) **2.** Central organs, administrations **3.** Baltic Fleet **4.** Black Sea Fleet **5.** Northern Fleet **6.** Pacific Fleet **7.** Flotillas **8.** Ground units **9.** Personal files **10.** Collections **11.** White Guard formations. Two appendixes Ship/Navy Record Groups not included here. Indexes: subject, places, ships. Abbreviations. Contents list in English and Russian.

In preparation
Guidebooks under the editorship of prominent American scholars J. Arch Getty, J. Burds, G. Freeze and W. Chase for key Russian archives which will include:
1) **Research Guide to the Russian Centre for the Preservation and Study of Documents of Contemporary History** (formerly Central Party Archive).
2) **Research Guide to the Central State Archive of the Russian Federation** (formerly the Central State Archive of the October Revolution). **Vol. I Pre-Revolutionary Period, Vol. II Central State Archive of the RSFSR.**

IMPERIAL ANTECEDENTS

DOCUMENTARY COLLECTIONS

8. Meshcheriakov M., Ed., <u>A.V. Suvorov. Dokumenty</u> **A.V. Suvorov. Documents**, Moscow, Voenizdat, Vols. I-IV 1949-1953. Vol. III 1791-1798; Vol. IV 1799-1800

9. Beskrovnyi L.G., Ed., <u>M.I. Kutuzov. Dokumenty</u> **M.I. Kutuzov. Documents**, Moscow, Voenizdat, Vols. I-V (vol. IV in two parts), 1950-1956. Vol. III 1808-1812; Vol. IV/1 June-October 1812, Vol.IV/2 October-December 1812.

10. Mordvinov R.N., Ed., <u>Materialy dlia istorii russkogo flota. Russkie flotovodtsy. Admiral Ushakov</u> **Materials for the history of the Russian navy. Russian naval commanders. Admiral Ushakov**, Moscow, Voenizdat, Vols. I-III 1951-56.

11. Fortunatov P.A., Ed., <u>Materialy po istorii russkoi armii P.A. Rumiantsev. Dokumenty</u> **Materials on the history of the Russian Army. P.A. Rumiantsev. Documents**, Moscow, Voenizdat, 1953-59. Vols. I-III. Vol. I 1756-1763; Vol II 1763-1775; Vol. III 1775-1796, edited by L.G. Beskrovnyi.

12. Maksakov V.V., Ed., <u>Sevastopol'skie vooruzhennoe vosstanie v noiabre 1905 goda. Dokumenty i materialy</u> **The Sevastopol armed insurrection in November 1905. Documents and materials**, Moscow, Voenizdat, 1957. 567 pp. Glav. arkhiv. uprav. MVD SSSR.

13. Lopatin V.S. <u>A.V. Suvorov. Pis'ma</u> **A.V. Suvorov. Letters**, Moscow, Nauka, 1986. 808 pp. Tirazh 100000. Endnotes, photographs, index of names, biographical chronology.

HISTORICAL STUDIES

14. Danilov Iu. N. <u>General ot infanterii. Na puti k krusheniiu. Ocherki iz poslednego perioda russkoi monarkhii</u> **On the road to ruin. Studies in the final period**

of the Russian monarchy, Moscow, Voenizdat, 1992. 287 pp. Tirazh 65000. Written by General Iu. Danilov, commander 5th Army Northern Front in 1917, in 1926. Printed from the copy in the Central State Military-Historical Archive. One appendix: Danilov Poslednie dni iiulia 1914 goda (1930).

15.   Zaionchkovskii A.M., General, Podgotovka Rossii k imperialisticheskoi voine. Ocherki voennoi podgotovki i pervonachalnykh planov. Po arkhivnym dokumentam **Preparation of Russia for the imperialist war. Studies of the military preparation and initial planning. Based on archives**, Moscow, Gosvoenizdat, Shtab RKKA, 1926. 428 pp. Tables, maps.

16.   Il'in-Zhenevskii A.F. Ot fevralia k zakhvatu vlasti. Vospominaniia o 1917 gode **From February to the seizure of power. Recollections of the year 1917**, Leningrad, 1927. Also Ilyin-Genevsky (sic) From February to October 1917, London, Modern Books, 1931. 122 pp.

17.   Khmelevskii G. Mirovaia imperialisticheskaia voina 1914-18 gg. Sistematicheskii ukazatel' knizhnoi i stateinoi voenno-istoricheskoi literatury za 1914-1935 gg. **The world imperialist war 1914-18. Sistematic guide of the books and articles of military-historical literature for 1914-18**, Moscow, Voennaia Akademiia RKKA, 1936. 280 pp. Index of names, subjects, sources.

18.   Beskrovnyi L.G., Ed., Khrestomatiia po russkoi voennoi istorii **Readings in Russian military history**, Moscow, Voenizdat, 1947. 639 pp.

19.   Zaionchkovskii P.A. Ed., Dnevnik D.A. Miliutina 1873-1875 **Diary of D.A. Miliutin 1873-1875**, Moscow, Lenin Library, Otdel rukopisei, 1947-50. 4 vols. **Vol. I 1947**, 252 pp. **Vol. II 1949**, 288 pp., **Vol. III 1950**, 333 pp., **Vol. IV 1950**, 202 pp. with index of names to all 4 vols.

20.   Barsukov E.Z. Artilleriia russkoi armii (1900-1917 gg.) **Artillery of the Russian Army (1900-1917)**, Tom I Organizatsiia artillerii **Organisation of the Artillery**, Moscow, Voenizdat, 1948. Tom II Artilleriiskoe snabzhenie **Artillery supplies**, 1949. Tom III Taktika i strel'ba artillerii **Tactics and artillery**, 1949. Tom IV a) Boevaia podgotovka artillerii b) Boevye deistviia artillerii 1914-1917 gg. **a) Combat training of artillery b) Artillery operations 1914-1917**, 1949. See also Russkaia artilleriia v mirovoi voiny **Russian artillery in the world war**, Moscow, Voenizdat, Vols. 1-2 1938-1940.

21.   Zaionchkovskii P.A. Voennye reformy 1860-1870 godov v Rossii **Military reforms in Russia during 1860-1870**, Moscow, Izd. Moskov. Univ., 1952. 370 pp. Based extensively on archives.

22.   Konovalov V.I. Ed., Revoliutsionnoe dvizhenie v armii v gody pervoi russkoi revoliutsii. Sbornik statei **Revolutionary movement in the army during the first Russian revolution. Collection of articles**, Moscow, Politizdat, 1955. 504 pp. Tirazh 10000. Footnotes with archival material.

23.   Beskrovnyi L.G. Ed., M.I. Dragomirov Izbranie trudy. Voprosy vospitaniia i obucheniia voisk **M.I. Dragomirov Selected works. Questions of troop edu-**

cation and training, Moscow, Voenizdat/Frunze Academy, 1956. 687 pp. Bibliography of Dragomirov's publications.

24. Beskrovnyi L.G. Ocherki po istochnikovedeniiu voennoi istorii Rossii **Essays on the sources of Russia's military history**, Moscow, Nauka, 1957. 453 pp. Tirazh 3500. Footnotes with archival material.

25. Pankov D.V. Ed., Razvitie taktiki russkoi armii. Sbornik statei **Development of tactics in the Russian Army. Collection of articles**, Moscow, Voenizdat, 1957. 331 pp. Footnotes with archival material, maps, illustrations, bibliography, index of names, places.

26. Punin L.N. Fel'dmarshal Kutuzov. Voenno-biograficheskii ocherk **Fieldmarshal Kutuzov. Military-biographical study**, Moscow, Voenizdat, 1957. 238 pp. Footnotes, photographs, maps.

27. Beskrovnyi L.G. Russkaia armiia i flot v XVIII veke (Ocherki) **The Russian Army and fleet in the XVIII century**, Moscow, Voenizdat, 1958. 645 pp. Footnotes with archival material, illustrations, maps supplement.

28. Fedorov A.V. Obshchestvenno-politicheskoe dvizhenie v russkoi armii 40-70 gg. XIX v. **Social-political movement in the Russian Army 1840-1870**, Moscow, Voenizdat, 1958. 231 pp. Footnotes with archival material, illustrations, bibliography.

29. Fedorov A.V. Russkaia armiia v 50-70 gg. XIX v. Ocherki **The Russian Army during 1850-1870. Studies**, Leningrad, Leningradskii universitet, 1959. 290 pp. Tirazh 2000. Based on archives, footnotes with archival material, tables, bibliography.

30. Beskrovnyi L.G., Liushkovskii R. Sh., Ed., Russkaia voenno-teoreticheskaia mysl' XIX i nachala XX vekov **Russian military-theoretical thought in the 19th and beginning of the 20th century**, Moscow, Voenizdat, 1960. 785 pp. Reproductions of Russian military texts.

31. Duz' P.D. Istoriia vozdukhoplavaniia i aviatsii v SSSR. Period pervoi mirovoi voiny (1914-1918 gg.) **The history of aeronautics and aviation in the USSR. Period of the First World War (1914-1918)**, Moscow, Oborongiz, 1960. 301 pp. Tirazh 2500. 2nd edn. (First edition deals with period up to 1914, published by Oborongiz in 1944.) Footnotes with archival material, tables, photographs, bibliography.

32. Beskrovnyi L.G. Ocherki voennoi istoriografii Rossii **Essays in Russian military historiography**, Moscow, Nauka, 1962. 318 pp. Tirazh 2500. Footnotes with archival material.

33. Beskrovnyi L.G. Pokhod russkoi armii protiv Napoleona v 1813 g. i osvobozhdenie Germanii. Sbornik dokumentov **Russian Army's campaign against Napoleon in 1813 and liberation of Germany. Collection of documents**, Moscow,

Nauka, 1964. 539 pp. Tirazh 2000. Appendixes, 340 documents, endnotes, index of names, of places, of documents.

34.   Pavlovich N.B., Rear Admiral, Ed., Flot v pervoi mirovoi voine. V dvukh tomakh **The fleet in the First World War**, in two volumes, Moscow, Voenizdat, 1964. See esp. Vol. I Deistviia russkogo flota **Operations of the Russian Fleet**, 647 pp. Maps, based on naval archives.

35.   Petrov V.A. Ocherki po istorii revoliutsionnogo dvizheniia v russkoi armii v 1905 g. **Studies in the history of the revolutionary movements in the Russian Army in 1905**, Moscow, Nauka, 1964. 427 pp. Tirazh 1200. Footnotes with archival material, tables, appendix.

36.   Panteleev Iu.A. Podvodnoe korablestroenie v Rossii 1900-1917. Sbornik dokumentov **Submarine construction in Russia 1900-1917. Collection of documents**, Leningrad, Sudostroenie, 1965. 403 pp. Tirazh 2000. Footnotes with archival material, endnotes, photographs, illustrations, 5 appendixes, index of names.

37.   Kostenko V.P. Na "Orle" v Tsusime **With the "Orel" at Tsushima**, Leningrad, Sudostroenie, 1968. 2nd edn. Ed. Admiral L.A. Vladimirskii. 492 pp. Tirazh 26700. Photographs, illustrations, bibliography.

38.   Shatsillo K.F. Russkii imperializm i razvitie flota nakanune pervoi mirovoi voiny (1906-1914 gg.) **Russian imperialism and development of the fleet on the eve of the First World War (1906-1914)**, Moscow, Nauka, 1968. 367 pp. Tirazh 2000. Footnotes with archival material, bibliography, index of names, appendix.

39.   Shunkov V.I. *et al*, Ed., Voprosy voennoi istorii Rossii XVIII i pervaia polovina XIX vekov **Issues of Russian military history in the XVIII and first half of the XIX century**, Moscow, Nauka, 1969. 445 pp. Tirazh 3300. Festschrift for Beskrovnyi. Footnotes with archival material, illustrations, has bibliography of Beskrovnyi's publications from 1931-1968.

40.   Arutiunian A.O. Kavkazkii front 1914-1917 gg. **The Caucasus Front 1914-1917**, Erevan, Aiastan, 1971. 415 pp. Tirazh 10000. Footnotes with archival material, bibliography, index of names, places, map supplement.

41.   Senchakova L.T. Revoliutsionnoe dvizhenie v russkoi armii i flote v kontse XIX - nachale XX v. (1879-1904 gg.) **Revolutionary movement in the Russian Army and Fleet at the end of the XIX - beginning of XX century (1879-1904)**, Moscow, Nauka, 1972. 216 pp. Tirazh 2550. Based on archives. Footnotes with archival material, index of names.

42.   Beskrovnyi L.G. Russkaia armiia i flot v XIX veke. Voenno-ekonomicheskii potentsial Rossii **Russian Army and Fleet in the XIX century. Russia's military-economical potential**, Moscow, Nauka, 1973. 616 pp. Tirazh 7000. Footnotes with archival material, tables, charts, index of names.

43.   Meshcheriakov G.P., Russkaia voennaia mysl' v XIX v. **Russian military thought in the 19th century**, Moscow, Nauka, 1973. 315 pp. Tirazh 3500. Extensive bibliography. Index of names.

44.   Zaionchkovskii P.A. Samoderzhavie i russkaia armiia na rubezhe XIX-XX stoletii 1881-1903 **Autocracy and the Russian Army at the cusp of XIX-XX centuries, 1881-1903**, Moscow, Mysl', 1973. 351 pp. Tirazh 11500. Footnotes with archival material, tables.

45.   Beskrovnyi L.G. Russkoe voennoe iskusstvo XIX v. **Russian military art in the 19th century**, Moscow, Nauka, 1974. 360 pp. Tirazh 13000. Footnotes with archival material.

46.   Miller V.I. Soldatskie komitety russkoi armii v 1917 g. (Vozniknovenie i nachal'nyi period deiatel'nosti) **Russian Army soldiers' committees in 1917. (The origin and initial period of activity)**, Moscow, Nauka, 1974. 312 pp. Tirazh 2000. Footnotes with archival material, tables, index of names.

47.   Shatsillo K.F. Rossiia pered pervoi mirovoi voinoi. (Vooruzhennye sily tsarizma v 1905-1914 gg.) **Russia before the First World War. (The armed forces of Tsarism in 1905-1914)**, Moscow, Nauka, 1974. 112 pp. Tirazh 40000. Endnotes with archival material.

48.   Strokov A.A. Vooruzhennye sily i voennoe iskusstvo v pervoi mirovoi voine **Armed forces and military art in the First World War**, Moscow, Voenizdat, 1974. 616 pp. Tirazh 12500. Footnotes, illustrations, maps, photographs, tables.

49.   Voronkova S.V. Materialy Osobogo soveshchaniia po oborone gosudarstva (istochnikovedcheskoe issledovanie) **Materials on the Special Conference on State Defence (study of sources)**, Moscow, Moscow University, 1975. 188 pp. Tirazh 2210. Footnotes with extensive archival material, appendix.

50.   Rostunov I.I. Russkii front pervoi mirovoi voiny **Russian Front during the First World War**, Moscow, Nauka, 1976. 387 pp. Tirazh 10600. Footnotes with archival material, tables, maps.

51.   Zhilin P.A. Ed., Russkaia voennaia mysl'. Konets XIX - nachalo XX v. **Russian military thought. End of XIX - beginning of XX century**, Moscow, Nauka, 1982. 252 pp. Tirazh 3700. Footnotes with archival material, bibliography.

52.   Stanislavskaia A.M. Politicheskaia deiatel'nost' F.F. Ushakova v Gretsii 1798-1800 gg. **F.F. Ushakov's political activity in Greece 1798-1800**, Moscow, Nauka, 1983. 303 pp. Tirazh 4400. Footnotes with archival material, index of names.

53.   Beskrovnyi L.G. Armiia i flot Rossii v nachale XX v. Ocherki voenno-ekonomicheskogo potentsiala **Russia's army and fleet at the beginning of XX century. Studies in military-economic potential**, Moscow, Nauka, 1986. 238 pp. Tirazh 18500. Footnotes with archival material, tables.

54. Duz' P.D. Istoriia vozdukhoplavaniia i aviatsii v Rossii (iiul' 1914 g.-oktiabr' 1917 g.) **History of aeronautics and aviation in Russia (July 1914-October 1917)**, 2nd edn. Moscow, Mashinostroenie, 1986. 366 pp. Tirazh 10000. New archival material. Footnotes with archival material, tables, photographs, bibliography, appendix.

55. Rostunov I.I. Ed., Istoriia Severnoi voiny 1700-1721 gg. **History of the Northern War**, Moscow, Nauka, 1987. 214 pp. Tirazh 14700. Chapter endnotes, maps, photographs, index of names, places, bibliography.

56. Keldysh M.V. *et al*, Aviatsiia v Rossii: Spravochnik **Aviation in Russia: A handbook**, 2nd edn. Moscow, Mashinostroenie, 1988. 367 pp. Tirazh 50000. Photographs, tables, illustrations, footnotes, appendix.

57. Laverychev V.Ia. Voennyi gosudarstvenno-monopolisticheskii kapitalizm v Rossii **Military state-monopolistic capitalism in Russia**, Moscow, Nauka, 1988. 336 pp. Tirazh 1800. Endnotes with archival material, index of names. Deals with the period 1914-1917.

58. Polikarpov V.D. Voennaia kontrrevoliutsiia v Rossii 1905-1917 **Military counter-revolution in Russia 1905-1917**, Moscow, Nauka, 1990. 383 pp. Tirazh 5000. Footnotes with archival material, index of names, appendix.

59. Shevyrev A.P. Russkii flot posle Krymskoi voiny: Liberal'naia biurokratiia i morskie reformy **The Russian Fleet after the Crimean War: the liberal bureaucracy and naval reforms**, Moscow, Moskovskii universitet, 1990. 184 pp. Tirazh 4385. For specialist historians. Endnotes with archival material, photographs, bibliography.

60. Begunova A. Sabli ostry, koni bystry...(iz istorii russkoi kavalerii) **Sharp sabres, fast horses...(from the history of Russian cavalry)**, Moscow, Molodaia gvardiia, 1992. 256 pp. Tirazh 50000. Coloured illustrations, bibliography.

61. Kersnovskii A.A. Istoriia russkoi armii v chetyrekh tomakh. Tom pervyi Ot Narvy do Parizha 1700-1814 gg **History of the Russian army in four volumes. Vol. One From Narva to Paris 1700-1814**, Moscow, Golos, 1992. 304 pp. Tirazh 100000. Publication continuing. Reprint of rare emigre history of the Russian army, first published in Belgrade, Tsarskii Vestnik, 1933-1938. Four volumes, 1014 pp.

BIOGRAPHIES AND MEMOIRS

BIOGRAPHIES

For a bibliographical guide to published biographies see Semanov S.N. <u>40 let ZhZL, Katalog 1933-1973</u> (Zhizn' Zamechatel'nykh Liudei. Seriia biographii) **40 years ZhZL catalogue (Life of significant individuals. Series of biographies)**, Moscow, Molodaia Gvardiia, 1974. 288 pp. Tirazh 100000. Summary of the series. This series was established by Maksim Gorkii in 1933.

For three composite biographical collections in the series <u>ZhZL: Polkovodtsyi grazhdanskoi voiny</u> **Leaders of the Civil War**, Moscow, Molodaia Gvardiia, 1960. 352 pp. Tirazh 90000. Bliukher, Frunze, Kamenev, *et al*. See also <u>Sovetskie polkovodtsy i voenachal'niki. Sbornik</u> **Soviet leaders and military commanders. Collection**, Moscow, Molodaia Gvardiia, 1988. 360 pp. Tirazh 150000. Batov, Kamenev, Konev, Kuznetsov, Rotmistrov, Tukhachevskii. Also <u>Polkovodtsi i voenachal'niki Velikoi Otechestvennoi voiny</u> **Military leaders and commanders of the Great Patriotic war**, Moscow, Molodaia Gvardiia, 1970. 448 pp. Tirazh 150000. A. Antonov, A. Golovko, L. Govorov, A. Khrulev, T. Khriukin, R. Malinovskii, K. Rokossovskii, P. Rybalko, V. Sokolovskii, N. Vatutin, N. Voronov, S. Zhavoronkov. Kumanev G.A. Ed. <u>Otchiznye slavnye syny. Stroiteli i polkovodtsy Sovetskikh Vooruzhennykh Sil. Stranitsy biographii: Rekomendatel'nyi bibliograficheskii spravochnik</u> **Famous sons of the Motherland. Creators and military leaders of the Soviet Armed Forces. Biographies: Recommended bibliographical handbook**, Moscow, Knizhnaia palata, 1987. 112 pp. Tirazh 40000.

The following entries are given in alphabetical order by subject, e.g. Antonov, Azin .....Zhukov.

***

62.   Gaglov I.I. <u>General Antonov</u> **General Antonov**, Moscow, Voenizdat, 1978. 132 pp. Tirazh 50000. Footnotes with archival material, photographs.

63. Kondrat'ev N. <u>Nachdiv Vladimir Azin</u> **Division Commander Vladimir Azin,** Moscow, Voenizdat, 1968. 236 pp. Tirazh 50000. Footnotes with archival material, photographs.

64. Bliukher V.K. <u>Stat'i i rechi</u> **Articles and speeches,** Moscow, Voenizdat, 1963. 232 pp. Tirazh 50000. Appendix of archival documents, endnotes.

65. Dushen'kin V. <u>Ot soldata do marshala</u> **From a soldier to a marshal**, Moscow, Politizdat, 1964. 224 pp. Tirazh 170000. Biography of Marshal **Blukher.** Footnotes with archival material, photographs, maps.

66. Kondrat'ev N. <u>Marshal Bliukher</u> **Marshal Blukher,** Moscow, Voenizdat, 1965. 296 pp. Tirazh 100000. Footnotes with archival material, photographs.

67. Rostunov I.I. <u>General Brusilov</u> **General Brusilov,** Moscow, Voenizdat, 1964. 246 pp. Tirazh 25000. Footnotes with archival material, bibliography, list of archives and documents.

68. Semanov S.N. <u>Brusilov</u> **Brusilov,** Moscow, Molodaia Gvardiia, 1980. 318 pp. Tirazh 100000. Based on historical material and documents. Photographs, map, short bibliography.

69. Rodin A.M. <u>A.S. Bubnov. Voennaia i politicheskaia deiatel'nost'</u> **A.S. Bubnov. Military and political activity,** Moscow, Voenizdat, 1988. 174 pp. Tirazh 50000. Footnotes with archival material, photographs.

70. Kuznetsov P.G. <u>General Cherniakhovskii</u> **General Cherniakhovskii,** Moscow, Voenizdat, 1969. 240 pp. Tirazh 50000. Footnotes with archival material, photographs.

71. Sharipov A. <u>Cherniakhovskii. Povestvovanie o polkovodtse</u> **Cherniakhovskii. Narrative about a leader**, Moscow, Voenizdat, 1971. 383 pp. Tirazh 100000. Material from archives, Institute of Military history, comrades in arms.

72. Bakhirev V.V., Kirillov I.I. <u>Konstruktor V.A. Degtiarev: Za strokami biographii</u> **Constructor V.A. Degtiarev: Following the lines of biography**, Moscow, Voenizdat, 1979. 192 pp. Tirazh 50000. Based on archives. Photographs, footnotes. 2nd ed. 1983. 240 pp. Tirazh 39000.

73. Pankov D.V. <u>Komkor Eideman</u> **Corps Commander Eideman,** Moscow, Voenizdat, 1965. 104 pp. Tirazh 61000. Photographs, footnotes with archival material.

74. Skryl'nik A.I. <u>General armii A.A. Epishev</u> **Army General Epishev,** Moscow, Voenizdat, 1989. 319 pp. Tirazh 50000. Photographs, footnotes with some archival material.

75. Obertas I.L. <u>Komandarm Fed'ko</u> **Army Commander Fed'ko,** Moscow, Voenizdat, 1973. 165 pp. Tirazh 50000. Based on archives. Photographs, footnotes with archival material.

76. Petrov F.N. Ed., <u>M.V. Frunze. Zhizn i deiatel'nost'</u> **M.V. Frunze. His life and work,** Moscow, Politizdat, 1962. 350 pp. Tirazh 80000. Photographs, footnotes with some achival material, bibliography of literature and archives.

77. Ivushkin N.B., Ed., <u>M.V. Frunze</u> **M.V. Frunze,** Moscow, Voenizdat, 1965. 328 pp. Tirazh 32000. Photographs, short biographies of contributors and mentioned persons.

78. Airapetian G.A. <u>Legendarnyi Gai</u> **Legendary Gai,** Moscow, Voenizdat, 1965. 176 pp. Tirazh 50000. Photographs, footnotes with archival material.

79. Zonin S.A. <u>Admiral L.M. Galler: Zhizn' i flotovodcheskaia deiatel'nost'</u> **Admiral L.M. Galler: Life and naval leadership,** Moscow, Voenizdat, 1991. 415 pp. Tirazh 50000. Footnotes with archival material, photographs.

80. Bogomolova-Gamarnik K.B. <u>Ian Gamarnik. Vospominaniia druzei i soratnikov</u> **Ian Gamarnik. Recollection of friends and comrades-in-arms,** Moscow, Voenizdat, 1978. 191 pp. Tirazh 65000. Photographs, some footnotes.

81. Idashkin Iu.V. <u>Nebo ego mechty. O Glavnom marshale aviatsii A.E. Golovanove</u> **The sky his dream. About the Air Chief Marshal A.E. Golovanov,** Moscow, Politizdat, 1986. 128 pp. Tirazh 200000. Two photographs.

82. Khametov M.I. <u>Admiral A.G. Golovko</u> **Admiral Golovko,** Moscow, Voenizdat, 1984. 205 pp. Tirazh 65000. Photographs.

83. Bychevskii B.V. <u>Marshal Govorov</u> **Marshal Govorov,** Moscow, Voenizdat, 1970. 176 pp. Tirazh 50000. Photographs, maps, footnotes with some archival material.

84. Babenko P. <u>I.E. Iakir (Ocherk boevogo puti)</u> **I.E. Iakir (Study of combat road),** Moscow, Politizdat, 1963. 80 pp. Tirazh 170000. Footnotes with archival material, photographs.

85. Iakir P.I., Geller Iu.A., <u>Komandarm Iakir. Vospominaniia druzei i soratnikov</u> **Army Commander Iakir. Recollections of friends and comrades in arms,** Moscow, Voenizdat, 1963. 248 pp. Tirazh 65000. Photographs.

86. Ponomarev A.N. <u>Konstruktor S.V. Il'iushin</u> **Designer S.V. Iliushin,** Moscow, Voenizdat, 1988. 400 pp. Tirazh 100000. Primarily for aviation specialists.

87. Rudnyi V., <u>Dolgoe, dolgoe plavanie. Ob admirale Flota Sovetskogo Soiuza I.S Isakove</u> **A long, long cruise. About Admiral of the Fleet of the Soviet Union I.S. Isakov,** 2nd ed. Moscow, Politizdat, 1984. 142 pp. Tirazh 200000. Based on personal archives of Isakov, recollection of colleagues. Photographs.

88. Kameneva N.S. <u>Put' polkovodtsa (Vospominaniia ob ottse)</u> **Commander's Road (Recollections about my father),** Kiev, Politizdat, 1982. 133 pp. Tirazh 25000. Daughter's account. Photographs, footnotes.

89.   Shiian I.S. General armii Khrulev **Army General Khrulev**, Moscow, Voenizdat, 1980. 112 pp. Tirazh 75000. Footnotes with some archival material, photographs.

90.   Astashenkov P.T. Glavnyi konstruktor **Chief designer**, Moscow, Voenizdat,
1975. 286 pp. Tirazh 200000. Life of **S.P. Korolev**. Based on documents. Photographs.

91.   Romanov A.P., Gubarev V.S., Konstruktory **Designers**, Moscow, Politizdat,
1989. 367 pp. Tirazh 200000. Life of **S.P. Korolev, M.K. Iangel', V.P.
Glushko.** photographs.

92.   Dragan I.G. Marshal N.I. Krylov **Marshal Krylov**, Moscow, Voenizdat, 1987.
239 pp. Tirazh 100000. Photographs, footnotes with some archival material.

93.   Gai D. Nebesnoe pritiazhenie. Zhizn' vydaiushchegosia konstruktora samoletov
Vladimira Mikhailovicha Miasishcheva **The pull of the sky. Life of prominent
designer of aeroplanes Vladimir Mikhailovich Miasishchev**, Moscow, Moskovskii Rabochii, 1984. 221 pp. Tirazh 75000. Photographs.

94.   Golubovich V.S. Marshal R.Ia. Malinovskii **Marshal Malinovskii**, Moscow,
Voenizdat, 1984. 215 pp. Tirazh 150000. Footnotes with archival material,
photographs. 1988: Kiev, Politizdat Ukrainy. 224 pp. Tirazh 100000.

95.   Tolubko V.F. Nedelin. Pervyi glavkom strategicheskikh **Nedelin. First commander of the Strategic Rocket Forces**, Moscow, Molodaia Gvardiia, 1979.
222 pp. Tirazh 100000. Photographs, footnotes with archival material, bibliography.

96.   Khorobrykh A.M. Glavnyi marshal aviatsii A.A. Novikov **Air Chief Marshal,
A.A. Novikov**, Moscow, Voenizdat, 1989. 287 pp. Tirazh 50000. Photographs,
footnotes.

97.   Gai D. Profil' kryla. Povest' o konstruktore samoletov Vladimire Mikhailoviche
Petliakove **The outline of the wings. Story about aircraft designer Vladimir
Mikhailovich Petliakov**, Moscow, Moskovskii rabochii, 1981. 192 pp. Tirazh
75000. Photographs.

98.   Tarasov E.P. Nikolai Il'ich Podvoiskii (Ocherk voennoi deiatel'nosti) **Nikolai
Ilich Podvoiskii (Study of his military activity)**, Moscow, Voenizdat, 1964.
176 pp. Tirazh 20000. Footnotes with archival material, photographs.

99.   Mel'nikov S.I. Marshal Rybalko. Vospominaniia byvshego chlena Voennogo
soveta 3-i gvardeiskoi tankovoi armii **Marshal Rybalko. Recollections of the
former member of the Military Soviet of the 3rd Guards Tank Army**, Kiev,
Politizdat, 1980. 255 pp. Tirazh 26500. Photographs, some footnotes.

100. Kardashov V.I. Rokossovskii **Rokossovskii**, Moscow, Molodaia Gvardiia, 1972.
448 pp. Tirazh 200000. Photographs, maps, tables.

101. Gorelik Ia.M. Marshal Sovetskogo soiuza Boris Mikhailovich Shaposhnikov: Kratkii ocherk zhizni i deiatel'nosti **Marshal of the Soviet Union Boris Mikhailovich Shaposhnikov: Short study of his life and work**, Moscow, Voenizdat, 1961. 109 pp. Tirazh 17000. Photographs, footnotes with some archival material.

102. Vasil'chikov V.S. Nachdiv Shchors (Boevoi put') **Division Commander Shchors (Combat road)**, Moscow, Voenizdat, 1957. 120 pp. Footnotes with archival material, maps, photographs, appendixes.

103. Karpenko V. Shchors **Shchors**, Moscow, Molodaia Gvardiia, 1974. 224 pp. Tirazh 100000. Based on archives and recollections of comrades in arms. Photographs, maps, short bibliography.

104. Volkogonov D.A. Triumf i tragediia. Politicheskii portret I.V. Stalina **Triumph and tragedy. Political portrait of I.V. Stalin,** in two books, four parts. Moscow, Novosti, 1989. **Book I,** part 1: 304 pp. Part 2: 336 pp. **Book II,** Part 1: 432 pp. Part 2: 272 pp. All parts: Tirazh 300000. Archival photographs, bibliography, index of names. English translation Stalin Triumph and tragedy London, Weidenfeld and Nicolson, 1991. 642 pp. Endnotes, index, subjects, names, photographs.

105. Kuz'mina L.M. Generalnyi konstruktor Pavel Sukhoi (Stranitsy zhizni) **Chief designer Pavel Sukhoi (Pages from his life)**, Minsk, Belarus', 1985. 239 pp. Tirazh 90000. Photographs.

106. Kuznetsov P.G. Lt.Gen. Marshal Tolbukhin **Marshal Tolbukhin,** Moscow, Voenizdat, 1966. 276 pp. Tirazh 75000. Photographs, maps, footnotes with some archival material.

107. Pliushchev V.A. Nikolai Tomin **Nikolai Tomin**, Moscow, Voenizdat, 1966. 148 pp. Tirazh 30000. Footnotes with archival material, photographs.

108. Todorskii A.I. Marshal Tukhachevskii **Marshal Tukhachevskii**, Moscow, Politizdat, 1963. 93 pp. Tirazh 150000. Photographs, some footnotes.

109. Nikulin L.V. Tukhachevskii. Biograficheskii ocherk **Tukhachevskii. Biographical study**, Moscow, Voenizdat, 1964. 200 pp. Tirazh 115000. Based on family's recollections and archives. Photographs.

110. Ivanov V.M. Marshal M.N. Tukhachevskii **Marshal M.N. Tukhachevskii**, Moscow, Voenizdat, 1985. 318 pp. Tirazh 100000. Photographs, footnotes with some archival material. 2nd ed. 1990. 320 pp. Tirazh 100000.

111. Shchetinov Iu.A., Starkov B.A., Krasnyi marshal: Istoricheskii portret Mikhaila Tukhachevskogo **The Red Marshal: Historical portrait of Mikhail Tukhachevskii,** Moscow, Molodaia Gvardiia, 1990. 303 pp. Tirazh 100000. Based on previously undisclosed archives. Photographs, footnotes, short bibliography.

112. Savost'ianov V.I. <u>Komandarm Uborevich. Vospominaniia druzei i soratnikov</u> **Army Commander Uborevich. Recollections of friends and comrades in arms,** Moscow, Voenizdat, 1964. 264 pp. Tirazh 65000. Collection of articles. Photographs, appendix.

113. Zakharov Iu.D. <u>General Armii N.F. Vatutin</u> **Army General N.F. Vatutin,** Moscow, Voenizdat, 1985. 192 pp. Tirazh 65000. Footnotes with some archival material, photographs.

114. Obertas I.L. <u>Nachdiv dvadtsatoi Velikanov</u> **Velikanov Division Commander of the 20th,** Moscow, Voenizdat, 1964. 160 pp. Tirazh 17000. Maps, photographs, footnotes, with some archival material.

115. Griaznov B.Z. <u>Marshal Zakharov</u> **Marshal Zakharov,** Moscow, Voenizdat, 1979. 152 pp. Tirazh 50000. Footnotes, photographs.

116. Iakovlev N.N. <u>Stranitsy zhizni marshala G.K. Zhukova. Povest'</u> **Pages of life of Marshal G.K. Zhukov. Story,** Moscow, Detskaia literatura, 1985. 239 pp. Tirazh 100000. Family and official photographs.

117. Iarovikov V.S. <u>Marshal Zhukov. Kakim my ego pomnim</u> **Marshal Zhukov. As we remember him,** Moscow, Politizdat, 1988. 398 pp. Tirazh 200000. Photographs, index of names, places.

118. Mirkina A.D., Iarovikov V.S. <u>Marshal Zhukov: polkovodets i chelovek. Sbornik. V dvukh tomakh</u> **Marshal Zhukov: leader and man. Collection. In two volumes,** Moscow, Novosti, 1988. Vol. I 384 pp. Vol. II 256 pp. Tirazh 50000. Articles by family members and friends, comrades in arms. Photographs, bibliography.

119. Iakovlev N.N. <u>Zhukov</u> **Zhukov,** Moscow, Molodaia Gvardiia, 1992. 459 pp. Tirazh 150000. Uses new archival material. Photographs.

MEMOIRS

For a bibliographical guide to memoir literature, see V.I. Ezhakov *et al*, <u>O voine, o tovarishchakh, o sebe. Velikaia Otechesvennaia voina v vospominani-iakh uchastnikov boevykh deistv. Annotirovannyi ukazatel' voenno-memuarnoi literatury (1941-1975)</u> **About the war, comrades and oneself. The Great Patriotic war as remembered by the participants of combat actions. Annotated index of military memoir literature (1941-1975),** Moscow, Voenizdat, 1977. 240 pp. Tirazh 50000. The following entries are given in alphabetical order.

120. Akhromeev S.F., Kornienko G.M., <u>Glazami marshala i diplomata. Kriticheskii vzgliad na vneshniuiu politiku SSSR do i posle 1985 goda</u> **Through the eyes of a marshal and of a diplomat,** Moscow, Mezhdunarodnye otnosheniia, 1992. 319 pp. Tirazh 9500.

121. Biriuzov S.S. <u>Surovye gody</u> **Hard (bleak) years**, Moscow, Nauka, 1966. 560 pp. Tirazh 50000. Coloured maps, photographs, index of names, footnotes.

122. Blagodatov A.V. Lt. General, <u>Zapiski o kitaiskoi revoliutsii 1925-1927 gg.</u> **Memoirs about the Chinese revolution 1925-1927,** Moscow, Nauka, 1979. 301 pp. Tirazh 15000. Maps, photographs, appendix.

123. Brusilov A.A. <u>Moi vospominaniia</u> **My recollections**, 1st edn. 1929. 2nd. ed., Moscow, Voenizdat, 1941. 248 pp. Maps, appendix. 1983 ed.: 256 pp. Tirazh 100000. Maps, footnotes. SEE ALSO <u>VOENNYE MEMUARY</u>

124. Budennyi S.M., Marshal, <u>Proidennyi put'</u> **The road I travelled**, Moscow, Voenizdat, 1959. 448 pp. Footnotes with archival material, maps, photographs.

125. Cherepanov A.I. <u>Zapiski voennogo sovetnika v Kitae</u> **Notes of a military adviser in China**, 2nd. ed. Moscow, Nauka, 1976. 648 pp. Tirazh 30000. Maps.

126. Chudodeev Iu.V., Ed., <u>Po dorogam Kitaia 1937-1945. Vospominaniia</u> **On the roads of China 1937-1945. Recollections**, Moscow, Nauka, 1989. 368 pp. Fourteen accounts of military specialists, advisers in China. Photographs, index of names.

127. Chuikov V.I., Marshal, <u>Missiia v Kitae. Zapiski voennogo sovetnika</u> **My mission in China. Memoirs of a military adviser**, Moscow, Nauka, 1981. 270 pp. Tirazh 50000. Endnotes.

128. Eremenko, see under Yeremenko

129. Golikov F.I., Marshal, <u>V Moskovskoi bitve. Zapiski komandarma</u> **In the battle for Moscow. Memoirs of Army Commander**, Moscow, Nauka, 1967. 200 pp. Tirazh 70000. Footnotes with archival material, photographs, coloured map.

130. Golovko A., Admiral, <u>With the fleet</u> **Vmeste s flotom,** Moscow, Progress publishers, 1988. 232 pp. Tirazh 4820. Endnotes, photographs.

131. Grabin V.G., Col. General, <u>Oruzhie pobedy</u> **The weapons of victory,** Moscow, Politizdat, 1989. 544 pp. Tirazh 200000. Development of new artillery weapons. Photographs.

132. Grechko A.A., Marshal, <u>Gody voiny 1941-1943</u> **The war years 1941-1943,** Moscow, Voenizdat, 1976. 574 pp. Tirazh 400000. Period Dnieper to Caucasus. Coloured maps, photographs, footnotes with archival material.

133. Iakovlev A.S. see under Yakovlev

134. Ignat'ev A.A., General, <u>Piat'desiat let v stroiu</u> **Fifty years in the ranks,** Moscow, Voenizdat, 1988. 752 pp. Tirazh 100000 Service in the Imperial Russian Army and the Red Army. Military-diplomatic account.

135. Kalashnikov M.T. Zapiski konstruktora-oruzheinika **Memoirs of a designer-gunsmith**, Moscow, Voenizdat, 1992. 300 pp. Tirazh 50000. Photographs.

136. Konev I.S. Marshal, Zapiski komanduiushchego frontom 1943-1944 **Memoirs of a Front commander 1943-1944,** Moscow, Nauka, 1972. 368 pp. Tirazh 50000. Appendixes, index of names, coloured maps, photographs, footnotes with archival material.

137. Leliushenko D.D., General, Moskva-Stalingrad-Berlin-Praga. Zapiski komandarma **Moscow-Stalingrad-Berlin-Prague. Memoirs of Army Commander**, 4th ed. Moscow, Nauka, 1985. 408 pp. Tirazh 50000. Footnotes with archival material, maps, photographs, index of names.

138. Malinovskii R.Ia., Marshal, Soldaty Rossii **Soldiers of Russia,** Moscow, Voenizdat, 1969. 452 pp. Tirazh 100000. Footnotes with some archival material.

139. Managarov I.M. V srazhenii za Khar'kov **In the battle for Kharkov,** Kharkov, Prapor, 1978. 256 pp. Tirazh 25000. Photographs, footnotes with some archival material, map.

140. Moskalenko K.S., Marshal, Na Iugo-zapadnom napravlenii **On the South-Western axis,** Moscow, Nauka, 1973. 2nd ed. Vol.II 644 pp. Tirazh 40000. Footnotes with archival material, coloured maps, photographs, index of names.

141. Meretskov K.A., Marshal, Na sluzhbe narodu. Stranitsy vospominaniia **In the service of people. Pages of recollections,** Moscow, Politizdat, 1969. 464 pp. Tirazh 200000. Photographs, some footnotes.

142. Novikov A.A., Air Chief Marshal, V nebe Leningrada **In the skies of Leningrad,** Moscow, Nauka, 1970. 308 pp. Tirazh 50000. Footnotes with archival material, coloured map, photographs, index of names.

143. Platonov V.I. Zapiski admirala **Memoirs of an admiral,** Moscow, Voenizdat, 1991. 319 pp. Tirazh 100000. Photographs.

144. Pern L., General, V vikhre voennykh let. Vospominaniia **In the whirlwind of military service. Recollections**, Tallin, Eesti Raamat, 1969. 244 pp. Tirazh 5000. Maps, photographs, footnotes.

145. Pliev I.A., General, Pod gvardeiskim znamenem **Under the Guards' banner**, Ordzhonikidze, 1976. 328 pp. Tirazh 15000. Footnotes with archival material, photographs.

146. Rokossovsky K.K., Marshal, A soldier's duty **Soldatskii dolg,** Moscow, Progress publishers, 1970. 341 pp. Photographs. Reprinted 1985.

147. Sandalov L.M., Col. General, Na moskovskom napravlenii **On the Moscow axis,** Moscow, Nauka, 1970. 368 pp. Tirazh 50000. Photographs, footnotes with some archival material, maps, index of names.

148. Semenov G.G. Tri goda v Pekine. (Zapiski voennogo sovetnika) **Three years in Peking. (Recollections of a military adviser)**, Moscow, Nauka, 1978. 296 pp. Tirazh 50000. Photographs.

149. Shakhurin A.I., People's Commissar for Aviation, Kryl'ia pobedy. Vospominaniia **The wings of victory. Recollections**, Moscow, Politizdat, 1990. 3rd ed. 302 pp. Tirazh 200000. Includes previously unpublished personal accounts, photographs.

150. Shaposhnikov B.M., Marshal, Vospominaniia. Voenno-nauchnye trudy **Recollection. Military-scientific works.** Moscow, Voenizdat, 1982. 2nd ed. 558 pp. Tirazh 100000. (1st ed 1974.) Footnotes, photographs, bibliography of author's works.

151. Svoboda L., General Ot Buzuluka do Pragi **From Buzuluk to Prague**, Moscow, Voenizdat. 1963. Translated from Czech. 406 pp. Tirazh 65000. Photographs, maps. 2nd edn. 1969. 436 pp.

152. Vasilevskii A.M., Marshal, Delo vsei zhizni **A life's work**, Moscow, Politizdat, 1974. 542 pp. Tirazh 600000. Footnotes with archival material, photographs, maps. 6th edition: 1989 in two volumes. SEE ALSO VM

153. Yakovlev A.S Tsel' zhizni (Zapiski aviakonstruktora). **The aim of a lifetime. (Memoirs of an aircraft designer)**, Moscow, Politizdat, 1968. 623 pp. Tirazh 100000. Photographs. Translated into English as The Aim of a Lifetime. The Story of Alexander Yakovlev, Designer of the YAK Fighter Plane Tsel' zhizni, Moscow, Progress publishers, 1972. 446 pp. Photographs, footnotes.

154. Yeremenko A.I., Marshal, Na zapadnom napravlenii. Vospominaniia o boevykh deistviiakh voisk Zapadnogo, Briianskogo fronta i 4-i udarnoi armii v pervom periode Velikoi otechestvennoi voine **On the western axis. Recollections of the combat troops of the Western, Bryansk Front and the 4th Shock Army in the first period of the Great Patriotic war,** Moscow, Voenizdat, 1959. 189 pp. Map supplement.

155. Yeremenko A.I., Marshal, Stalingrad. Zapiski komanduiushchego frontom **Stalingrad. Memoirs of the Front Commander,** Moscow, Voenizdat, 1961. 504 pp. Tirazh 100000. Separate appendix of 22 coloured maps, photographs, footnotes.

156. Yeremenko A.I., Marshal, V nachale voiny **At the beginning of the war**, Moscow, Nauka, 1964. 512 pp. Tirazh 15500. Coloured maps, photographs, endnotes with archival material.

157. Yeremenko A.I., Marshal, Gody vozmezdiia 1943-1945 **The years of retribution 1943-1945**, Moscow, Nauka, 1969. 598 pp. Tirazh 50000. Footnotes with archival material, coloured maps, photographs, index of names.

158.   Yeremenko A.I., Marshal, Pomni voinu. Avtobiograficheskii ocherk **Remember the war. Autobiographical study,** Donetsk, Donbass, 1971. 296 pp. Tirazh 165000. Photographs.

159.   Zhukov G.K., Marshal, Vospominaniia i razmyshleniia **Recollections and reflections,** Moscow, Novosti, 1969, 1971. 704 pp. Tirazh 500000. Coloured maps, footnotes with archival material, photographs.

160.   Zhukov G.K., Marshal, The Memoirs of Marshal Zhukov, London, Jonathan Cape, 1971. 703 pp. Photographs, coloured maps, footnotes, index. New York, Delacourt.

161.   Zhukov G.K., Marshal, Vospominaniia i razmyshleniia **Recollections and reflections,** 2nd enlarged ed. Moscow, Novosti, 1975. Vol. I 432 pp. Tirazh 200000. Vol. II 448 pp. Tirazh 200000. Photographs, footnotes with archival material, coloured maps.

162.   Zhukov G.K., Marshal, Vospominaniia i razmyshleniia **Recollections and reflections,** 5th ed. in three volumes, Moscow, Novosti, 1983. Vol. I: 303 pp. Vol. II: 328 pp. Vol. III: 352 pp. Tirazh 400000. Photographs, maps, footnotes with some archival material.

163.   Zhukov G.K., Marshal, Vospominaniia i razmyshleniia **Recollections and reflections,** 10th ed. in three volumes, Moscow, Novosti, 1990. Vol.I 384 pp. Vol. II 368 pp. Vol. III 384 pp. Tirazh 300000. Maps, photographs, footnotes with archival material, index of names.

VOENNYE MEMUARY

The series Voennye Memuary **Military Memoirs,** begun in the 1950s, presently numbers several hundred volumes. The listing below is intended to present merely a profile representing date of publication, authors, subject matter, spanning 1958-1991.

The series **VM** is now superseded by Biblioteka izbrannykh voennykh memuarov. 50 let pobedy **Library of selected military memoirs. 50 years of victory.** The first reprint in this new series is I.S. Konev, Zapiski komanduiushchego frontom **Notes of the front commander,** Moscow, Voenizdat, 1991. 602 pp. Tirazh 100000. Photographs. Additional material from author's archive.

Scheduled for re-issue with author's archival material: A.K. Babadzhanian, I.Kh. Bagramian, P.I. Batov, A.P. Beloborodov, S.S. Biriuzov, A.M. Vasilevskii, N.N. Voronov, A.G. Golovko, A.I. Yeremenko, G.K. Zhukov, M.E. Katukov, K.A. Meretskov, K.K. Rokossovskii, V.I. Chuikov, S.M. Shtemenko *et al.*

The following entries are given in chronological order.

164.   Samoilo A.A., Lt. General, Dve zhizni **Two lives,** Moscow, Voenizdat, 1958. 276 pp. Photographs, footnotes, map. Spans period from last decade of 19th century to post-1945.

165. Verkhovskii A.I. Na trudnom perevale **On a difficult crossing**, Moscow, Voenizdat, 1959. 447 pp. Endnotes.

166. Lobachev A.A., Major General, Trudnymi dorogami **On hard roads**, Moscow, Voenizdat, 1960. 336 pp. Photographs.

167. Mel'kumov Ia.A. Turkestantsy **The fighting men of Turkestan,** Moscow, Voenizdat, 1960. 272 pp. Photographs, footnotes, map.

168. Popel' N.K., Lt. General, Tanki povernuli na zapad **The tanks turned westwards,** Moscow, Voenizdat, 1960. 382 pp. Photographs.

169. Tiulenev I.V., General, Cherez tri voiny **Through three wars**, Moscow, Voenizdat, 1960. 256 pp. Photographs, footnotes with some archival material.

170. Brusilov A.A. Moi vospominaniia **My recollections**, Moscow, Voenizdat, 1963. 288 pp. Tirazh 50000. Maps, footnotes. A controversial text published in the VM series.

171. Bonch-Bruevich M.D., Lt. General, Vsia vlast' Sovetam **All power to the Soviets,** Moscow, Voenizdat, 1964. 260 pp. Tirazh 50000. Footnotes.

172. Fediuninskii I.I., General, Podniatye po trevoge **Summoned by combat alert**, Moscow, Voenizdat, 1964. 2nd ed. 248 pp. Tirazh 65000. Photographs, some footnotes.

173. Krasovskii S.A., Air Marshal, Zhizn' v aviatsii **Life in the Air force**, Moscow, Voenizdat, 1968. 376 pp. Tirazh 75000. Photographs.

174. Shtemenko S.M., Army General, General'nyi shtab v gody voiny **The General Staff during the war**, Moscow, Voenizdat, 1968. 416 pp. Tirazh 200000. Vol. II was published separately, 1973, 511 pp. Tirazh 400000. Re-issued 1981 Book I 480 pp. Book II 503 pp. Tirazh 100000. Photographs, maps, footnotes. English translation **The Soviet General Staff at War 1941-1945,** in two volumes. Moscow, Progress, 1985, 1986.

175. Batov P.I., General, V pokhodakh i boiakh **In campaigns and battles**, Moscow, Voenizdat, 1974. 528 pp. Tirazh 200000. Photographs, footnotes.

176. Katukov M.E., Marshal, Na ostrie glavnogo udara **At the spearhead of the main attack,** Moscow, Voenizdat, 1974. 429 pp. Tirazh 100000. Photographs, footnotes with some archival material. 2nd ed. 1976. Reprinted by Vysshaia Shkola in 1985. 432 pp. Tirazh 150000.

177. Panteleev Iu.A., Admiral, Polveka na flote **Half a century in the fleet,** Moscow, Voenizdat, 1974. 319 pp. Tirazh 100000. Photographs, some footnotes.

178. Poplavskii S.G., General, Tovarishchi v bor'be **Comrades in battle**, 2nd ed. Moscow, Voenizdat, 1974. 296 pp. Tirazh 100000. Photographs, some footnotes.

179. Iakubovskii I.I., Marshal, Zemlia v ogne **The earth in flames**, Moscow, Voenizdat, 1975. 567 pp. Tirazh 300000. Photographs, footnotes with archival material.

180. Chechneva M.P. Nebo ostaetsia nashim **The sky remains ours**, Moscow, Voenizdat, 1976. 2nd ed. 238 pp. Tirazh 100000. Photographs.

181. Lobanov M.M., Lt. General, My - voennye inzhenery **We -military engineers**, Moscow, Voenizdat, 1977. 223 pp. Tirazh 65000. On Soviet radar development. Photographs.

182. Golovko A.G., Admiral Vmeste s flotom **With the fleet,** 2nd ed., Moscow, Voenizdat, 1979. 285 pp. Tirazh 100000. Footnotes, photographs, appendix.

183. Rotmistrov P.A. Stal'naia gvardiia **The steel Guard**, Moscow, Voenizdat, 1984. 272 pp. Tirazh 100000. Footnotes with archival material, photographs. An unfinished work by the senior armoured warfare commander and expert, owing to his sudden death. A postscript has been added by Major General I. Krupchenko.

184. Vasilevskii A.M., Marshal, Delo vsei zhizni **A life's work**, 5th ed. Moscow, Voenizdat, 1984. 496 pp. Tirazh 150000. Footnotes with archival material, coloured maps, photographs.

185. Chuikov V.I., Marshal, Ot Stalingrada do Berlina **From Stalingrad to Berlin**, Moscow, Sovetskaia Rossiia, 1985. 704 pp. Tirazh 200000. Maps, footnotes with some archival material.

186. Rudenko S.I., Air Marshal, Kryl'ia pobedy **The wings of victory**, Moscow, Mezhdunarodnye otnosheniia, 1985. 2nd ed. 400 pp. Tirazh 150000. Footnotes with archival material. 1st ed. Voenizdat 1976.

187. Tributs V.F., Admiral, Baltiitsi srazhaiutsia **Men of the Baltic join battle**, Moscow, Voenizdat, 1985. 463 pp. Tirazh 150000. Photographs.

188. Bagramian I.Kh., Marshal, Tak shli my k pobede **Our road to victory**, Moscow, Voenizdat, 1988. 638 pp Tirazh 100000. In two parts. Footnotes with archival material, photographs, biographical sketch.

189. Ustinov D.F., Marshal, Vo imia pobedy. Zapiski narkoma vooruzheniia **In the name of victory. Notes of a People's Commissar for Armament**, Moscow, Voenizdat, 1988. 320 pp. Tirazh 150000. Photographs, footnotes with some archival material.

190. Kuznetsov N.G., Admiral of the Fleet, Kursom k pobede **On course to victory**, Moscow, Voenizdat, 1989. 495 pp. Tirazh 100000. Footnotes with archival material, photographs, list of fleet commanders.

191. Zakharov M.V., Marshal, General'nyi shtab v predvoennye gody **The General Staff during the pre-war period**, Moscow, Voenizdat, 1989. 318 pp. Tirazh

65000. Written in 1969, only published in 1989. Based on documents and personal recollections. Footnotes with archival material, photographs, 2 appendixes.

192. Ivanov S.P., General, <u>Shtab armeiskii, shtab frontovoi</u> **Army Staff, Front Staff,** Moscow, Voenizdat, 1990. 480 pp. Tirazh 50000. Footnotes with archival material, photographs.

193. Liashchenko N.G., General, <u>Vremia vybralo nas</u> **Events chose us,** Moscow, Voenizdat, 1990. Photographs, footnotes with archival material, maps.

194. Riabyshev D.I., Lt.General, <u>Pervyi god voiny</u> **The first year of war,** Moscow, Voenizdat, 1990. 255 pp. Tirazh 50000. Footnotes with archival material.

REFERENCE,
DICTIONARIES

REFERENCE

195. Sovetskaia voennaia entsiklopediia **Soviet military encyclopedia**, Moscow, Sovetskaia entsiklopediia, 1932. Vol. I 959 pp. Illustrations, tables, coloured maps, photographs. Vol II 925 pp. Published 1933. Subject index vols I and II, coloured photographs and maps, tables, illustrations.

196. Spravochnik dlia takticheskikh i operativnykh zaniatii starshego i vysshego nach-sostava RKKA Part IV Inostrannye armii sosednikh gosudarstv **Guide for the tactical and operational studies of the senior and higher command of the Red Army Part IV Foreign armies of neighbouring countries**, Moscow, Leningrad, Narkom, 1934. 103 pp. Tables, illustrations (no text).

197. Grechko A.A., Marshal, Ed., Vols. 1-2; Ogarkov N.V., Marshal, Ed., Vols. 3-8, Sovetskaia voennaia entsiklopediia **Soviet military encyclopedia**, Moscow, Voenizdat, Vol. 1 A-B, 1976, 640 pp., Vol. 2 V-G, 1976, 640 pp., Vol. 3 G-I, 1977, 672 pp. Vol. 4 K-L, 1977, 656 pp., Vol. 5 L-O, 1978, 688 pp., Vol. 6 O-R 1978, 671 pp., Vol. 7 R-T 1979, 687 pp. Vol. 8 T-Ia 1980, 687 pp. All vols. Tirazh 100000. Illustrations, photographs, coloured maps.

198. Klassifikator soderzhatl'nykh informatsionnykh potrebnostei po voenno-politiche-skoi informatsii **Classifier of the data requirements regarding military-political information**, Moscow, Lenin Military Politial Academy, 1979. Pt. I 146pp. Pt, II 24 pp.

199. Kir'ian M.M. Ed., Istoriia otechestvennoi voenno-entsiklopedicheskoi literatury **History of native Russian military-encyclopedic literature**, Moscow, Nauka, 1980. 174 pp. Tirazh 2150. Footnotes, bibliography.

200. Ogarkov N.V. Marshal, *et al* Ed., Voennyi entsiklopedicheskii slovar' **Military encyclopedic dictionary**, Moscow, Voenizdat, 1983. 863 pp. Tirazh 300000. Coloured illustrations and maps, photographs, chronology, list of maps, illustrations.

201. Kozlov M.M. General, *et al*, Ed., <u>Velikaia Otechestvennia voina 1941-1945:</u> <u>entsiklopediia</u> **The Great Patriotic War 1941-1945: Encyclopedia**, Moscow, Sovetskaia entsiklopediia, 1985. 832 pp. Tirazh 500000. Coloured maps and illustrations, photographs, tables.

202. Akhromeev S.F., Marshal, *et al*, Ed., <u>Voennyi entsiklopedicheskii slovar'</u> **Military encyclopedic dictionary**, Moscow, Voenizdat, 1986. 2nd edn. 863 pp. Tirazh 150000. Coloured illustrations and maps, photographs, chronology, list of maps.

203. Khromov S.S. *et al*, Ed., <u>Grazhdanskaia voina i voennaia interventsiia v SSSR:</u> <u>Entsiklopediia</u> **Civil war and military intervention in the USSR: Encyclopedia**, Moscow, Sovetskaia Entsiklopedia, 1987. 720 pp. Tirazh 100000. Coloured maps and illustrations, photographs, tables, bibliography.

204. Moiseev M.A., General, *et al*, Ed., <u>Sovetskaia voennaia entsiklopediia</u> **Soviet military encyclopedia**, Moscow, Voenizdat, 1990. In eight volumes. Vol. I 543 pp. Tirazh 100000. Coloured maps and illustrations, tables, photographs, list of illustrations. Revised edition of the Grechko/Ogarkov publication.

DICTIONARIES

205. <u>Kratkii slovar' operativno-takticheskikh i obshchevoennykh slov (terminov)</u> **Concise dictionary of operational-tactical and general military words (terms)**, Moscow, Voenizdat, 1958. 323 pp.

206. Sudzilovskii G.A. <u>Anglo-russkii slovar' po protivozdushnoi i protivoraketnoi</u> <u>oborone</u> **English-Russian dictionary of air defence and anti-missile defence**, Moscow, Voenizdat, 1961. 724 pp. Tirazh 8500. Ten appendixes of technical drawings.

207. Oleinik A.A. *et al*, <u>Slovar' osnovnykh voennykh terminov</u> **Dictionary of basic military terms**, Moscow, Voenizdat, 1965. 248 pp. Tirazh 27000. English language version published in the Soviet Military Thought series under the auspices of the United States Air Force, No. 9: <u>Dictionary of Basic Military Terms. A</u> <u>Soviet View</u> 256 pp. Index.

208. Skuibeda P.I. <u>Tolkovyi slovar' voennykh terminov</u> **Explanatory dictionary of military terms**, Moscow, Voenizdat, 1966. pp. 528. Tirazh 35000. Appendix of abbreviations.

209. Neliubin L.L. <u>Illiustrirovannyi voenno-tekhnicheskii slovar'. Russkii, angliiskii,</u> <u>nemetskii, frantsuzskii i ispanskii iazyki</u> **Illustrated military-technical dictionary. Russian, English, German, French and Spanish languages**, Moscow, Voenizdat, 1968. 484 pp. Tirazh 30000. Illustrations, index of names, subjects.

210. Sudzilovskii G.A. et.al. <u>Anglo-russkii voennyi slovar'</u> **English-Russian military dictionary**, 2nd edn. Moscow, Voenizdat, 1968. 1064 pp. Tirazh 19000. Fifty thousand words, index of co-ordinates, abbreviations.

211. Nadysev M.A. *et al*, Russko-angliiskii voenno-tekhnicheskii slovar'. Okolo 35000 terminov **Russian-English military-technical dictionary. Around 35000 terms**, Moscow, Voenizdat, 1975. 619 pp. Tirazh 18500.

212. Elagin N.M. Russko-angliiskii voenno-morskoi slovar'. Okolo 40000 terminov **Russian-English naval dictionary. About 40000 terms**, Moscow, Voenizdat, 1976. 782 pp. Tirazh 14500. Four appendixes.

213. Murashkevich A.M., Vladimirov O.N., Anglo-russkii slovar' sokrashchenii po aviatsionnoi i raketno-kosmicheskoi tekhnike: Okolo 30000 sokrashchenii **English-Russian aviation and space-rocket abbreviations dictionary: about 30000 abbreviations,** Moscow, Voenizdat, 1981. 621 pp. Tirazh 9000.

214. Neliubin L.L., Dormidontov A.A., Vasil'chenko A.A., Uchebnik voennogo perevoda. Angliiskii iazyk, Obshchii kurs **Text-book of military translating. English language. General course**, Moscow, Voenizdat, 1981. 444 pp. Tirazh 30000.

215. Favorov P.A. Anglo-russkii morskoi slovar' sokrashchenii: Okolo 22000 sokrashchenii **English-Russian naval dictionary of abbreviations, about 22000 abbreviations,** Moscow, Voenizdat, 1983. 632 pp. Tirazh 13000. For specialists, translators, lecturers.

216. Parparov L.F., Azarkh L.S., Nemetsko-russkii slovar' voennykh sokrashchenii. Okolo 15000 sokrashchenii **German-Russian dictionary of military abbreviations. Around 15000 abbreviations,** Moscow, Voenizdat, 1983. 320 pp. Tirazh 9500. For translators, military students.

217. Shevchuk V.N. Proizvodnye voennye terminy v angliiskom iazyke. Affiksalnoe slovoproizvodstvo **Coined military terms in the English language. Affix-coined words**, Moscow, Voenizdat, 1983. 231 pp. Tirazh 9000. Bibliography.

218. Novichkov N.N., Pimenov G.S. Anglo-russkii voennyi slovar' po radioelektronike, lazernoi i infrakrasnoi tekhnike: Okolo 30000 terminov **English-Russian dictionary of radioelectronics, laser and infrared engineering: Around 30000 terms,** Moscow, Voenizdat, 1984. 639 pp. Tirazh 10000. For military and civilian specialists, translators.

219. Pasechnik G.A. Anglo-Ruskii uchebnyi slovar' - minimum voennoi terminologii **English-Russian Dictionary - military terminology minimum**, Moscow, Voenizdat, 1986. 232 pp. Tirazh 25000.

220. Solov'ev V.I., Shitova T.Iu., Anglo-russkii slovar' po sviazi **English-Russian communications dictionary**, Moscow, Voenizdat, 1986. 800 pp. Tirazh 19000. Has 45000 terms, 3 appendixes.

221. Dmitrichev T.F., Ushomirsky M.Y., English-Russian dictionary on disarmament. About 12000 terms **Anglo-russkii terminologicheskii slovar' po voprosam razoruzheniia. Okolo 12000 terminov**, Moscow, Russky Yazyk Publishers, 1987. 377 pp. Bibliography, 6 appendixes.

222. Shevchuk V.N., Poliukhin V.M., Anglo-russkii voennyi slovar' v dvukh tomakh **English-Russian military dictionary in two volumes**, Moscow, Voenizdat, 1987. Vol. I 655 pp. Tirazh 20000. Vol.II 688 pp. Tirazh 20000. Appendixes. Both 70000 terms.

223. Zheltov L.M., Kniazev V.S., Anglo-russkii i russko-angliiskii slovar' po morskomu pravu **English-Russian and Russian-English Law of the Sea Dictionary,** Moscow, Voenizdat, 1988. 207 pp. Tirazh 10000. For naval officers, specialists. Three appendixes.

224. Novichkov N.N., Volkova A.N., Smirnova M.V., Anglo-russkii slovar' po protivoraketnoi i protivo-kosmicheskoi oborone: Okolo 25000 terminov **English Russian dictionary of antimissile and antisatellite defence. About 25000 terms**, Moscow, Voenizdat, 1989. 592 pp. Tirazh 10000. For translators of military and scientific-technical literature.

225. Plekhov A.M. Slovar' voennykh terminov **Dictionary of military terms**, Moscow, Voenizdat, 1989. 335 pp. Tirazh 65000. For instructors of recruits. 2800 frequently used terms.

226. Voroiskii F.S. *et al*, Anglo-russkii slovar' sokrashchenii po sviazi i radio-elektronike: Okolo 30000 sokrashchenii **Anglo-Russian dictionary of communications and radio-electronics abbreviations: Around 30000 abbreviations**, Moscow, Voenizdat, 1989. 680 pp. Tirazh 20000. Appendix.

227. Dmitrichev T.F. Russko-angliiskii terminologicheskii slovar' po voprosam razoruzheniia **Russian-English dictionary on disarmament terminology**, Moscow, Russkii iazyk, 1990. 560 pp. Tirazh 11000. Six appendixes.

BIBLIOTEKA OFITSERA

Three series of *Biblioteka komandira* published in the 1920s and 1930s preceded the post-1945 volumes in *Biblioteka ofitsera*. The latter are presented here in the three series (1957-62, 1965-73 and 1980-88).

SERIES 1957-1962

228. Engel's F. Izbrannye voennye proizvedeniia **Selected military works**, Moscow, Voenizdat, 1957. 844 pp.

229. Levanov I.N. Ed., Marksizm-Leninizm o voine i armii **Marxism-Leninism on war and the army**, Moscow, Voenizdat, 1957. 288 pp. Also 1958.

230. Lenin o voine, armii i voennoi nauke. Sbornik v 2-kh tomakh **V.I. Lenin on war, the army and military science. Two volume collection**, Tom I **Vol. I**, Moscow, Voenizdat, 1957. 616 pp. Tom II **Vol. II** Moscow, Voenizdat, 1958. 704 pp.

231. Kalinin M.I. O komunisticheskom i voennom vospitanii. Sbornik statei i rechei **On communist and military education. Collection of articles and speeches**, Moscow, Voenizdat, 1958. 622 pp.

232. Platonov S.P., Lt. General, Ed., Vtoraia mirovaia voina 1939-1945 gg. Voenno-istoricheskii ocherk **Second World War 1939-1945. Military-historical study**, Moscow, Voenizdat, 1958. 932 pp. Bibliography. Vol. II. Thirty-one coloured maps, index of main theatres of war events.

233. Nevskii N.A. Voenno-morskoi flot **The Navy**, Moscow, Voenizdat, 1959. 328 pp.

234. Glukhov M.K., Major General, Voenno-vozdushnye sily **Air forces**, Moscow, Voenizdat, 1959. 203 pp.

235. Demidov P.K. Ed., Voiska Protivovozdushnoi oborony strany **Air Defence Troops (PVO)**, Moscow, Voenizdat, 1960. 219 pp.

236. Egorov P.T. Reaktivnoe oruzhie **Rocket weapons** Moscow, Voenizdat, 1960. 224 pp. Illustrations, bibliography.

237. Listov K.M., Trofimov K.N. Radio i radiolokatsionnaia tekhnika i ikh primenenie **Radio and radar technology and their application**, Moscow, Voenizdat. 1960. 424 pp.

SERIES 1965-1973

238. Frunze M.V. Izbrannye proizvedeniia **Selected works**, Moscow, Voenizdat, 1965. 528 pp. Tirazh 27000.

239. Lenin V.I. O voine, armii i voennoi nauke **On war, the army and military science**, Moscow, Voenizdat, 1965. 836 pp. Tirazh 29000.

240. Radzievskii A.I., Col. General, Ed., Slovar' osnovnykh voennykh terminov **Dictionary of the basic military terms**, Moscow, Voenizdat, 1965. 248 pp. Tirazh 27000.

241. Semenov N.R. et al, Organizatsiia i vooruzhenie armii i flotov kapitalisticheskikh gosudarstv **Organisation and armament of the capitalist armies and fleets**, Moscow, Voenizdat, 1965. 548 pp. Tirazh 31000. Photographs of weapons and equipment, tables.

242. Sushkov N.Ia., Major General, Tiushkevich S.A., Ed., Marksizm-Leninizm o voine i armii **Marxism-Leninism on war and the army**, 4th edn., Moscow, Voenizdat, 1965. 384 pp. Tirazh 50000.

243. Barabanshchikov A.V. Ed., Voennaia pedagogika **Military pedagogy**, Moscow, Voenizdat, 1966. 375 pp. Tirazh 40000. Bibliography.

244. Pobezhimov I.F., Major General, et al Osnovy sovetskogo voennogo zakonodatel'stva **Basics of Soviet military law**, Moscow, Voenizdat, 1966. 432 pp. Tirazh 40000.

245. Reznichenko V.G., Major General, Ed., Taktika **Tactics**, Moscow, Voenizdat, 1966. 408 pp. Tirazh 40000. Subject index, bibliography, illustrations, tables.

246. Strokov A.A. Ed., Istoriia voennogo iskusstva **History of military art**, Moscow, Voenizdat, 1966. 656 pp. Tirazh 35000. Maps, illustrations.

247. D''iachenko M.I., Fedenko N.F., Ed., Voennaia psikhologiia **Military psychology**, Moscow, Voenizdat, 1967. 260 pp. Tirazh 50000. For commanders, political workers. Tables, photographs, bibliography.

248. Kalinin M.I., <u>O komunisticheskom vospitanii i voinskom dolge. Sbornik rechei, dokladov, statei</u> **On Communist education and military duty. Collection of speeches, reports, articles**, Moscow, Voenizdat, 1967.

249. Khmel' A.E. Ed., <u>Partiino-politicheskaia rabota v Sovetskikh Vooruzhennykh Silakh</u> **Party-political work in the Soviet Armed Forces**, Moscow, Voenizdat, 1968. 352 pp. Tirazh 65000.

250. Safronov I.V., Lt. General Rt. Ed., <u>Spravochnik ofitsera po voiskovomu khoziaistvu</u> **Officer's handbook on military management**, Moscow, Voenizdat, 1968. 272 pp. Tirazh 32000. Illustrations, tables.

251. Sokolovskii V.D., Marshal, <u>Voennaia strategiia</u> **Military strategy**, 3rd. edn. Moscow, Voenizdat, 1968. 464 pp. Tirazh 30000.

252. Kozlov S.N. Major General, *et al*, <u>Spravochnik ofitsera</u> **Officer's handbook**, Moscow, Voenizdat, 1971. 400 pp. Tirazh 83000.

253. Druzhinin V.V., Kontorov D.S., <u>Ideia, algoritm, reshenie. (Priniatie reshenii i avtomatizatsiia)</u> **Idea, algorithm, solution. (Decision making and automation)**, Moscow, Voenizdat, 1972. 328 pp. Tirazh 30000.

254. Lomov N.A., Colonel-General, Ed., <u>Nauchno-tekhnicheskii progress i revolutsiia v voennom dele</u> **Scientific-technical progress and the revolution in military affairs**, Moscow, Voenizdat, 1973. Tirazh 40000.

SERIES 1980-1988

255. Zhelatov A.S. Ed., <u>V.I. Lenin i Sovetskie Vooruzhennye Sily</u> **Lenin and the Soviet Armed Forces**, Moscow, Voenizdat, 1980. 3rd edn. 558 pp. Tirazh 75000.

256. Brezhnev L.I., Marshal, <u>Na strazhe mira i sotsializma</u> **Protecting peace and socialism**, Moscow, Politizdat, 1981. 815 pp. Tirazh 100000. Reprint of 1979 edn.

257. Savinkin N.I., Bogoliubov K.M., <u>KPSS o Vooruzhennykh Silakh Sovetskogo Soiuza: Dokumenty 1917-1981</u> **The Communist Party on the Soviet Armed Forces: Documents 1917-1981**, Moscow, Voenizdat, 1981. 622 pp. Tirazh 95000.

258. Bublik L.A. *et al*, <u>Partiino-politicheskaia rabota v Sovetskoi Armii i Voenno-Morskom Flote</u> **Party-political work in the Soviet Army and Navy**, Moscow, Voenizdat, 1982. 256 pp. Tirazh 100000.

259. Frunze M.V. <u>Izbranie proizvedeniia</u> **Selected works**, Moscow, Voenizdat, 1984. 559 pp. Tirazh 80000. Reprint of 1977 edn.

260. Reznichenko V.G. *et al*, <u>Taktika</u> **Tactics**, Moscow, Voenizdat, 1984. 271 pp. Tirazh 55000. 2nd edn. 1987.

261. Verbitskii A.D. <u>Armii stran Varshavskogo Dogovora: Spravochnik</u> **Warsaw Pact Armies: Handbook**, Moscow, Voenizdat, 1985. 223 pp. Tirazh 50000.

262. Zhilin P.A., Lt. General, Ed., <u>Istoriia voennogo iskusstva</u> **History of military art**, Moscow, Voenizdat, 1986. 446 pp. Tirazh 90000.

MILITARY MANUALS, FIELD REGULATIONS

Presented in chronological order.

263. Polevoi ustav RKKA Pt.I Manevrennaia voina **Red Army Field Manual Pt.I Manoeuvre war**, Moscow, Dated 22 Dec. 1918. 336 pp.

264. Vremennyi polevoi ustav RKKA Chast' II (diviziia i korpus) Shtab RKKA (Upravlenie po issledovaniiu i ispol'zovanniiu opyta voin) **Provisional Field Manuals of the Red Army. Part II (division and corps) Red Army Staff**, Moscow, Voennyi Vestnik, 1926. 391 pp. Five appendixes.

265. Rukovodstvo po boevoi podgotovke tankovykh chastei RKKA **Instruction for the combat training of Red Army tank units**, Moscow, Gosvoenizdat, 1930. 236 pp.

266. Vremennyi ustav vnutrennoi sluzhby RKKA (1924) **Provisional regulations of Red Army internal service (1924)**, Moscow, Voenizdat, 1931. 175 pp. Also NKO SSSR 1935.

267. Boevoi ustav mekhanizirovannykh voisk RKKA Pt. 2 Boevoe primenie tankov **Combat regulations of the Red Army mechanised forces Pt 2 Combat employment of tanks**, Moscow, Uprav. mekh. i motorizatsii RKKA, 1932. 175 pp.

268. Boevoi ustav RKKA **Combat regulations of the RKKA**, Pt.I 1928; Pt. II 1927; Moscow, Voenizdat, 1933.

269. Polevoi ustav RKKA (1929) PU-29 **Red Army Field Manual 1929**, Moscow, Voenizdat, 1933 (also 1934) 184 pp. Tirazh 50000. (Original PU 29 21 June 1929 RVS SSR Order No. 154).

270. Vremennoe nastavlenie po polevoi sluzhbe voiskovyikh shtabov, **Provisional manual for field service of troop staffs**, Moscow, Narkom/Red Army General Staff, 1935. 224 pp. Three appendixes.

271. Ivanov N. Kratkii takticheskii spravochnik **Short handbook on tactics**, Moscow, Gosvoenizdat. Narkom, 1936. 3rd edn. 212 pp. Tirazh 100000. Mostly tables, 14 appendixes.

272. Vremennyi polevoi ustav RKKA (PU 36) **Red Army provisional Field Service Regulations 1936**, Moscow, Narkom, 1937. 215 pp. Tirazh 90000.

273. Sluzhba obshchevoiskovykh shtabov v boiu. (Polk-diviziia) **The work of all-arms staffs in battle. (Regiment-division)**, Moscow, Frunze Academy, 1940. 368 pp.

274. Boevoi ustav pekhoty RKKA (BUP-38) **Red Army infantry combat regulations (BUP-38) Pt.I Soldier, platoon, section**, Moscow, Voenizdat, 1942. 167 pp. (Original 8.12.1938 NKO Order No. 254). Dated 8 June 1942.

275. Polevoi ustav RKKA. Proekt **Red Army Field Service Regulations. Draft**, Moscow, Voenizdat, 1944 and 1945. Each 399 pp.

276. Stroevoi Ustav Vooruzhennyikh Sil Soiuza SSR **Drill manual of the Armed Forces of the Soviet Union**, Moscow, Voenizdat, 1962. 176 pp. Six appendixes, illustrations. Voenizdat, 1970, 1972.

277. Ustav garnizonnoi i karaul'noi sluzhb Vooruzhennykh Sil SSSR **Regulations of garrison and sentry duties of the Soviet Armed Forces**, Moscow, Voenizdat, 1964. 240 pp. Also 1972, 1973.

278. Barabolia P.D. *et al*, Voenno-morskoi Mezhdunarodno-pravovoi spravochnik **Handbook of Naval International Maritime Law**, Moscow, Voenizdat, 1966. 500 pp. Tirazh 15000. Legal enactments and appendixes, bibliography.

279. Kalendar' voina 1968 **Soldier's diary 1968**, Moscow, Voenizdat, 1967. 240 pp. Tirazh 100000. First issue. Thereafter published annually.

280. Ustav vnutrennei sluzhby Vooruzhennykh Sil Soiuza SSR **Manual of unit administration of the Soviet Armed Forces**, Moscow, Voenizdat, 1967. 248 pp. Eighteen appendixes. Also Voenizdat, 1969, 1972, 1973.

281. Kushnirenko K.F. Kratkii spravochnik po goriuchemu, tekhnicheskim sredstvam i skladam **Short handbook on fuel, technical equipment and stores**, Moscow, Voenizdat, 1968. 272 pp. Tirazh 32000. Subject index, short bibliography, illustrations. Also 1973 (2nd ed.)

282. Nastavlenie po strelkovomu delu; 9-mm pistolet Makarova (PM) **Instruction on shooting; 9 mm Makarov pistol (PM)**, 4th ed. Moscow, Voenizdat, 1970. 104 pp. Tirazh 100000. Illustrations, appendix.

283. Odintsov A.I., Lt. General, Ed., Uchebnoe posobie po nachal'noi voennoi podgotovke **Handbook for pre-military training**, Moscow, Voenizdat, 1970. 336 pp. Tirazh 300000

284. Distsiplinarnyi ustav Vooruzhennyikh Sil Soiuza SSR **Discipline regulations of the Soviet Armed Forces**, Moscow, Voenizdat, 1971. 48 pp. Four appendixes. Also 1973

285. Borisov V.V. Abberviatsiia i akronimiia. Voennye i nauchno-tekhnicheskie sokrashcheniia v inostrannyikh iazykakh **Abbreviations and acronyms. Military and scientific-technical abbreviations in foreign languages**, Moscow, Voenizdat, 1972. 320 pp. Tirazh 10000.

286. Kamkov I.A., Konoplianik V.M., Voennye akademii i uchilishcha. Dlia tekh kto khochet v nikh uchit'sia. Spravki, sovety **Military academies and schools. For those who wish to study in them. Information, advice**, Moscow, Voenizdat, 1972. 312 pp. Tirazh 83000. Math, photographs, tables, 2 appendixes.

287. Dukachev M.P. Ed.,Obshchevoinskie ustavy Vooruzhennykh Sil SSSR. Ustav vnutrennei sluzhby. Distsiplinarnyi ustav. Ustav garnizonnoi i karaul'noi sluzhb. Stroevoi ustav **Troop regulations of the Soviet Armed Forces. Internal service. Discipline. Garrison and guard. Drill.** Moscow, Voenizdat, 1973. 480 pp. Repeat publications to 1986.

288. Odintsov A.I. Ed., Uchebnoe posobie po nachal'noi voennoi podgotovke **Text book on pre-military training**, Moscow, DOSAAF, 1975. 6th ed. 320 pp. Tirazh 900000. Illustrations, tables.

289. Govorukhin A.M. *et al*, Spravochnik po voennoi topografii **Handbook on military topography**, Moscow, Voenizdat, 1973. 264 pp. Tirazh 50000. For generals, officers. Illustrations, coloured maps, tables, photographs, math, appendixes. Also 1980, 352 pp. Tirazh 110000.

290. Poleznye sovety voinu **Useful advice for the soldier**, Moscow, Voenizdat, 1975. 416 pp. Tirazh 100000. 3rd ed. Illustrations, tables.

291. Spravochnik starshini i michmana VMF **Handbook for the Soviet Navy petty officer and warrant officer**, Moscow, Voenizdat, 1976. 255 pp. Tirazh 57000. Tables, illustrations, appendix, short bibliography, subject index.

292. Lebedev V.Ia. Spravochnik ofitsera nazemnoi artillerii **Handbook for surface-to-surface artillery officer**, Moscow, Voenizdat, 1977. 453 pp. Tirazh 32000. Illustrations, tables, math. Also 1984, 400 pp. Tirazh 30000. Subject index.

293. Spravochnik plovtsa-podvodnika **Handbook for frogmen**, Moscow, Voenizdat, 1977. 255 pp. Tirazh 100000. Tables, illustrations, math, subject index. 8 appendixes.

294. Spravochnik po strel'be beregovoi artillerii VMF **Handbook for Soviet Navy coastal artillery firing**, Moscow, Voenizdat, 1977. 351 pp. Tirazh 8000. Tables, illustrations 8 appendixes, bibliography, math, subject index.

295. V pomoshch' postupaiushchemu v vysshee voenno-politicheskoe uchilishche **An aid for the candidates of higher military-political schools**, Moscow, Voenizdat, 1977. 135 pp. Tirazh 30000. Short bibliography.

296. Spravochnik propagandista i agitatora armii i flota **Handbook for a propagandist and agitator of army and fleet**, Moscow, Voenizdat, 1978. 264 pp. Tirazh 90000. Tables. Also 1983.

297. Spravochnik voennogo stroitelia **Handbook of a military construction engineer**, Moscow, Voenizdat, 1978. 367 pp. Tirazh 30000. Tables, appendix, bibliography.

298. Abchuk V.A. *et al*, Spravochnik po issledovaniiu operatsii **Handbook on operations research**, Moscow, Voenizdat, 1979. 368 pp. Tirazh 26000. For officers. Math, tables, appendix, bibliography, subject index.

299. Gorshkov G.S., Melkov G.M., Predotvrashchenie zagriazneniia morskoi sredy. Spravochnik **Pollution prevention of sea ways**, Moscow, Voenizdat, 1979. 288 pp. Tirazh 16000. For command staff. Bibliography, subject index, tables, math.

300. Bukharov A.I. *et al*, Spravochnik voennogo elektrika: Elektro-snabzhenie voennykh ob''ektov **Handbook for military electrician: Electricity supply for military installations**, Moscow, Voenizdat, 1980. 351 pp. Tirazh 32000. Math, tables, illustrations, subject index, bibliography.

301. Soshnev V.G. Sputnik sekretaria armeiskoi partiinoi organizatsii. Konsul'tatsii po voprosam organizatsionno-partiinoi raboty v Sovetskoi armii i voenno-morskom flote **Companion for Party organization secretary of army. Advice regarding Party organization work in the Soviet army and navy**, Moscow, Voenizdat, 1980. 222 pp. Tirazh 65000. Also 1984, 223 pp. Tirazh 50000.

302. Anashkin I.N., Belokur M.N., Spravochnik serzhanta artillerii **Artillery sergeant's handbook**, Moscow, Voenizdat, 1981. 232 pp. Tirazh 20000. Illustrations, tables, appendix.

303. Mikhailovskii N.N. *et al*, Spravochnik po korabel'nym vspomagatel'nym mekhanizmam **Handbook on ship's auxiliary mechanisms**, Moscow, Voenizdat, 1981. 367 pp. Tirazh 20000. Math, tables, illustrations, subject index, bibliography.

304. Droblenkov V.F. *et al*, Spravochnik po teorii korablia **Handbook on ship theory**, Moscow, Voenizdat, 1984. 589 pp. Tirazh 18000. For command staff. Math, illustrations, appendix, bibliography, subject index.

305. Iakimov V.A. *et al*, Spravochnik po zhivuchesti korablia **Handbook on ship's combat survivability**, Moscow, Voenizdat, 1984. 398 pp. Tirazh 19000. Math, tables, illustrations, bibliography, 2 appendixes, subject index.

306. Obshchevoinskie ustavy Vooruzhennykh Sil SSSR. Ustav vnutrennei sluzby. Distsiplinarnyi ustav. Ustav garnizonnoi i karaul'noi sluzb. Stroevoi ustav **All arms regulations of the Soviet Armed Forces. Internal regulations. Disciplinary regulations. Regulations of the garrison and sentry duties. Drill regulations,** Moscow, Voenizdat, 1984. Also 1977, 1981.

307. Rumiantsev N.I. Spravochnik korabel'nogo inzhinera-mekhanika **Handbook for ship's engineer-mechanic,** Moscow, Voenizdat, 1984. 559 pp. Tirazh 23000. For command staff. Math, tables, illustrations, index of tables, 55 appendixes, bibliography.

308. Gorshkov G.S., Major General, *et al*, Mezhdunarodnoe morskoe pravo. Spravochnik **International maritime law. Handbook,** Moscow, Voenizdat, 1985. 430 pp. Tirazh 25000. For officers. Subject index, bibliography.

309. Pombrik I.D., Shevchenko N.A., Karta ofitsera **Officer's map,** Moscow, Voenizdat, 1985. 176 pp. Tirazh 150000. Illustrations, 2 appendixes.

310. Kamanin V.I. *et al*, Shturman flota. Spravochnik po korablevozhdeniiu **Fleet navigator. Handbook of ship navigation,** Moscow, Voenizdat, 1986. 539 pp. Tirazh 30000. For officers. Tables, math, illustratons, subject index, bibliography.

311. Merimskii V.A. Ed., Spravochnik serzhanta motostrelkovykh (tankovykh) voisk **Handbook for motor rifle (tank) troops sergeant,** Moscow, Voenizdat, 1987. 367 pp. Tirazh 55000. Illustrations, tables, subject index, appendix.

312. Zimin G.V. *et al*, Spravochnik ofitsera protivovozdushnoi oborony **Handbook for the air defence officer,** Moscow, Voenizdat, 1987. 512 pp. Tirazh 30000. Math, illustrations, tables, subject index.

313. Boevoi ustav sukhoputnykh voisk **Ground Forces Field Manual, Pt. III Platoon, Squad, Tank crew,** Moscow, Voenizdat, 1989. 320 pp. Tactical diagrams, 20 appendixes.

314. Red Army Combat Orders. Combat regulations for Tank and Mechanized Forces, 1944 Translated from Russian. Ed. R. Armstrong. London, Frank Cass, 1991. 163 pp.

PART TWO

REVOLUTION AND CIVIL WAR

DOCUMENTS

315. <u>Grazhdanskaia voina. Materialy po istorii Krasnoi Armii,</u> Kommissiia po issledovaniiu i ispol'zovaniiu opyta mirovoi i grazhdanskoi voiny, 1923. 509 pp. Tirazh
3000. Collection of material on history and formation of the Red Army. In three
parts: 1) The Red Guard; 2) The Old Army; 3) Formation of the Red Army; last
part contains pieces by Spil'nichenko, Pugachevski and Kovtiukh.

316. Kakurin N.E. <u>Razlozhenie armii v 1917 godu</u> **The disintegration of the army
in 1917**, Moscow, Leningrad, Gosizdat, 1925. 202 pp. Index to archives, maps.

Gaponenko L.S. Ed. <u>Velikaia Oktiabr'skaia sotsialisticheskaia revoliutsiia. Dokumenty i materialy. Revoliutsionnoe dvizhenie v Rossii posle sverzheniia samo-
derzhaviia</u> **The Great October socialist revolution. Documents and materials.
Revolutionary movement in Russia after the overthrow of autocracy**,
Moscow, Nauka, 1957. 857 pp. Tirazh 6500. See ch. 5 on the army and the
navy. Endnotes, index of names, places, documents, list of archival sources.

317. Golikov G.N. Ed., <u>Oktiabr'skoe vooruzhennoe vosstanie v Petrograde</u> **October
armed rising in Petrograd,** Moscow, Nauka, 1957. 1043pp. Tirazh 6500. One
thousand three hundred 87 documents, appendix containing endnotes, index of
names, places, businesses, factories, institutions, military units, list of sources,
documents. See under Armies, battalions, batteries, brigades, garrisons, divisions, corps, detachments, regiments, navy, fleets, naval ministry, Naval General Staff, ships.

318. Institut Marksizma-Leninizma <u>Dekrety Sovetskoi vlasti</u> **Soviet Government
decrees,** <u>Tom I 25 oktiabria 1917 g. - 16 marta 1918 g.</u> **Vol I. 25 October
1917-16 March 1918**, Moscow, Politizdat, 1957. 626 pp. Tirazh 30000. Two
appendixes, subject index, illustrations. This series continues at least as far as
<u>Tom XIII fevral' - mart 1921g.</u> **Vol. XIII February - March 1921**, Moscow,
Politizdat, 1989. 572 pp. Two appendixes, index of places, subjects, illustrations.

319. Oktiabr'skaia revoliutsiia v Latvii. Dokumenty i materiialy **October revolution in Latvia. Documents and data**, Riga, Nauka, 1957. 460 pp. Tirazh 1500. Threehundred 72 documents, 177 endnotes, index of places, list of documents, footnotes.

320. Shumeiko G.V. Ed. Boevoe sodruzhestvo trudiashchikhsia zarubezhnykh stran s narodami Sovetskoi Rossii, (1917- 1922) **Combat co-operation of the workers from foreign countries with the people of the Soviet Russia, (1917-1922),** Moscow, Sovetskaia Rossiia 1957, 573 pp. Tirazh 12000. Documentary materials, international units of the Red Army.

321. Tashliev Sh. Ed., Turkmenistan v period inostrannoi voennoi interventsii i grazhdanskoi voiny (1918-1920 gg.) Sbornik dokumentov **Turkmenistan during the period of foreign military intervention in the Civil War (1918-1920). Collection of documents,** Ashkhabad, Turkmengosizdat, 1957. 569 pp. Tirazh 5000. Illustrations, index of documents, army units, maps; chronology.

322. Tron'ko P.T. Ed., Bor'ba za vlast' Sovetov na Kievshchine (mart 1917-fevral'1918). Sbornik documentov i materiialov **Struggle for power of the Soviets in the Kievshchina (March 1917-February 1918). Collection of documents and data,** Kiev, Politizdat, 1957. 660 pp. Tirazh 5000. Index of organizations and institutions, of geographical names, enterprises, documents.

323. Gerasin F.V. Ed., Simbirskaia guberniia v gody grazhdanskoi voiny (mai 1918 g.-mart 1919 g.) Sbornik dokumentov Tom I **Simbirsk province during the Civil War (May 1918-March 1919) Collection of documents,** Ul'ianov, Ul'ianovskoe knizhnoe izdatel'stvo, 1958. 488 pp. Tirazh 3000. Endnotes, maps, photographs, index of names, places, subjects, all 290 documents.

324. Il'ina I. Ed., Bol'shevistskie voenno-revoliutsionnye komitety **Bolshevik military-revolutionary committees,** Moscow, Gospolitizdat, 1958. 567 pp. Tirazh 20000. List of all 730 documents.

325. Naida S.F. Ed., Iz istorii grazhdanskoi voiny v SSSR. Sbornik dokumentov i materialov v trekh tomakh **From the history of the Civil War in the USSR. Collection of documents and materials in three volumes,** Moscow, Sovetskaia Rossiia, 1960. Tom pervyi Mai 1918-mart 1919 **Vol. I May 1918-March 1919,** 831 pp. Tom vtoroi Mart 1919-fevral' 1920 **Vol. II March 1919-February 1920,** Moscow, 1961. 895 pp. Tom tretii Fevral' 1920-oktiabr' 1922 **Vol. III February 1920-October 1922,** Moscow, 1961, 875 pp. All vols. Tirazh 10000. Endnotes, index of archival sources.

326. Gorlenko A.F., Prokopenko N.R., Ed., Severnyi front. Bor'ba Sovetskogo naroda protiv inostrannoi interventsii i belogvardeishchiny na Sovetskom Severe (1918-1920) Dokumenty **The Northern Front. Fight of the Soviet people against the foreign intervention and the White guards in the Soviet North (1918-1920) Documents,** Moscow, Voenizdat, 1961. 296 pp. Tirazh 5000. Index of names, list of sources, 3 appendixes.

327. Partiino-politicheskaia rabota v Krasnoi Armii (aprel' 1918-fevral' 1919) Doku-
      menty. **Party-political work in the Red Army (April 1918 - February 1919)
      Documents.** Moscow, Voenizdat, 1961. 360 pp. Tirazh 9000. Endnotes, list of
      the archival sources.

328. Krastyn' Ia.P. *et al*, Ed., Latyshskie strelki v bor'be za Sovetskuiu vlast' v
      1917-1920 godakh; Vospominaniia i dokumenty. **Latvian riflemen in the fight
      for Soviet power in 1917-1920; Recollections and documents,** Riga, Izda-
      tel'stvo Akademii Nauk Latviiskoi SSR, 1962. 528 pp. Tirazh 1500. List of
      documents.

329. Tron'ko P.T. Ed., Kievshchina v gody grazhdanskoi voiny i inostrannoi voennoi
      interventsii (1918-1920) Sbornik dokumentov **Kievshchina during Civil War
      and foreign military intervention (1918-1920). Collection of documents,**
      Kiev, Politizdat 1962. 538 pp. Tirazh 5000. Endnotes; Chronology of events;
      index of places, names, organizations, businesses; list of sources: archives,
      newspapers, journals, documents, index of 510 documents.

330. Chugaev D.A., Ed., Protokoly i postanovleniia Tsentralnogo komiteta Baltiisko-
      go flota (1917-1918) **Minutes and decisions of the Central Committee of the
      Baltic Fleet (1917-1918),** Moscow, Leningrad, Nauka, 1963. 480 pp. Tirazh
      1400. Two hundred thirty-five documents, Baltic Fleet Central Committee
      constitution, 110 endnotes, index of names.

331. Inostrannaia voennaia interventsiia i grazhdanskaia voina v Srednei Azii i
      Kazakhstane Mai 1918 g-sentiabr' 1919g. **Foreign intervention and Civil War
      in Central Asia and Kazakhstan May 1918-September 1919,** Alma-Ata,
      Akad. Nauk Kazakhstan, 1963. Vol.I 702 pp. Tirazh 4500. Five hundred and
      forty six documents, 169 endnotes, footnotes, index of places, list archives,
      journals, Lenin, published documentary literature. Vol.II: Sentiabr' 1919-dek-
      abr' 1920 **September 1919-December 1920,** 1964, 724 pp. Tirazh 4240. Six
      hundred and twelve documents, maps, footnotes, 83 endnotes, index of places,
      list of archives, journals, published works.

332. Moriaki v bor'be za vlast' sovetov na Ukraine (noiabr' 1917-1920 gg) Sbornik
      dokumentov. **Sailors in the battle for Soviet rule in the Ukraine (November
      1917-1920) Collection of documents.**   Kiev, Izdatel'stvo Akademii nauk
      Ukrainskoi SSR, 1963. 686 pp. Tirazh 1000. Endnotes, index of names, places,
      list of ships, military units, of archives used in the book, of newspapers referred
      to in the volume.

333. Nikiforov P.M. Zapiski prem'era DVR. Pobeda leninskoi politiki v bor'be s
      interventsiei na Dal'nem Vostoke (1917-1922 gg) **Memoirs of the premier of
      the Far East Republic. Victory of leninist policy in the battle with the
      intervention in the Far East (1917-1922),** Moscow, Gospolitizdat, 1963. 287
      pp. Tirazh 23000. Footnotes with archival material.

334. Partiino-politicheskaia rabota v Krasnoi Armii (mart 1919-1920 gg.) Doku-
      menty. **Party-political work in the Red Army (March 1919-1920) Docu-**

ments. Moscow, Voenizdat, 1964. 536 pp. Tirazh 4500. End notes, list of archival sources.

335. Chugaev D.A. *et al*, Ed., Petrogradskii voenno-revoliutsionnyi komitet. Dokumenty i materialy V trekh tomakh, **Petrograd military revolutionary committee. Documents and materials.** In three volumes, Moscow, Nauka, Vol. I 1966. 583 pp. Photocopies, 1546 documents. Vol. II 1966. 558 pp. One thousand 392 documents. Vol. III 1967. 743 pp. Appendixes, 1529 documents, index of names, places, establishments. Tirazh all vols. 7200. See especially Richard Pipes, Kritika, Cambridge, Mass. spring 1968, Vol. IV, No. 3: 21-32.

336. Sidorov A.L., Ed., Revoliutsionnoe dvizhenie v armii i na flote v gody pervoi mirovoi voiny, 1914-fevral', 1917. Sbornik Dokumentov **Revolutionary Movement in the Army and the Fleet during the First World War, February 1914 -1917, Collection of Documents,** Moscow, Nauka, 1966. 468 pp. Tirazh 2000. Endnotes, list of legal definitions, index of names.

337. Bor'ba za pobedu Sovetskoi vlasti v Azerbaidzhane 1918-1920, Dokumenty i materialy **Battle for victory of the Soviet rule in Azerbaidzhan 1918-1920, Documents and   materials,** Baku, Izdatel'stvo Akademii Nauk Azerbaidzhanskoi SSR, 1967. 571 pp. Tirazh 1200. End notes, list of documents.

338. Korolivskii S.M. *et al*, Ed., Grazhdanskaia voina na Ukraine 1918-1920. Sbornik dokumentov i materialov v trekh tomakh, chetyrekh knigakh **Civil War in the Ukraine 1918-1920. Collection of documents and materials in three volumes, four books,** Tom pervii, kniga pervaia Osvoboditel'naia voina ukrainskogo naroda protiv nemetsko-avstriiskikh okkupantov. Razgrom burzhuazno-natsionalisticheskoi direktorii **Vol. I book 1 Liberation war of the Ukrainian people against the German-Austrian occupiers. Defeat of the bourgeois-nationalist directory,** 875 pp. Kniga 2 Bor'ba rabochikh i krest'ian za osvobozhdenie Ukrainy ot interventov Antanty i denikintsev Noiabr' 1918-aprel' 1919 **Book 2 Workers' and peasants' fight for the liberation of the Ukraine from the Antante intervenionists and Denikin's forces November 1918-April 1919** 491 pp. Tom vtoroi Bor'ba protiv denikinshchiny i petliurovshchiny na Ukraine Mai 1919 g.-fevral' 1920 g. **Vol. II Fight against the forces of Denikin and Petliura in the Ukraine May 1919-February 1920,** 918 pp. Tom tretii Krakh belopol'skoi interventsii. Razgrom ukrainskoi natsionalisticheskoi kontrrevoliutsii i belogvardeiskikh voisk Vrangelia mart-noiabr' 1920 g. **Vol. III Failure of Polish intervention. Destruction of the Ukrainian nationalist contra-revolution and Wrangel's White Guards troops March-November 1920,** 910 pp. All vols. Kiev, Naukova dumka, 1967. Tirazh 4500. Endnotes, index of names, places, army/navy units, documents.

339. Korolivskii S.M., Rubach M.A., Suprunenko N.I., Pobeda Sovetskoi vlasti na Ukraine **Victory of the Soviet government in the Ukraine,** Moscow, Nauka, 1967. 580 pp. Tirazh 7000. Chapter endnotes with archival material, index of names, places, list of illustrations, photographs.

340. Baltiiskie moriaki v bor'be za vlast' Sovetov. (noiabr' 1917-dekabr' 1918) **Baltic sailors in the fight for Soviet power (November 1917-December 1918),** Len-

ingrad, Nauka, 1968. 367 pp. Tirazh 4000. Three hundred 68 documents, 162 endnotes, footnotes, index of names, ships, units, list of archives, bibliography.

341. Gaponenko L.S. Ed., Revoliutsionnoe dvizhenie v Russkoi armii, 27 fevralia-24 oktiabra 1917 goda. Sbornik Dokumentov. **Revolutionary movement in the Russian Army, 27 February-24 October 1917. Collection of Documents.** Moscow, Nauka, 1968. 622 pp. Tirazh 1900. Endnotes, index of military units, index of names.

342. Vengerskie internatsionalisty v Oktiabr'skoi revoliutsii i grazhdanskoi voine v SSSR Sbornik dokumentov **Hungarian internationalists in the October revolution in USSR Collection of documents**, Moscow, Politizdat, 1968. Vol.I: 507 pp. Tirazh 5000. Index of names, of Hungarian revolutionary organizations, places, of documents by chapters, photographs, footnotes. Vol. II. 516 pp. Tirazh 5000. Bibliography by themes, index of documents.

343. Belov P.A. *et al*, Ed., Direktivi glavnogo komandovaniia Krasnoi Armii (1917-1920). **Directives of the Red Army High Command (1917-1920)**, Moscow, Voenizdat, 1969. 884 pp. Tirazh 10000. Seven hundred and fifty one documents.

344. Badalian Kh.A. Iz istorii inostrannoi interventsii v Armenii v 1918 g. Dokumenty i materialy **From the history of foreign intervention in Armenia in 1918. Documents and materials**, Erevan, Izd. Erevanskogo universiteta, 1970. 249 pp. Tirazh 5000. Turkish intervention.

345. Azarov A.I. Ed. *et al*, Bor'ba za Sovetskuiu vlast' v Belorussii. 1918-1920 gg Sbornik documentov i materialov v dvukh tomakh. Tom vtoroi (Fevral' 1918-1920g) **Battle for the Soviet power in Belorussia. 1918-1920. Collection of documents and data in two volumes. Vol. II (February 1919- 1920)**, Minsk, Belarus', 1971. 632 pp. Tirazh 4000. Endnotes, chronology, index of names, places, published documents, decrees.

346. Azovtsev N.N. *et al* Ed.Direktivy komandovaniia frontov Krasnoi Armii (1917-1922 gg.) Sbornik Dokumentov v 4-kh Tomakh. **Directives of the Red Army Front commands (1917-1922) Collection of documents in 4 volumes**, Tom I: Noiabr' 1917g.- Mart 1919g. **Volume I: November 1917-March 1919**, Moscow, Voenizdat, 1971. 788 pp. Tirazh 5200. Tom II: Mart 1919 g.- Aprel' 1920 g. **Volume II: March 1919-April 1920**, 1972, 804 pp. Tirazh 4500. Tom III: Aprel' 1920g.- 1922g. **Volume III: April 1920-1922**, 1974, 768 pp. Tirazh 4500. Tom IV: Materialy, ukazateli. **Data, Indexes**, 1978, 728 pp. Tirazh 4500.

347. Rybalki I.K. Ed. Khar'kovshchina v period grazhdanskoi voiny i inostrannoi voennoi interventsii 1918-1920 gg Sbornik dokumentov i materialov **"Kharkovshchina" during the Civil War and the foreign military intervention 1918-1920, Collection of documents**, Khar'kov, Prapor, 1973. 324 pp. Tirazh 3000. Endnotes.

348. Gaponenko L.S. Ed., Oktiabr'skaia Revoliutsia i armiia, 25 oktiabria 1917g.-mart 1918g. Sbornik dokumentov, **October Revolution and the Army, 25 Oc-**

tober 1917-March 1918. Collection of Documents, Moscow, Nauka, 1973. 456 pp. Tirazh 3500. Footnotes, endnotes, index of army units, names.

349.   Voenno-Morskoi revoliutsionnyi komitet. Sbornik dokumentov **Navy-revolutionary committee. Collection of documents,** Leningrad, Nauka, 1975. 296 pp. Tirazh 2700. Five hundred and 39 documents, 201 end notes, footnotes, list of ships, units, archives, bibliography.

350.   Vovk A.A. *et al* Ed., Chernigovshchina v gody grazhdanskoi voiny 1919-1920. Sbornik dokumentov i materialov **Chernigov (district) during the Civil War 1919-1920. Collection of documents and materials,** Kiev, Naukova dumka, 1975. 456 pp. Tirazh 4200. Based on archives, photographs, appendix, endnotes, index of names, places.

351.   Uchastie iugoslavskikh trudiashchikhsia v Oktiabr'skoi revoliutsii i grazhdanskoi voine v SSSR, **Participation of the Yugoslav workers in the October revolution and the Civil War in the USSR,** Moscow, Nauka, 1976, 555 pp. Tirazh 1200.

352.   Gavrilov L.M., Tishin I.G., Ed., Voenno-revoliutsionnye komitety deistvuiushchei armii. 25 oktiabria 1917 g.-mart 1918 g. **Military-revolutionary committees of the field army. 25 October 1917-March 1918,** Moscow, Nauka, 1977. 647 pp. Tirazh 2600. Collection of 606 documents. Endnotes, footnotes with archival material, appendix.

353.   Krastyn' Ia.P. *et al* Ed., Glavnokomanduiushchii vsemi Vooruzhennymi Silami respubliki I.I. Vatsietis. Sbornik dokumentov **Commander-in-Chief of all the Armed Forces of the republic I.I. Vatsietis. Collection of documents,** Riga, Zinatne, 1978. 364 pp. Tirazh 2000. Endnotes, footnotes with archival material, short bibliography, index of names, units, photographs.

354.   Voennye moriaki v bor'be za vlast Sovetov na severe, (1917 -1920 gg.) Sbornik dokumentov. **Navymen in the fight for Soviet power in the north (1917-1920). Collection of documents,** Leningrad, Nauka, 1982. 408 pp. Tirazh 4200. Four hundred and thirty four documents, 215 endnotes, index of names, ships, military units, list of archives, bibliography.

CIVIL WAR BIBLIOGRAPHY

355.   Gorodetskii E.N., Ed., Sovetskaia strana v period Grazhdanskoi voiny 1918-1920, bibliograficheskii ukazatel' dokumental'nykh publikatsii. **Soviet state during the Civil War 1918-1920, bibliographical index of published documents,** Moscow, Izdatel'stvo vsesoiuznoi knizhnoi palat, 1961. 496 pp. Tirazh 3000. See esp. Ch. VIII Bor'ba sovetskovo naroda s inostrannoi voennoi interventsiei i vnutrennei kontrrevoliutsiei. pp. 179 -254. Ch. IX   Stroitel'stvo Krasnoi Armii i Flota. pp. 255 - 285.

LENIN V.I.

356. Lenin V.I. <u>Voennaia perepiska (1917-1920).</u> **(Military correspondence)** Moscow, Voenizdat, 1956. 276 pp. Footnotes.

357. Grinishin D.M. <u>Voennaia deiatel'nost' V.I. Lenina</u> **Lenin's military work,** Moscow, Voenizdat, 1957. 363 pp. Footnotes with archival material.

358. Ignat'ev V., Ed. <u>Lenin i Krasnaia Armiia</u> **Lenin and the Red Army,** Moscow, Gospolitizdat, 1958. 88 pp. Articles written by participants in the October Revolution.

359. Vlasov I.I. <u>V.I. Lenin i stroitel'stvo Sovetskoi Armii</u> **Lenin and the creation of the Soviet Army,** Moscow, Voenizdat, 1958. 207 pp. Footnotes with archival material.

360. Danilevskii A.F. <u>V.I. Lenin i voprosy voennogo stroitel'stva na VIII sezde RKP(b),</u> **V.I. Lenin and problems of military development at the VIII congress of the Communist Party,** Moscow, Voenizdat, 1964. 96 pp. Tirazh 8700. Footnotes.

361. Tsvetkov V.G. <u>O voenno-teoreticheskom nasledenii V.I. Lenina</u> **Military-theoretical inheritance of Lenin,** Moscow, Voenizdat, 1964. 287 pp. Tirazh 20000. Footnotes with some archival material.

362. Lenin V.I <u>Voennaia perepiska 1917-1922gg</u> Moscow, Voenizdat, 1966. 453 pp. Tirazh 13000. Expansive end notes, subject index.

363. Lenin V.I. <u>Alfavitnyi ukazatel' proizvedenii, voshedshikh v polnoe sobranie sochinenii V.I. Lenina; Predmetnyi ukazatel' k novym proizvedeniiam V.I Lenina, vklyuchenym v polnoe sobranie sochinenii.</u> **Alphabetical index of works included in the complete works of Lenin; subject index of the new works of V.I. Lenin included in the complete works.** Moscow, Politizdat, 1966. 758 pp. Tirazh 100000. (See under Krasnaia Armiia; see also Vsevobuch and Kontrrevoliutsiia).

364. Iarovenko I.S. <u>Voenno-teoreticheskoe nasledie V.I. Lenina - v massy voinov. Metodicheskie i bibliograficheskie materialy</u> **Military-theoretical inheritance of Lenin in the military services. Bibliography and method,** Moscow, Voenizdat, 1969. 184 pp. Tirazh 35000. Illustrations, photographs.

365. Grinishin D.M. <u>O voennoi deiatel'nosti V.I. Lenina</u> **On Lenin's military work,** Kiev, Izdatel'stvo Kievskogo universiteta, 1970. 259 pp. Tirazh 21500. Footnotes, photographs, illustrations, bibliography, map.

366. Korablev Iu.I. <u>V.I. Lenin i sozdanie Krasnoi Armii</u> **V.I. Lenin and the creation of the Red Army,** Moscow, Nauka, 1970. 463 pp. Tirazh 11000. Footnotes with documentary and archival material. Index of names.

367. Novikov M.S., Lt. General, Ed., <u>V.I. Lenin i tyl Sovetskikh Vooruzhennykh Sil</u>
      Lenin and the Soviet Armed Forces Rear Services, Moscow, Voenizdat, 1970.
      106 pp. Tirazh 30000. Footnotes.

368. <u>Voennye voprosy v trudakh V.I. Lenina.</u> **Military issues in the works of
      Lenin.** Moscow, Voenizdat, 1972. 456 pp. Tirazh 20000. Documents from the
      collected works of Lenin. Alphabetical index of Lenin's speeches, telegrams,
      letters and other works used in this bibliographical volume.

369. Zverev B.I. <u>V.I. Lenin i flot, (1918-1920)</u> **V.I. Lenin and the fleet (1918-
      1920),** Moscow, Voenizdat, 1978. 296 pp. Tirazh 18000. Footnotes.

370. Moroz I.M., Col. General, Ed., <u>V.I.Lenin i Sovetskaia aviatsiia. Dokumenty,
      materialy, vospominaniia</u> **Lenin and Soviet aviation. Documents, materials,
      recollections,** Moscow, Voenizdat, 1979. 238 pp. Tirazh 15000. Illustrations, 8
      appendixes, footnotes.

371. Selianichev A.K. <u>V.I. Lenin i stanovlenie Sovetskogo voenno-morskogo flota</u>
      Lenin and the formation of the Soviet navy, Moscow, Nauka, 1979. 230 pp.
      Tirazh 5650. Footnotes with archival material, bibliography.

372. Azovtsev N.N. <u>V.I. Lenin i Sovetskaia voennaia nauka</u> **Lenin and Soviet mili-
      tary science,** Moscow, Nauka, 1981. 2nd edn. 351 pp. Tirazh 7100. Chapter
      endnotes with archival material, index of names.

TROTSKII L.

373. Trotskii L. <u>Kak vooruzhalas' revoliutsiia (na voennoi rabote) Materialy i
      dokumenty po istorii Krasnoi Armii v trekh tomakh</u> **How the revolution armed
      (on military work) Data and documents about the history of the Red Army
      in three volumes,** Moscow, Vysh. voennii redaktsionnyi sovet, 1923-25. Three
      volumes in 5 parts. Vol. I **The year 1918,** 1923, 431 pp. Tirazh 10000. Vol. II
      1919-1920, (1) 1924, 475 pp. Tirazh 15000. Maps. (2) 1924, 320 pp. Tirazh
      15000. Maps. Vol.III **1921-1923,** (1) 1924, 330. pp. Tirazh 15000. Maps. (2)
      1925, 343 pp. Tirazh 15000.

374. Majer J.M., Ed., <u>The Trotsky papers 1917-1922</u> London, The Hague, Mouton.
      Vol. I 1964; Vol. II 1971.

375. Trotsky L. <u>How the Revolution Armed</u> translation annotations by Brian Pearce,
      London, New Park Publishers, 1979-1981. Five vols. The military writings and
      speeches of Leon Trotsky. See above.

REVOLUTION AND CIVIL WAR 1917-1922

376. Gusev S.I. <u>Grazhdanskaia voina i Krasnaia Armiia. Sbornik voenno-teoretiche-
      skikh i voenno-politicheskikh statei (1918-1924 gg.)</u> **The Civil War and the
      Red Army. Collection of military-theoretical and military-political essays**

(1918-1924), Moscow, Gosizdat, 1925. See also Gusev S.I. Grazhdanskaia voina i Krasnaia Armiia **Civil War and the Red Army**, Moscow, Voenizdat, 1958. 224 pp. Photographs.

377. Alekseev S.A., Ed., Denikin, Iudenich, Vrangel **Denikin, Iudenich, Wrangel**, Moscow, Gosizdat, 1927. Also Revoliutsiia i grazhdanskaia voina v opisaniiakh belogvardeitsev. Denikin, Iudenich, Vrangel **Revolution and the Civil War in the writings of the White Guard. Denikin, Iudenich, Wrangel**, Moscow, Izdatel'stvo Otechestvo, 1991. 512 pp. Tirazh 100000. Illustrations.

378. Shatagin N.I. Organizatsiia i stroitel'stvo Sovetskoi Armii v period inostrannoi voennoi interventsii i grazhdanskoi voiny (1918-1920gg.) **Organization and development of the Soviet Army during the foreign military intervention and the Civil War (1918-1920)**, Moscow, Voenizdat, 1954. 248 pp. Footnotes with archival material.

379. Kapustin M.I. Soldaty Severnogo fronta v bor'be za vlast' sovetov **Soldiers of the Northern Front in the battle for Soviet government**, Moscow, Gospolitizdat, 1957. 320 pp. Tirazh 15000. Footnotes with archival material, photographs, maps.

380. Naida S.F. *et al*, Ed., Istoriia grazhdanskoi voiny v SSSR Tom tretii Uprochenie Sovetskoi vlasti. Nachalo inostrannoi voennoi interventsii i grazhdanskoi voiny. (noiabr' 1917-Mart 1919 g.) **History of the Civil War in the USSR Vol III Consolidation of Soviet power. Beginning of foreign military intervention and of the Civil War,** Moscow, Politizdat, 1957. 402 pp. Tirazh 40000. Coloured maps, photographs, endnotes, index of names. Dates of events. Tom chetvertyi Reshaiushchie pobedy Krasnoi Armii nad ob"edinennymi silami Antanty i vnutrennei kontrrevoliutsii. (mart 1919g.-fevral' 1920 g.) **Vol. IV Decisive victories of the Red Army against the united forces of the Entente and internal contra-revolution. (March 1919-February 1920)**, Moscow, Politizdat, 1959. 446 pp. Tirazh 40000. Coloured maps, photographs, dates of events, endnotes, index of names.

381. Papin L.M. Krakh kolchakovshchiny i obrazovanie Dal'nevostochnoi respubliki **Defeat of Kolchak's forces and formation of the Far-Eastern republic**, Moscow, Moskovskii Universitet, 1957. 224 pp. Tirazh 3000. Footnotes with archival material.

382. Kuz'min G.V. Grazhdanskaia voina i voennaia interventsiia v SSSR. Voenno-politicheskii ocherk **Civil War and military intervention in the USSR. Military-political study**, Moscow, Voenizdat, 1958. 360 pp. Maps, photographs, footnotes.

383. Naida S.F. O nekotorykh voprosakh istorii grazhdanskoi voiny v SSSR **Some historical questions of the Civil War in the USSR**, Moscow, Voenizdat, 1958. 244 pp. Footnotes with archival material.

384. Belan Iu. Ia. Otechestvennaia voina ukrainskogo naroda protiv nemetskikh okkupantov v 1918 godu **The Patriotic war of the Ukrainian people against the**

German occupation in 1918, Kiev, Izdatel'stvo Kievskogo Universiteta, 1960. 330 pp. Tirazh 5000. Footnotes with archival material, bibliography.

385. Kadishev A.B. Interventsiia i grazhdanskaia voina v Zakavkaz'e **Intervention and the Civil War in the TransCaucasus**, Moscow, Voenizdat, 1960. 510 pp. For officers. Footnotes with archival material, maps, photographs, index of names, places, bibliography.

386. Naida S.F., Kovalenko D.A., Ed., Reshaiushchie pobedy sovetskogo naroda nad interventami i belogvardeitsami v 1919 g. **The decisive victories of the Soviet people over the interventionists and the White Guard in 1919**, Moscow, Gospolitizdat, 1960. 661 pp. Tirazh 10000. Footnotes with archival material, maps.

387. Fridman V.G. et al, Ed., Gody ognevye, gody boevye. Sbornik vospominanii **Years of fire, years of combat. Collection of recollections**, Irkutsk, Irkutskoe knizhnoe izdatel'stvo, 1961. 303 pp. Tirazh 3000. Photographs, footnotes, index of names, places.

388. Glebov S.S. Pobeda sovetskoi vlasti v Iuzhnom Zaural'e **Victory of the Soviet power in the South Urals**, Kurgan, Sovetskoe Zaural'e, 1961. 147 pp. Tirazh 3000. Footnotes with archival material, illustrations, map.

389. Lyu Yun-An' Ed., Kitaiskie dobrovol'tsy v boiakh za Sovetskuiu vlast' (1918-1922 gg.) **Chinese volunteers in the battle for Soviet power (1918-1922)**, Moscow, Vostochnaia literatura, 1961. 180 pp. Tirazh 3200. Documents, photographs.

390. Shamagdiev Sh.A. Ocherki istorii grazhdanskoi voiny v Ferganskoi doline **Historical studies of the Civil War in the Fergana valley**, Tashkent, Akademiia Nauk Uzbekskoi SSR, 1961. 388 pp. Tirazh 1000. Footnotes with archival material, map, photographs, 22 pp. bibliography, 36 appendixes.

391. Strod I. V Taige, **In the taiga**, Iakutsk, Iakutskoe Knizhnoe Izdatel'stvo, 1961, 125 pp. Tirazh 5000.

392. Stishov M.I. Bol'shevistskoe podpol'e i partizanskoe dvizhenie v Sibiri v gody grazhdanskoi voiny, **The Bol'shevik underground and partisan movement in Siberia during the Civil War,** Moscow, Izd. Mosk. Univ. 1962, 420 pp. Tirazh 2750.

393. Irkaev M. Istoriia grazhdanskoi voiny v Tadzhikistane **History of the Civil War in Tadzhikistan**, Dushanbe, Tadzhik State University, 1963. 760 pp. Tirazh 1000. Footnotes with archival material, maps, photographs, 16 pp. bibliography.

394. Polikarpov V.D. Ed., Etapi bol'shogo puti, Vospominaniia o grazhdanskoi voine. **Phases of the great road, Recollections about the Civil War,** Moscow, Voenizdat, 1963. 528 pp. Tirazh 40000. Contains articles from 20 contributors: S.S. Kamenev, M.N. Tukhachevski, I.E Yakir, R.I. Berzin, V.N. Egor'ev, V.P Zatonskii, V.M. Primakov, A.S. Bubnov, I.I. Vatsetis, M.S. Kedrov, N.N. Kuz'min, R.P. Eideman, V. K. Putna, I.P. Belov, S.A. Mezheninov, E.I

Kovtyukh, V.K. Blyukher, A.I. Kork, G.D. Gai, P.E. Dybenko, covers wide range of topics. Provides additional notes on some of the individuals mentioned in the book.

395. Fraiman A.L. Revoliutsionnaia zashchita Petrograda v fevrale-marte 1918g. **Revolutionary defence of Petrograd in February-March 1918,** Moscow - Leningrad, Nauka, 1964. 324 pp. Tirazh 1300. Footnotes with substantial archival material. Index of names, places.

396. Gorodetskii E.N. Rozhdenie Sovetskogo gosudarstva (1917-1918 gg) **The birth of the Soviet state (1917-1918),** Moscow, Nauka, 1965. 531 pp. Tirazh 4000. Index.

397. Kliatskin S.M. Na zashchite Oktiabria, Organizatsiia reguliarnoi armii i militsionnoe stroiteli'stvo v Sovetskoi Respublike, 1917-1920 **In defence of October, Organization of the regular army and militia establishment in the Soviet Republic, 1917-1920,** Moscow, Nauka, 1965. 476 pp. Tirazh 5000. Based on archives; organizational charts of military administration; index of names.

398. Startsev V.I. Ocherki po istorii Petrogradskoi Krasnoi Gvardii i rabochei militsii (mart 1917 - aprel' 1918 g.) **Studies about the history of the Petrograd Red Guards and the workers' militia,** Moscow, Leningrad, Nauka, 1965, 312 pp. Tirazh 1500. Footnotes, appendixes.

399. Ochak I.D. Iugoslavianskie internatsionalisty v bor'be za pobedu sovetskoi vlasti v Rossii (1917-1921 gody) **Yugoslav internationalists in the fight for Soviet government victory in Russia (1917-1921),** Moscow, Izd. Moskovskogo universiteta, 1966. 338 pp. Tirazh 1500. Substantial archival footnotes, photographs, bibliography, index of names, places.

400. Petrash V.V. Moriaki Baltiiskogo Flota v bor'be za pobedu Oktiabria. **Sailors of the Baltic Fleet in the battle for victory of October (revolution),** Moscow, Leningrad, Nauka, 1966. 268 pp. Tirazh 2800. Footnotes with archival material.

401. Petrov F.N. *et al* Ed., Geroicheskie gody bor'by i pobed. (Dal'nii Vostok v ogne grazhdanskoi voiny) **The heroic years of battles and victories. (Far East in the blaze of the Civil War),** Moscow, Nauka, 1966. 390 pp. Tirazh 7000. Footnotes with archival material, photographs, bibliography, appendix.

402. Golub P.A. Oktiabr' na fronte. Vospominaniia **October at the front. Recollections,** Moscow, Voenizdat, 1967. 296 pp. Tirazh 40000. Photographs.

403. Iroshnikov M.P. Sovet narodnykh komissarov i narodnye komissariaty oktiabr' 1917 g. - ianvar' 1918 g. **Soviet of the people's commissars and people's commissariats October 1917 - January 1918,** Leningrad, Nauka, 1967. 1st edn. 298 pp. 2nd edn. 302 pp. Tirazh 4300.

404. Manusevich A.Ia. *et al,* Ed., Internatsionalisty. Trudiashchiesia zarubezhnykh stran - uchastniki bor'by za vlast' sovetov **The internationalists. Workers of**

the foreign countries -participants in the battle for Soviet power, Moscow, Nauka, 1967. 614 pp. Tirazh 3400. Footnotes with archival material, photographs, index of names.

405. Mints I.I. *et al*, Ed., Pobeda sovetskoi vlasti v Srednei Azii i Kazakhstane **Victory of the Soviet power in Central Asia and Kazakhstan**, Tashkent, Fan, 1967. 771 pp. Tirazh 5000. Footnotes with archival material, photographs, maps, index of names, places, bibliography.

406. Spreslis A.I. Latyshskie strelki na strazhe zavoevanii Oktiabria. 1917-1918 gg. **Latvian riflemen protect the gains of October. 1917-1918**, Riga, Zinatne, 1967. 243 pp. Tirazh 1500. Footnotes with archival material, photographs, maps, index of names, bibliography.

407. Pozhiakov K.I. Krasnyi tyl - frontu. Deiatel'nost' kommunisticheskoi partii po ukrepleniiu tyla Krasnoi Armii v period razgroma vrangelevshchiny (na materialakh Ukrainy) **The Red rear - for the front. Activities of the Communist Party in strengthening the rear of the Red Army at the time of Wrangel's defeat (based on Ukrainian material)**, Khar'kov, Izdatel'stvo Khar'kovskogo Universiteta, 1968. 218 pp. Tirazh 3000. Footnotes with archival material, illustrations.

408. Spirin L.M. Klassy i partii v grazhdanskoi voine v Rossii (1917-1920) **Classes and parties during the Civil War in Russia (1917-1920)**, Moscow, Mysl', 1968. 438 pp. Tirazh 5000. Footnotes with archival material, photographs, appendix.

409. Beskrovnyi L.G. *et al*, Ed., Bor'ba Bol'shevikov za armiiu v trekh revoliutsiiakh **Bolsheviks' battle for the army in the three revolutions** Moscow, Politizdat, 1969. 271 pp. Tirazh 20000. Bibliography.

410. Kovalenko D.A. Oboronnaia promyshlennost' Sovetskoi Rossii v 1918-1920 gg. **Defence industry in Soviet Russia during 1918-1920**, Moscow, Nauka, 1970. 416 pp. Tirazh 1800. Footnotes with documentary and archival material, index of names, places.

411. Mints I.I. Ed., Sverzhenie samoderzhaviia. Sbornik statei. **Overthrow of the autocracy. Collection of articles,** Moscow, Nauka, 1970. 328 pp. Tirazh 3700. (19 essays).

412. Khesin S.S. Oktiabr'skaia Revoliutsiia i flot. **October Revolution and the fleet,** Moscow, Nauka, 1971, 486 pp. Tirazh 2800. Index of names.

413. Poznanskii V.S. Sibirskii krasnyi general **Siberian Red general**, (Lt. General Baron A.A. von Taube) Novosibirsk, Nauka, 1972. 270 pp. Tirazh 21000. Footnotes with archival material, photographs, appendix, index of names.

414. Mel'chin A.I. Ed., Oktiabrskaia Revoliutsiia i grazhdanskaia voina v Severnoi Osetii **October Revolution and the Civil War in Northern Ossetia**, Ordzhonikidze, Ir, 1973. 299 pp. Tirazh 2000. Footnotes with archival material.

415. Shurygin A.P. *et al*, Ed., Grazhdanskaia voina na Dal'nem Vostoke (1918-1922) Vospominaniia veteranov **Civil War in the Far East (1918-1922) Recollections of veterans**, Moscow, Nauka, 1973. 351 pp. Tirazh 15300. Photographs, maps, some footnotes.

416. Iakushevskii A.S. Propagandistskaia rabota bol'shevikov sredi voisk interventov v 1918-1920 gg. **Propaganda work of the Bol'sheviks amongst the interventionist troops in the years 1918-1920**, Moscow, Nauka, 1974, 186 pp. Tirazh 3400.

417. Shershevskii B.M. V bitvakh za Dal'nii Vostok (1920-1922 gg.) **In the battles for the Far East (1920-1922)**, Novosibirsk, Nauka, 1974. 187 pp. Tirazh 4300. Substatial archival footnotes, photographs.

418. Andreev A.M. Soldatskie massy garnizonov russkoi armii v Oktiabr'skoi revoliutsii **The soldier masses in the Russian army garrisons during the October revolution**, Moscow, Nauka, 1975. 343 pp. Tirazh 3800. Footnotes with archival material, tables, appendix, index of names.

419. Iakupov N.M. Bor'ba za armiiu v 1917 godu (Deiatel'nost bol'shevikov v prifrontovykh okrugakh), **The struggle for the Army in the year 1917 (The activity of the Bol'sheviks in military districts in front line areas)**, Moscow, Mysl', 1975. 294 pp. Tirazh 6000.

420. Polikarpov, V.D. Prolog grazhdanskoi voiny v Rossii, oktiabr' 1917-fevral' 1918 **Prologue of the Civil War in Russia, October 1917-February 1918**, Moscow, Nauka, 1976. 416 pp. Tirazh 9000. Footnotes, maps, index of names.

421. Tokarev Iu.S. Petrogradskii sovet rabochikh i soldatskikh deputatov v marteaprele 1917. **Petrograd soviet of the workers' and soldiers' deputies in March-April 1917**, Leningrad, Nauka, Leningradskoe otdelenie, 1976. 208 pp. Tirazh 2200. Footnotes, with some archival material. Index of names.

422. Tsypkin G.A., Tsypkina R.G., Krasnaia gvardiia - udarnaia sila proletariata v Oktiabr'skoi revoliutsii **The Red Guard - striking power of the proletariat in the October revolution**, Moscow, Nauka, 1977. 376 pp. Tirazh 5650. Based on material from the Central industrial region of Urals and Povolozhe. Two appendixes.

423. Artem'ev S.A. Partiia bol'shevikov i Sovety rabochikh i soldatskikh deputatov v 1917 g. iiul'-oktiabr', **The Bolshevik Party and the Soviets of worker and soldier deputies in 1917 July - October,** Moscow, Izdatel'stvo Moskovskogo Universiteta, 1978. 213 pp. Tirazh 3300.

424. Batalov A.N. Bor'ba bol'shevikov za armiiu v Sibiri (1916-fevral'1918) **Battle of the Bolsheviks for the Army in Siberia**, Novosibirsk, Nauka, 1978. 284 pp. Tirazh 2500. Based on archives. Footnotes with archival material, photographs, index of names.

425. Kuz'mina T.F. Revoliutsionnoe dvizhenie soldatskikh mass tsentra Rossii naka-nune Oktiabria. (Po materialam Moskovskogo voennogo okruga) **Revolutionary movement of Central Russia soldiers on the eve of October. (Data from the Moscow Military District)** Moscow, Nauka, 1978, 312 pp. Tirazh 1900. Index of names.

426. Shishkin V.I. Revoliutsionnye komitety Sibiri v gody grazhdanskoi voiny (avgust 1919-mart 1921). **Revolutionary committees of Siberia in the Civil War (August 1919- March 1921),** Novosibirsk, Nauka, Sibirskoe Otdelenie, 1978. 336 pp. Tirazh 1500. Footnotes with archival material, index .

427. Zlokazov G.I. Petrogradskii Sovet na puti k Oktiabriu. **Petrograd Soviet on the road to the October revolution,** Moscow, Nauka, 1978. 344 pp. Tirazh 2550. Footnotes, some archival material.

428. Gizzatullin I.G. Zashchishchaia zavoevaniia Oktiabria. Tsentral'naia musul'man-skaia voennaia kollegiia 1918-1920 **Defending the gains of October. Moslem Central Military Collegium 1918-1920,** Moscow, Nauka, 1979. 159 pp. Tirazh 1950. Footnotes with archival material, index of names, bibliography.

429. Lipitskii S.V. Leninskoe rukovodstvo oboronoi strany. Sozdanie i deiatel'nost' vysshikh organov rukovodstva oboronoi Sovetskoi respubliki, 1917-1920 **Lenin's leadership in the defence of the country. Formation and activity of the higher organs of defence leadership in the Soviet republic, 1917-1920,** Moscow, Politizdat, 1979. 304 pp. Tirazh 50000. Footnotes with archival material.

430. Smol'nikov A.S. Bol'shevizatsiia XII armii Severnogo fronta v 1917 g. **The Bolshevisation of the Twelfth Army of the Northern Front in 1917,** Moscow, Izdatel'stvo Moskovskogo universiteta, 1979. 200 pp. Tirazh 970. Footnotes with archival material, photographs.

431. Azovtsev N.N. et al, Ed., Grazhdanskaia voina v SSSR, v dvukh tomakh. Tom pervyi Podavlenie vnutrennei kontrrevolutsii. Sryv otkrytoi interventsii mezh-dunarodnogo imperializma (oktiabr' 1917-mart 1919 g.) **Civil War in the USSR in two volumes. Vol. I Suppression of internal counter-revolution. Failure of intervention by international imperialism (October 1917-March 1919),** Moscow, Voenizdat, 1980. 368 pp. Tirazh 50000. Footnotes with some archival material, photographs, map, tables, chronology of events, index of names, places. Tom vtoroi Reshaiushchie pobedy Krasnoi Armii. Krakh imperialistiche-skoi interventsii (Mart 1919-oktiabr' 1922g.) **Vol. II Decisive victories of the Red Army. Collapse of imperialist intervention (March 1919-October 1922),** Moscow, Voenizdat, 1986. 447 pp. Tirazh 43000. Footnotes with archival material, photographs, tables, map, index of names, places, chronology of events.

432. Petrov V.I. Otrazhenie stranoi Sovetov nashestviia germanskogo imperializma v 1918 godu **Repulse of German imperialism's invasion by the Soviets in 1918,** Moscow, Nauka, 1980. 416 pp. Tirazh 3400. Footnotes with archival material, index of names.

433. Polikarpov V.D. Nachal'nyi etap grazhdanskoi voiny, (Istoriia izucheniia) **The initial phase of the Civil War, (History of the studies)**, Moscow, Nauka, 1980. 372 pp. Tirazh 2850. Footnotes, index of names. Photographs of Svechin, Tukhachevskii, Krylenko etc.

434. Khokhlov A.G. Krakh antisovetskogo banditisma v Belorussii v 1918-1925 godakh. **Break-up of anti-Soviet banditry in Belorussia in 1918-1925**, Minsk, Belarus', 1981. 176 pp. Tirazh 5000. Endnotes with archival material. LE 20 July 1994

435. Selianichev A.K. Flot pod krasnym flagom revoliutsii **Fleet under the red banner of the revolution**, Moscow, Prosveshchenie, 1983. 176 pp. Tirazh 20000.

436. Svatachev, M.I. Imperialisticheskaia interventsiia v Sibiri i na Dal'nem Vostoke, (1918-1922gg.) **Imperialist intervention in Siberia and the Far East, (1918-1922)**, Novosibirsk, Nauka, Sibirskoe otdelenie, 1983. 336 pp. Tirazh 1600. Endnotes with references from British, Japanese, USA publications. Also archival material.

437. Korablev Iu.I., Shishkin V.I. Ed., Iz istorii interventsii i grazhdanskoi voiny v Sibiri i na Dal'nem Vostoke 1917-1922 gg. **From the history of intervention and the Civil War in Siberia and the Far East 1917-1922**, Novosibirsk, Nauka, 1985. 232 pp. Tirazh 2900. Endnotes with archival material.

438. Portnov V.P., Slavin M.M., Pravovye osnovy stroitel'stva Krasnoi Armii 1918-1920 gg. Istoriko-iuridicheskoe issledovanie **Legal foundation of Red Army organisation 1918-1920. Historical juridical studies**, Moscow, Nauka, 1985, 289 pp. Tirazh 2600.

439. Sobolev G.L. Petrogradskii garnizon v bor'be za pobedu Oktiabria **Petrograd garrison in the battle for October (revolution) victory**, Leningrad, Nauka, 1985. 311 pp. Tirazh 1900. Endnotes (33pp.) with archival material, tables, index of names, military: units, institutions.

440. Kavtaradze A.G. Voennye spetsialisty na sluzhbe Respubliki Sovetov 1917-1920 gg. **Military specialists in the service of the Soviet Republic 1917-1920**, Moscow, Nauka, 1988. 280 pp. Tirazh 10000. Based on substantial archival material. Five appendixes, photographs, index of names.

441. Nenarokov, A.P. Ed., Revvoensovet Respubliki, 6 sentiabria 1918g./28 avgusta 1923g **Revolutionary Soviet of the Republic, 6 September 1918/28 August 1923**, Moscow, Izdatel'stvo politicheskoi literatury, 1991. 464 pp. Tirazh 15000. Compilation of articles about the 23 members of the first Revolutionary Military Soviet of the Republic: L.D. Trotskii, E.M. Sklyanski, I.I. Vatsetis, S.S. Kamenev, V.M. Al'tfater, V.A. Antonov-Ovseenko, D.I. Ralov, S.I. Gusev, K.Kh. Danishevskii, P.A. Kobozev, D.I. Kurskii, K.A. Mekhonoshin, V.I. Nevski, A.I. Okulov, N.I. Podvoiskii, F.F. Raskol'nikov, A.P. Rozengol'ts, A.I. Rykov, L.P. Serebyakov, I.T. Smilga, I.N. Smirnov, I.V. Stalin, K.K. Yurenev. Chronology of the activities of Revvoensovet.

CIVIL WAR MILITARY OPERATIONS

442. Anishev A. Ocherki istorii grazhdanskoi voiny 1917-1920 gg. **Historical studies of the Civil War 1917-1920**, Leningrad, Voenno-politcheskaia Akademiia Tolmacheva, 1925. 288 pp. Maps.

443. Podshivalov I. Grazhdanskaia voina na Urale 1917-1918 **Civil War in the Urals 1917-1918**, Moscow, Voennyi Vestnik, 1925. 221 pp.

444. Antonov-Ovseenko V.A. Zapiski o grazhdanskoi voiny. Tom vtoroi **Notes on the Civil War Vol. II**, Moscow-Leningrad, Vysh. Voen. Redak. Sovet, 1928. 297 pp. Tirazh 4000. Map supplement. Ukraine and Donbas operations 1918. Also Vol. I 1924 and Vol. III 1932. Vol. IV 1933. Moscow-Leningrad, Gosizdat/Gosvoen-izdat.

445. Bubnov A.S., Kamenev S.S., Eideman R.P., Ed., Grazhdanskaia voina 1918-1921 V tri tomakh **Civil War 1918-1921 In three volumes**, Tom 1 **Vol. I**, Boevaia zhizn' Krasnoi Armii **Combat life of the Red Army**, Moscow, Voennyi Vestnik, 1928. 374 pp. Tom 2, **Vol. II**, Voenno iskusstvo Krasnoi Armii **Military art of the Red Army**, 351 pp. Tom 3, **Vol. III**, Operativno-strategicheskii ocherk boevykh deistvii Krasnoi Armii **Operational-strategic study of the combat actions of the Red Army**, Moscow, Leningrad, Gosvoenizdat, 1930. 560 pp. Tirazh all vols. 10000.

446. Sapozhnikov V.I. Podvig baltiitsev v 1918 gody **Feat of the Baltic sailors in 1918**, Moscow, Voenizdat, 1954. 99 pp. Maps, footnotes with archival material, photographs.

447. Bogdanov A.V. Moriaki-Baltiitsy v 1917 g. **Baltic Sailors in the year 1917**, Moscow, Voenizdat, 1955. 242 pp.

448. Cherepanov A.I. Pod Pskovom i Narvoi. Fevral' 1918 g. **At Pskov and Narva. February 1918**, Moscow, Voenizdat, 1957. 140 pp. Footnotes with archival material, maps, photographs.

449. Spirin L.M. Razgrom armii Kolchaka **The defeat of Kolchak's army**, Moscow, Gospolitizdat, 1957. 296 pp. Tirazh 40000. Footnotes with archival material, photographs, maps, bibliography.

450. Kuz'min N.F. Krushenie poslednogo pokhoda Antanty **The defeat of the Entente's last campaign**, Moscow, Gospolitizdat, 1958. 344 pp. Tirazh 15000. Footnotes with archival material, photographs, maps.

451. Lipatov N.P. 1920 god na Chernom more. Voenno-morskie sily v razgrome Vrangela **The year of 1920 on the Black Sea. Naval forces during Wrangel's defeat**, Moscow, Voenizdat, 1958. 344 pp. Footnotes with archival material, photographs, maps, tables.

452. Tarasov V.V. Bor'ba s interventami na severe Rossii (1918-1920 gg.) **Battle with the interventionists in the north of Russia (1918-1920)**, Moscow, Go-

spolitizdat, 1958. 312 pp. Tirazh 10000. Footnotes with archival material, photographs, maps, tables, bibliography.

453. Shelestov D.K. Bor'ba za vlast' sovetov na Altae v 1917-1919 gg **Struggle for power of the Soviets in the Altai in 1917-1919,** Moscow, Izd. Mosk. Univ., 1959. 136 pp. Tirazh 3000. Footnotes.

454. Draudin T.Ia. Boevoi put' Latyshskoi strelkovoi divizii v dni Oktiabria i v gody grazhdanskoi voiny, (1917-1920). **Combat road of the Latvian Rifle Division in the days of the October revolution and the Civil War,** Riga, Izdatel'stvo Akademii Nauk Latviskoi SSR, 1960. 156 pp. Tirazh 3000. Endnotes.

455. Eikhe, G.Kh. Ufimskaia avantiura Kolchaka (mart-aprel' 1919 g.) **Kolchak's Ufim adventure (March-April 1919),** Moscow, Voenizdat, 1960. 296 pp. Footnotes, endnotes, with archival material. Thirteen maps. Orders of battle of the Eastern Front and 2nd and 3rd Armies.

456. Makeev P.V. Na Denikina! Rol' Latyshskikh strelkov v razgrome Denikinskikh polchishch **Fight Denikin! Role of the Latvian riflemen in the defeat of the Denikin horde,** Riga, Latviiskoe Gosudarstvennoe Izdatel'stvo, 1960. 120 pp. Tirazh 2000. Footnotes, photographs.

457. Agureev K.V. Razgrom Belogvardeiskikh voisk Denikina (Oktiabr' 1919-mart 1920 goda), **Defeat of Denikin's White Guard (October 1919-March 1920),** Moscow, Voenizdat, 1961. 224 pp. Tirazh 5000. Operational maps, footnotes with archival material, bibliography.

458. Antonov A.E. Boevoi vosemnadtsatyi god. (Voennyie deistviia Krasnoi Armii v 1918 - nachale 1919 g.) **1918, the year of combat. (Military actions of the Red Army in 1918 - beginning of 1919),** Moscow, Voenizdat, 1961. 262 pp. Tirazh 11500. Footnotes with archival material, photographs, maps.

459. Britov V.V. Rozhdenie Krasnoi Armii **The birth of the Red Army,** Moscow, Uchpedgiz, 1961. 280 pp. Tirazh 24000. Footnotes with archival material, illustrations, maps, photographs.

460. Kaimin' Ia. Latyshskie strelki v bor'be za pobedu Oktiabr'skoi revoliutsii 1917-1918 **Latvian riflemen in the fight for victory of the October revolution,** Riga, Latviiskoe gosudarstvennoe izdatel'stvo, 1961. 422 pp. Tirazh 3000. Footnotes with archival material, photographs, bibliography.

461. Morozov K.A. Onezhskaia Flotiliia v gody grazhdanskoi voiny i inostrannoi interventsii (1918-1920) **The Onega Flotilla during the Civil War and the international intervention (1918-1920),** Petrozavodsk, Gosudarstvennoe izdatel'stvo Karel'skoi ASSR, 1961. 128 pp. Tirazh 2000. Footnotes, photographs, maps.

462. Sukhorukov V.T. XI Armiia v boiakh na severnom Kavkaze i nizhnei Volge. (1918-1920 gg.) **XI Army in the battle in the North Caucasus and Lower Volga. (1918-1920).** Moscow, Voenizdat, 1961. 288 pp. Tirazh 9500. Maps,

photographs, footnotes with archival material, bibliography, list of archives, index of names, their commands and ranks.

463. Kesarev S.P., Korolev A.N., Pichugov S.G., Osobaia brigada (Istoricheskii ocherk) **Special brigade (Historical study)**, Moscow, Voenizdat, 1962. 243 pp. Tirazh 10500. Footnotes with archival material, maps, photographs, index of names.

464. Lipkina A.G. 1919 god v Sibiri (Bor'ba s kolchakovshchinoi) **1919 in Siberia (Struggle with Kolchak forces)**, Moscow, Voenizdat, 1962. 234 pp. Tirazh 9500. Footnotes with archival material, photographs, maps.

465. Mordvinov R.N. Kursom Avrory. Formirovanie Sovetskogo Voenno-morskogo Flota i nachalo ego boevoi deiatel'nosti (1917-1919) **Aurora's course. Formation of the Soviet Navy and the beginning of its combat actions (1917-1919)**, Moscow, Voenizdat, 1962. 398 pp.

466. Zharov F.I. Podvigi krasnykh letchikov **The feats of the Red pilots**, Moscow, Voenizdat, 1963. 120 pp. Tirazh 26000. Footnotes with archival material, photographs, bibliography.

467. Eikhe G.Kh. Oprokinutyi tyl, **The rear (was) overrun,** Moscow, Voenizdat, 1966, 384 pp. Tirazh 20000. Footnotes, endnotes, with archival material. Substantial statistical demographic information.

468. Gorlov V.P. Geroicheski pokhod (Voenno-istoricheskii ocherk o geroicheskom boevom puti Tamanskoi armii). **Heroic march (Military-historical study of the heroic combat road of the Taman Army),** Second edition, revised and enlarged. Moscow, Voenizdat, 1967. 240 pp. Tirazh 50000. Footnotes with archival material, maps, photographs.

469. Dushen'kin V.V, Vtoraia konnaia, voenno-istoricheskii ocherk **Second Cavalry (Army) military-historical study,** Moscow, Voenizdat, 1968. 216 pp. Tirazh 25000. Photographs, maps.

470. Nenarokov A.P. Vostochnyi front 1918 **Eastern Front 1918,** Moscow, Nauka, 1969. 280 pp. Tirazh 7300. Based on archives. Photographs, index of names, places.

471. Spirin L.M. Razgrom Kolchaka. Vospominaniia **The defeat of Kolchak. Recollections,** Moscow, Voenizdat, 1969. 296 pp. Tirazh 50000. Photographs, footnotes.

472. Tairian I. XI Krasnaia Armiia v bor'be za ustanovlenie i uprochenie Sovetskoi vlasti v Armenii **XI Red Army in the struggle for establishment and consolidation of Soviet power in Armenia,** Erevan, Izdatel'stvo Aiastan, 1971. 320 pp. Tirazh 4000.

473. Krastynia Ia.P. Ed., Istoriia Latyshskikh strelkov (1915-1920) **The history of the Latvian riflemen (1915-1920),** Riga, Zinatne, 1972. 618 pp. Tirazh 10000.

Endnotes, bibliography with archival material, maps, photographs, index of names.

474. Azovtsev N.N. Krakh pervogo nashestviia imperialistov na Stranu Sovetov **The collapse of the first invasion of the imperialists of Soviet Lands**, Moscow, Voenizdat, 1973. 440 pp. Tirazh 30000. Recommended text military: personnel, students. Footnotes with archival material, maps, photographs.

475. Selivanov P.A. Voennoe stroitel'stvo v Belorussii v period razgroma pokhodov Antanty **Military structure in Belorussia during the rout of the Entente offensives**, Minsk, Izdatel'stvo Nauka i tekhnika, 1973. 208 pp. Tirazh 1400. Footnotes.

476. Pospelov P.N. Ed., Krakh kontrrevoliutsionnoi avantiury. Vospominaniia **Defeat of the counter-revolutionary adventure. Recollections**, Leningrad, Lenizdat, 1978. 288 pp. Tirazh 15000. Kronstadt mutiny. Photographs, 2 appendixes.

477. Akhmiranova-Kulish A.S., Zul'pukarov Z.G. Pomoshch' Krasnoi Armii v sotsialisticheskom stroitel'stve v Azerbaidzhane **Red Army assistance in the creation of socialist Azerbaidzhan**, Moscow, Nauka, 1981. 184 pp. Tirazh 1650. Footnotes with archival material, index of names, bibliography.

478. Mints I.I. Boevoe sodruzhestvo sovetskikh respublik 1919-1922 gg. **Combat cooperation of the Soviet republics 1919-1922**, Moscow, Nauka, 1982. 248 pp. Tirazh 3800. Footnotes with archival material.

479. Denikin A.I., Lt. General, Pokhod na Moskvu (Ocherki russkoi smuty) **March on Moscow (Studies in Russian time of troubles)** Moscow, Voenizdat, 1989. 288 pp. Tirazh 50000.

SOVIET-POLISH WAR: 1920

480. Egorov A. Marshal, L'vov-Varshava 1920 god. Vzaimodeistvie frontov **Lwów-Warsaw in 1920. Co-ordination of front**, Moscow, Leningrad, Gosizdat Otdel voennoi literatury, 1929. 198 pp. Tirazh 3000. Documentary appendix.

481. Kakurin N.E., Melikov V.A. Voina s belopoliakami 1920 g. So skhemami i prilozheniiami **War with the White Poles 1920. With illustrations and appendixes**, Moscow, Gosvoenizdat, 1925. 527 pp. Tirazh 5000.

482. Pilsudskii protiv Tukhachevskogo: Sbornik **Pilsudski against Tukhachevskii: Collection**, Moscow, Voenizdat, 1991. 254 pp. Tirazh 12000.

MILITARY REFORM, DOCTRINE, OPERATIONS, 1922–1940

FRUNZE AND MILITARY REFORM 1922-1928

483. Kulchak M. Novaia organizatsiia mestnogo voennogo upravleniia **New organization of local military administration**, Moscow, Gosizdat, 1926. 192 pp. Introduction by M.N. Tukhachevskii.

484. Pil'niak B. Povest nepogashennoi luny **Tale of an unextinguished moon**, Moscow, Novyi Mir, 1926. Reprinted, Russian text, Ubiistvo komandarma **Murder of an army commander**, B. Pil'nyak. London, Flegon Press, 1965. 48 pp. See also *Gibel' Narkoma Frunze*, Krasnaia Zvezda, 23 October 1993.

485. Frunze M.V. Sobranie sochinenii **Collected works**, Ed. A.S. Bubnov, Moscow-Leningrad, Gosizdat, 1926-29. Vol. I 1905-1923 gody **1905-1923**, 1926. 692 pp. Photographs. Vol. II 1924 god **1924**, 1926. 323 pp. Photographs. Vol. III 1925 god **1925**, 1927. 402 pp.

486. Frunze M.V. Izbrannye proizvedeniia **Selected works**, Moscow, Partizdat, 1934. 598 pp. Maps, photographs.

487. Frunze M.V. Izbrannye proizvedeniia **Selected works**, Moscow, Voenizdat, 1951. 584 pp. Endnotes.

488. Frunze M.V. Izbrannye proizvedeniia **Selected works**, Moscow, Voenizdat, 1957. Tom I **Vol. I** 472 pp. Endnotes. Index of documents. Tom II **Vol. II** 500 pp. Endnotes.

489. Berkhin I.B. Voennaia reforma v SSSR, (1924-1925) **Military reform in the USSR, (1924-1925)**, Moscow, Voenizdat, 1958. 460 pp. Footnotes, archival study.

490. Frunze M.V. Izbrannye proizvedeniia **Selected works**, Moscow, Voenizdat, 1965. 528 pp. Tirazh 27000. Details of Frunze's family and career. Endnotes. Appears in series Biblioteka Ofitsera.

491. Mikhail Vasil'evich Frunze 1885-1925 Bibliograficheskii ukazatel' **Mikhail Vasilevich Frunze 1885-1925. Bibliographical index,** Kishinev, Izdateljstvo Karta Moldoveniaske, 1974. 216 pp. Tirazh 2000. List of authors, editors compilers translators, reviewers, mentioned in the book. Cites Ia. G. Zimin article in Voenno-istoricheski Zhurnal: *"M.V. Frunze o reorganizatsii Krasnoi Armii v 1924 godu".* Unpublished papers.

492. Frunze M.V. Izbrannye proizvedeniia **Selected works,** Moscow, Voenizdat, 1977. 480 pp. Tirazh 65000. Apendix on Frunze's family details and his career. Subject index.

493. Gareev M.A. M.V. Frunze - Voennyi teoretik. Vzgliady M.V. Frunze i sovremennaia voennaia teoriia **M.V. Frunze - Military theoretician. Frunze's views and contemporary military theory.** Moscow, Voenizdat, 1985. 448 pp. Tirazh 50000. Subject index, maps, footnotes.

MILITARY DOCTRINE

494. Osipov K. Shto takoe okhranenie i kak ego neset pekhota. 'Biblioteka pekhotnitsa' **What is protection and how does the infantry carry it out,** Moscow, Polit. uprav. RVSR, 1920 23 pp.

495. Tukhachevskii M.N., Marshal, Strategiia natsional'naia i klassovaia. Lektsiia chitannaia v Akademii Krasnogo General'ogo shtaba RKKA 24 dek. 1919 g. **National and class strategy. Lecture given at the Academy of the Red General Staff 24.12.1919,** Rostov-on-Don, Izd. otdel shtab. Kavkaz. fronta, 1920. 19 pp.

496. Tukhachevskii M.N., Marshal, Voina klassov. Stat'ei 1919-1920 **Class war. Articles 1919-1920,** Otdel voen. lit. pri RVSR. Gosizdat, 1921. (signed by Tukhachevskii, Smolensk 21 Jan. 1921) 140 pp.

497. Tukhachevskii M.N., Marshal, Ed., Budushchaia voina **Future war,** Moscow, IV Directorate Red Army Staff, 1928. 735 pp. Tirazh 80. Pt. I Predislovie. Obschaia obstanovka **Introduction. General situation,** Pt. II Liudskie resursy i ikh ispol'zovanie **Manpower resources and their utilisation,** Pt.III Ekonomicheskie faktory **Economic factors,** Pt. IVa Tekhnicheskie faktory **Technical factors,** Pt. IVb Tekhnicheskie faktory **Technical factors,** Pt. V Politicheskie faktory **Political factors,** Operativnye i organizatsionnye problemy **Operational and organizational problems.**

498. Tukhachevskii M.N., Marshal, Voina kak problema vooruzhennoi bor'by **War as a problem of armed struggle,** reprint of Bol'shaia Sovetskaia Entsiklopediia 1928, vol. 12, col. 576-598.

499. Tukhachevskii M.N., Marshal, O strategicheskikh vzgliadakh prof. Svechina: Protiv reaktsionnykh teorii na voenno-nauchnoi fronte **Professor Svechin's views on strategy: Against the reactionary theories on the military-scientific front,** Moscow, Gosvoenizdat, 1931. See pp. 3-16.

500. Tukhachevskii M.N., Marshal, Novye voprosy voiny. Pt. I Vooruzhennye sily i ikh ispol'zovanie **New questions on war. Pt. I Armed forces and their utilisation**, Moscow, unpublished manuscript, 1932. 227 pp.

501. Tukhachevskii M.N., Marshal, Voennye plany nyneshnei Germanii **Military plans of the present day Germany**, Leningrad, Lenoblizdat, 1935. 20 pp.

502. Tukhachevskii M.N., Marshal, Izbrannye proizvedeniia **Selected works.** In 2 vols. Moscow, Voenizdat, 1964. Vol. I 320 pp. Vol. II 264 pp. Tirazh 12500. Vol. I covers period of 1919-1927. Vol. II covers period of 1928-1937; list of Tukhachevskii's publications, (122 items). pp 260 263.

503. Batovskii M. Podgotovka plana voiny i operatsii **Preparation of the war plan and operations plans,** Voen-ucheb. zaved. Zapadnyi front (Smolensk) 1921. 76 pp.

504. Berngardi F. O voine budushchego **On future war**, Moscow, Gosudarstvennoe izdatel'stvo, 1921. 171 pp. Translation from German. English version: General von Bernhardi The War of the Future. In the light of the lessons of the World War, London, Hutchison, 1920. 272 pp.

505. Smilga I. Ocherednye voprosy stroitel'stva Krasnoi Armii. 1) Militsionnaia sistema 2) PUR i Glavpolitprosvet **Immediate questions regarding the establishment of the Red Army. 1) Militia System 2) PUR (Political Administration of REVVOENSOVET) and Main Political Education,** Moscow, Gosudarstvennoe izdatel'stvo, 1921. 30 pp.

506. Vatsetis I.I. O voennoi doktrine budushchego **On the military doctrine of the future,** Moscow, Gosizdat, 1923. 146 pp. Tirazh 4000. "Future" features, chemical warfare, women in war.

507. Zaionchkovskii A.M. Lektsii po strategii ...chitannye v Voennoi Akademii RKKA v 1922-1923 gg. Pts. 1, 155 pp. and 2, 102 pp. **Lectures on strategy delivered at the Red Army Academy 1922-1923**, Moscow, VAF, 1923. Tirazh 800. Diagrams, 12 maps.

508. Svechin A. Ed., Strategiia v trudakh voennykh klassikov Lloid, Napoleon, Medem, Vilzen, Leval', Verdi-diu Vernua, Fon-der-Gol'ts, Fosh, Shlifen **Strategy in the works of military classic writers Lloyd, Medem, Wilson, Leval, Verdi de Vernua, Von der Goltz, Foch, Schlieffen**, Vol.I Moscow, Vysshii Voennyi Redaktsionnyi Sovet, 1924. 367 pp. Tirazh 5000. Footnotes, index of names.

509. Svechin A. Strategiia **Strategy.** Moscow, Voennyi Vestnik, 1927. 263 pp.

510. Svecin A. Strategija Beograd, Vojno Delo, 1956. In the series Vojna Biblioteka Inostrani pisci. 440 pp. Tirazh 3000.

511. Svechin Aleksandr A. Strategy Minneapolis, East View Publications, 1992. 374 pp. Introductory essays by Andrei A. Kokoshin, Valentin Larionov, Vladimir N. Lobov, Jacob W. Kipp. Index.

512. Verkhovskii A.I. Istoricheskie primery k kursu obshchei taktiki **Historical examples for the course in general tactics**, Moscow, Vysshii voennyi redaktsionnyi sovet, 1924. 90 pp. List of publications of same publisher at the back.

513. Lebedev P.P. Gosudarstvennaia oborona **State defence**, Moscow, Gosvoenizdat, 1925. 47 pp. Tirazh 6000.

514. Sergeev P. Tekhnika voenno-nauchnoi raboty **Technique and technology in military scientific work**, Moscow, Voennyi Vestnik, 1925. 68 pp. Bibliography.

515. Unshlikht, Ipat'ev, Baranov, Zof, Budennyi, Voina budushchego **Future war**, Moscow, Voenizdat, 1925. 72 pp. Stenographic report from RVS SSSR.

516. Vedenie operatsii. Rabota komandovaniia i polevogo upravleniia **The conduct of operations. The work of the command and the field administration**, Moscow, Biblioteka Tolmacheva, 1925. (Typescript) Papers from N. Varfolomev, N. Sapozhnikov, A. Verkhovskii, Lapchinskii et al.

517. Baranovskii V.G. Spravochnaia knizhka po taktike **Handbook on tactics**, Moscow, Voenizdat, 1926. 822 pp. Tables, 115 illustrations. (Last chapter: on war games).

518. Bushe A. Osnovy podgotovki velikoi voiny **Preparation for large scale war**, Moscow, Izdanie Narkomvoenmor i RVS SSSR, 1927. 119 pp. Tirazh 3000. Maps.

519. Kapustin N. Operativnoe iskusstvo v pozitsionnoi voine **Operational art in positional war**, Moscow, Leningrad, Gosizdat Otdel. voen. lit., 1927. 290 pp.

520. Lebedev P. Boevaia podgotovka v territorial'nykh voiskakh **Combat training in the territorial forces**, Moscow, Voennyi Vestnik, 1927. 69 pp.

521. Shaposhnikov B.M., Marshal, Mozg armii **The Brain of the Army**, Moscow, Voennyi Vestnik, 1927. Vol. I 259 pp. Tirazh 5000. Vol. II Gosizdat, Otdel Voen. lit. Moscow-Leningrad, 1929. 262 pp. Tirazh 4000. Vol. III Gosizdat, 1929. 377 pp. Tirazh 4000.

522. Verkhovskii A.I. Obshchaia taktika. Posobie dlia voennykh shkol i komsostava **General tactics. Handbook for military schools and officers**, Moscow, Voennyi Vestnik, 1927. 3rd edn. 400 pp. Tirazh 15000. Illustrations.

523. Baranovskii V.G. Boevye deistviia voisk. Obshchaia taktika **Troop combat action. General tactics**, Leningrad, Voenizdat, 1928. 162 pp. Illustrations.

524. Lapchinskii A. Krasnyi vozdushnyi flot 1918-1928 **The Red Air Fleet 1918-1928**, Moscow, Voennyi Vestnik, 1928. 48 pp.

525. Oborona SSSR i Krasnoi Armii. Katalog knig **Defence of the USSR and the Red Army. Catalogue of books**, Moscow, Leningrad, Gosizdat, 1928. 242pp.

526. Uborevich I. Podgotovka komsostava RKKA **Preparation of Red Army command staff**, Moscow, Leningrad, Otdel voen. lit., 1928. 180 pp. (Nauchno-ustavnyi otdel Shtaba RKKA)

527. Slashcher Ia. Mysli po voprosam obshchei taktiki. Iz lichnogo opyta i nabliudenii **Thoughts on the problems of general tactics. From personal experience and observation**, Moscow, Leningrad, Voen. lit. Gosizdat, 1929. 100 pp. Tirazh 5000.

528. Aleksandrov A.P. Kritika teorii vladeniia morem **Critique of the theory of command of the sea**, Leningrad, Voenno-morskaia akademiia, 1930. 80 pp. Tirazh 350.

529. Belitskii S.M. Strategicheskie rezervy **Strategic reserves**, Moscow, Gosizdat, 1930. 298 pp.

530. *Komakad.* Sektsiia po izucheniiu problemy voiny. Zapiski. Tom pervyi. Communist Academy. Section for studying the problems of war. **Notes.** Vol. I. Moscow, Komakad, 1930. 232 pp. Contributors: Tukhachevskii, Bubnov, Belitskii, Gorev, Geronimus, Zhbikovskii, Iasinskii, Dombrovskii, Varga, Bocharov. Bibliography.

531. Golubev A. Ed., M.V. Frunze o kharaktere budushchei voiny **M.V. Frunze on the character of the future war**, Moscow, Voenizdat, 1931. 126 pp.

532. Volkov V. Boevaia sluzhba legkikh tankov **Combat employment of light tanks**, Moscow, Leningrad, Gosvoenizdat, 1931. 94 pp. Tirazh 20000.

533. Krasil'nikov S.N. Organizatsiia krupnykh obshchevoiskovykh soedinenii. Proshedshee, nastoiashchee i budushchee **Organization of large all-arms formations. Past, present and future**, Moscow, Gosvoenizdat, 1933. 315 pp. Tirazh 5150. Bibliography, 126 diagrams, tables.

534. Voenno-bibliograficheskii biulleten' **Military-bibliographical bulletin**, Moscow, Biblioteka Lenina, 1933. 74 pp. Tirazh 300.

535. Gromychenko A. Ocherki taktiki tankovykh chastei **Studies in tactics of tank units**, Moscow, Voenizdat, 1935. 320 pp.

536. Smirnov S.A. Taktika. Uchebnik dlia voennykh shkol RKKA. Kurs obshchii **Tactics. Textbook for Red Army military schools. General course**, Moscow, Voenizdat, 1935. 3rd edn. 232 pp.

537. Tsiffer R. Taktika pekhoty. Upravlenie strelkovym i pulemetnym vzvodami. Uchebnik dlia pekhotnikh shkol RKKA **Infantry tactics. The control of rifle and machine-gun sections. Text book for infantry schools in the Red Army**, Moscow, Voenizdat, 1935. 184 pp.

538. Voenno-inzhenernaia akademiia Odnostoronnaia komandnaia voennaia igra. Vstrechnyi boi SK na perepravakh **One party war game. Meeting engagement of Rifle Corps in assault river crossing**, Moscow, Voenno-inzhenernaia akademiia RKKA, 1935. 12 pp. Tirazh 116. Table. Far Eastern Theatre.

539. Alekin B., Bykov P. Morskaia taktika. Uchebnik dlia Voenno-morskogo uchilishche im. M.V. Frunze **Naval tactics. Textbook for Frunze Naval School**, Moscow, Gosvoenizdat, 1936. 208 pp. Tirazh 10000.

540. Due Dzh. (Douhet Giulio) Gospodstvo v vozdukhe **The command of the air**, original Il dominio del l'aria, 1921. Moscow, Ogiz, series "*Biblioteka komandira*", 1936. 608 pp. Foreword V.V. Khripin.

541. Kirei V. Artilleriia ataki i oborony. Vyvody iz primeneniia artillerii na russkom fronte v 1914-1917 gg. **Artillery in the attack and defence. Conclusions from the use of artillery on the Russian front 1914-1917**, Moscow, Gosvoenizdat, 1936. 2nd edn. 134 pp. Fourteen diagrams, tables appended, index.

542. Triandafillov V.K. Kharakter operatsii sovremennykh armii **The Nature of the Operations of Modern Armies**, Moscow, Gosudarstvennoe voennoe izd. Narkomata, 1936. 259 pp. Tables, illustrations, author's bibliography. English translation by W.A. Burhans, edited by Jacob W. Kipp, Frank Cass, London, 1994. 234 pp.

543. Butyrskii V.S., Ed., Boi pulemetnoi roty **Machine-gun company in battle**, Kiev, Gosvoenizdat, 1937. 110 pp.

544. Figner N. Boevaia rabota artilleriiskogo samoleta **Combat task of artillery spotter aircraft**, Moscow, Gosvoenizdat, 1937. 46pp. plus 6 appendixes.

545. Nikolaev A.B. Batal'onnaia artilleriia **Battalion artillery**, Moscow, Gosvoenizdat, 1937. 2nd edn. 235 pp. Tables.

546. Melikov V.A. Strategicheskoe razvertyvanie (Po opytu pervoi imperialisticheskoi voiny 1914-1918 gg. i Grazhdanskoi voiny v SSSR) Tom I Pervaia imperialisticheskaia voina 1914-1918 **Strategic deployment (According to the experience of the First Imperialist War 1914-1918 and the Civil War of the USSR) Vol.I First Imperialist War 1914-1918**, 2nd edn. Moscow, Voenizdat, 1939. 527 pp. Footnotes, tables, maps, illustrations. Supplement of 21 maps. Original edition published by Frunze Academy 1935, 617 pp. Tirazh 3000, bibliography.

547. Nikiforov N.N., Sobolevskii A.V., Smirnov V.A., Uchebnik mladshego komandira artillerii **Text book for the junior artillery commander**, Bk.1 Moscow, Voenizdat, 1940. 254 pp. Two appendixes. Bk. 2 Voenizdat NKO, 1941. 304 pp. Appendixes including Morse code.

548. Teplinskii B.L. Osnovy obshchei taktiki voennykh vozdushnykh sil. Tekhnika i taktika vidov aviatsii **The basics of general tactics in the air forces. Technology and tactics of branches of aviation**, Moscow, Gosvoenizdat, 1940. 208 pp.

549. Sbornik form boevykh dokumentov Pt. I Formy prikazov i prikazanii **Collection of pro-formas of military documents. Pt. I Forms of orders and commands**, Moscow, Voenizdat, 1941. 247 pp. Tables, coloured maps, illustrations, appendix.

550. Talenskii N.A. Boevye deistviia pekhotnoi divizii. Sbornik istoricheskikh primerov **Combat actions of an infantry division. Collection of historical examples**, Moscow, Voenizdat, 1941. 274 pp. Illustrations, tables, maps.

551. Ivlev A.A. Ed., Sovetskoe voennoe iskusstvo (Strategiia, operativnoe iskusstvo, taktika) Bibliograficheskii ukazatel' literatury za 1936-1944 gg. **Soviet military art (Strategy, operational art, tactics) Bibliographical guide to the 1936-1944 literature**, Moscow, Frunze Academy, 1956. 386 pp. Index of names, bibliography.

552. Kamenev S.S. Zapiski o grazhdanskoi voine i voennom stroitel'stve, Izbrannye stat'i **Notes about the Civil War and military development, Selected essays**, Moscow, Voenizdat, 1963. 264 pp. Tirazh 35000. List of Kamenev's other works.

553. Shaposhnikov B.M., Marshal, Vospominaniia. Voenno-nauchnye trudy **Recollections. Military-scientific works**, 1st edn. Moscow, Voenizdat, 1974. 574 pp. Tirazh 50000. 2nd edn. 1982. 560 pp. Tirazh 100000.

MILITARY OPERATIONS

554. Kak my bili Iaponskikh samuraev. Sbornik statei i dokumentov **How we defeated Japanese samurais. Collection of articles and documents**, Moscow, Molodaia Gvardiia, 1938.

555. Boevye epizody. Sbornik statei i materialov o sobytiiakh u ozero Khasan **Battle episodes. Collection of articles and materials about the events at the Lake Khasan**, Moscow, Gos. Voen. Izdat. Narkom, 1939.

556. Kuz'min N.F. Na strazhe mirnogo truda (1921-1940 gg) **Protecting peaceful labour (1921-1940)**, Moscow, Voenizdat, 1959. 294 pp. Footnotes, tables, photographs. Album of 15 maps.

557. Dzhenchuraev D. Po sledam basmachei **On the trail of the Basmachis**, Frunze, Kirgizskoe Gosudarstvennoe izdatel'stvo, 1964. 2nd edn. 207 pp. Tirazh 75000.

558. Voronov N.N. *et al*, Ed., Pod znamenem Ispanskoi Respubliki. 1936-39. Vospominaniia **Under the flags of Spanish Republic 1936-39. Recollections**, Moscow, Nauka, 1965. 576 pp. Tirazh 20000. Footnotes, photographs, illustrations, coloured map.

559. Kazanin M.I. V shtabe Bliukhera. Vospominaniia o Kitaiskoi revoliutsii 1925-1927 godov **On Bliukher's Staff. Recollections about the Chinese Revolution during 1925-1927**, Moscow, Nauka, 1966. 168 pp. Tirazh 30000.

560. Kuznetsov N.G. Na dalekom meridiane. Vospominaniia uchastnika natsional'no-revoliutsionnoi voiny v Ispanii **On the far meridian. Recollections of participants in the national-revolutionary war in Spain**, Moscow, Nauka, 1966. 264 pp. Tirazh 16000. Photographs, footnotes, map, index of names.

561. Zyrianov P.I. Ed., Pogranichnye voiska SSSR 1929-1938. Sbornik dokumentov i materialov **USSR Frontier troops 1929-1938. Collection of documents and materials**, Moscow, Nauka, 1972. 775 pp. Tirazh 20000. Photographs, endnotes, list of 748 documents.

562. Forpost Geroev. Geroicheskie povestvovaniia o podvigakh dal'nevostochnikov **The outpost of heroes. Tales of heroic deeds of the Far Eastern veterans**, Khabarovsk, Khabarovsk knizhnoe izdatel'stvo, 1973. 736 pp. Tirazh 25000. Memoirs of Far Eastern commanders and the creation of ODVA (Special Far Eastern Army); conflict with the Chinese Eastern railway.

563. Cherepanov A.I. Zapiski voennogo sovetnika v Kitae. **Memoirs of a military adviser in China**, Moscow, Glavnaia redaktsiia vostochnoi literatury, 1976. 648 pp. Tirazh 30000. Maps of military operations.

564. Blagodatov A.V. Zapiski o kitaiskoi revoliutsii 1925-1927 gg. **Notes about the Chinese revolution 1925-1927**, Moscow, Nauka, 1979. 304 pp. Tirazh 15000. Photographs, footnotes, maps. Endnotes with composition of Chiang Kai-Shek's Army, Chinese military activists, and Soviet military advisers.

565. Chudodeev Iu.V. Ed., V nebe Kitaia. 1937-1940. Vospominaniia sovetskikh letchikov-dobrovol'tsev **In China skies. 1937-1940. Recollections of Soviet volunteer pilots**, Moscow, Nauka, 1980. 381 pp. Tirazh 30000. Photographs, index of names.

566. Zhilin P.A., Ed., Pobeda na reke Khalkhin-Gol **Victory on the river Khalkin-Gol**, Moscow, Nauka, 1981. 144 pp. Tirazh 23000. Footnotes with archival material, 10 appendixes, bibliography.

567. Forpost na Vostoke: Literaturno-khudozhestvennyi i istoriko-publitsisticheskii sbornik. **Outpost in the East: Literary-belles-lettres and historical-journalistic collection**, Irkutsk, Vostochno-Sibirsko knizhnoe izdatel'stvo, 1985. 512 pp. Tirazh 40000. Some documents, biographies of Far Eastern commanders.

568. Krasnoznamennyi Dal'nevostochnyi: Istoriia Krasnoznamennogo Dal'nevostochnogo voennogo okruga. **Far Eastern Red Banner: History of the Red Army Far Eastern Military District**, Moscow, Voenizdat, 1985. 352 pp. Tirazh 50000. Photographs, maps, footnotes with archival material, list of the most important events.

569. Semiryaga, M.I. The Winter War. Looking Back After Fifty Years **Zimniaia voina. Vzgliad 50 let spustia**, Moscow, Novosti, 1990. 64 pp. Soviet-Finnish war.

570. Dvoinykh L.V., Eliseeva N.E., Konflikt. Komplekt dokumentov o Sovetsko-finliandskoi voine (1939-1940 gg.) **Conflict. A set of documents on the Soviet-Finnish War (1939-1940)**, Minneapolis, East View Publications, 1992. 173 pp. Eleven maps, 171 documents.

THE GREAT
PATRIOTIC WAR,
1941–1945

BIBLIOGRAPHIES

571. Izuchai vraga. Ukazatel' literatury **Study the enemy. Bibliography**, Moscow, Vsesoiuznaia knizhnaia palata, 1942. 79pp. Tirazh 3500. Index of literature concerning strategy and operational-tactical manuals of the German Army from 1914-1918 war to the Second World War, with special attention given to the preparations of operations against the USSR.

572. Korobkov N.M. Geroicheskii Sevastopol' 1854-1855 gg. 1941-1942 gg. Ukazatel' literatury **Heroic Sevastopol 1854 - 1855 1941-1942. Bibliography**, Moscow, Vsesoiuznaia knizhnaia palata, 1942. 47 pp. Tirazh 30000. Divided into 2 parts: first contains books and journals concerned with 1854-1855 period; second lists newspapers' articles, reports from Sevastopol front, and articles from journals during 1941-1942.

573. Miasnikov M.A. Major General, Ed., Pekhota. Istoria, organizatsiia, vooruzhenie i taktika. Ukazatel' literatury, **Infantry. History, organization, armament and tactics Bibliography**, Moscow, Vsesoiuznaia knizhnaia palata, 1942. 83 pp. Tirazh 3500. Register of the most significant books, articles from journals and newspapers, about infantry printed in Russian since 1937 up to and including 1942.

574. Miasnikov M.A. Major General, Voiska sviazi. Ukazatel' literatury **Signals troops. Bibliography,** Moscow, Vsesoiuznaia knizhnaia palata, 1942. pp. 32. Tirazh 30000.

575. Paikin Ia. Ed., Osobennosti i kharakter Velikoi Otechestvennoi voiny. Ukazatel' literatury, **Singularities and character of the Great Patriotic War. Bibliography,** Moscow, Vsesoiuznaia knizhnaia palata, 1942. 52 pp. Tirazh 30000. Index of books, articles, remarks, speeches published in Russian from June 23, 1941 to September 1, 1942.

576. Petrukhin I.S. Marksizm-Leninizm o voinakh i zashchite sotsialisticheskogo otechestva. Ukazatel' literatury **Marxism-Leninism about wars and the defence of the socialist fatherland. Bibliography**, Moscow, Vsesoiuznaia knizhnaia palata, 1942. 71 pp. Survey of literature about types of war, and working class and Communist Party's attitude to them; also index of basic literature dealing with Soviet people's patriotic wars.

577. Safr B.G., Ed., Velikaia Otechestvennaia voina Sovetskogo naroda. Ukazatel' literatury **The Great Patriotic War of the Soviet people. Bibliography.** Moscow, Vsesoiuznaia knizhnaia palata, 1942. 327 pp. Tirazh 30000. Index of Soviet books and articles which appeared in journals, from 23 June 1941 to 1 June 1942, newspaper articles from 23 June till 1 April 1942.

578. Vostokova M.P., Kaufman I.M., Geroicheskii Leningrad. Kratkii annotirovannyi spisok literatury **Heroic Leningrad. Short annotated list of literature**, Moscow, Lenin library, 1943. pp. 40. Tirazh 1500.

579. Olishev V.G. Ed., Velikaia Otechestvennia voina. Ukazatel' literaturi za iiul' - sentiabr' 1942 goda **The Great Patriotic War. Bibliography for July - September 1942.** Moscow, Lenin library, 1943. pp. 81. Tirazh 20000. Covers books and articles from journals and newspapers from July to September 1942. Includes bibliography concerning other "freedom loving" nations.

580. Tolkachev N.T. Voenno-inzhenernoe delo. Ukazatel' literatury **Military-engineering soldiering. Bibliography,** Moscow, Vsesoiuznaia knizhnaia palata, 1943. pp. 83. For commanders of engineer troops. Covers period from 1937, with the greatest emphasis on the Great Patriotic War.

581. Timofeev A.S. Voenno-morskoi flot. Ukazatel' literatury **The Navy. Bibliography** Moscow, Vsesoiuznaya knizhnaia palata, 1943. pp. 104. Tirazh 3500. (Intended for command personnel of the Navy. Contains entries of books and articles from 1935 to 1942).

582. Tolkachev N.T. Voennoe iskusstvo. Strategiia, operativnoe iskusstvo, obshevoiskovaia taktika. Ukazatel' literatury **Military art. Strategy, operational art, combined armed tactics. Bibliography** Moscow, Vsesoiuznaia knizhnaia palata, 1943. pp. 204. Tirazh 1500. (Intended for the command personnel of the Red Army. Contains index of fundamental books, articles from journals and newspapers of the 6 preceding years).

583. Efebovskii I.V. Ed., Velikaia Otechestvennaia voina Sovetskogo Soiuza (1941-1945 gg.) Rekomendatel'nyi ukazatel' literatury **The Great Patriotic War of the Soviet Union (1941-1945). Recommended bibliography** Moscow, "Kniga", 1965. pp 250. Tirazh 20000. Histories, memoirs, art literature covering military actions in the war.

584. Golovanova L.G. *et al*, Velikii podvig. Rekomendatel'nyi ukazatel' literatury o Velikoi Otechestvennoi voine Sovetskogo Soiuza **The great feat. Recommended bibliography about the Great Patriotic War of the Soviet Union.**

Moscow, "Kniga", 1970. 216 pp. Tirazh 15000. Index of names, books, articles. Continuation of the bibliography published by "Kniga" in 1965.

585. Margolina E.B. Narodnoe khoziaistvo SSSR v gody Velikoi Otechestvennoi voiny (iiun' 1941 - mai 1945 gg.) Bibliograficheskii ukazatel' knizhnoi i zhurnal'noi literatury na russkom iazyke (1941-1968 gg.) **National economy of the USSR during the Great Patriotic War (June 1941 - May 1945). Bibliography of books and journals written in Russian (1941-1968).** Moscow, "Nauka", 1971. pp. 460. Tirazh 3200. (Based on 29 other bibliographies).

586. Markovskaia G.M. *et al*, Ed., Istoria SSSR Ukazatel' Sovetskoi literatury za 1917-1967 gg. Tom III; Istoria Sovetskogo obshchestva; SSSR v god Velikoi Otechestvennoi Voiny (iiun' 1941 - sentiabr' 1945 g.) Ukazatel' Sovetskoi literatury za 1941-1967 gg. **History of the USSR Bibliography of Soviet literature for the period 1917-1967. Volume III; History of Soviet society; USSR during the Great Patriotic War (June 1941 - September 1945) Bibliography of Soviet literature for period 1941-1967.** Moscow, "Nauka", 1971. pp. 693. Tirazh 2000. (Contains 7940 entries. Photo-offset) This bibliography has two supplements 1) SSSR v gody Velikoi Otechestvennoi voiny (iiun' 1941-sentiabr' 1945 g.) Ukazatel' Sovetskoi literatury za 1941-1967 gg. Prilozhenie. Skhema klassifikatsii vspomagatel'nye ukazateli **USSR during the Great Patriotic War (June 1941 September 1945). Bibliography of Soviet literature for 1941-1965. Appendix. Classification plan, auxiliary bibliography.** Moscow, "Nauka", 1977. pp. 175. Tirazh 6200. (Photo-offset). 2) SSSR v gody Velikoi Otechestvennoi voiny (iiun' 1941 - sentiabr' 1945 g.) Geroi fronta i tyla; Ukazatel' Sovetskoi literatury za 1941-1967 gg. **USSR during the Great Patriotic War (June 1941 - September 1945); Heroes of the front and the rear; Bibliography of Soviet literature from 1941 to 1967.** Moscow, "Nauka", 1981. pp. 215. Tirazh 50000.

587. Dokuchaev G.A. Sibir' v Velikoi Otechestvennoi voine. Bibliograficheskii ukazatel' rabot, opublikovannykh v 1941-1971 gg. **Siberia in the Great Patriotic War. Bibliography of writings published during 1941-1971.** Novosibirsk, Akademiia Nauk, 1972. pp. 159. Tirazh 600. (Photo-offset).

588. Baiburina G.Ia. Bashkiriia v gody Velikoi Otechestvennoi voiny (1941-1945 gg.). Bibliograficheskii ukazatel' **Bashkir in the Great Patriotic War (1941-1945). Bibliography.** Ufa, Bashkirskaia Respublikanskaia Biblioteka, 1975. pp. 197. Tirazh 250. (Covers printed material in Russian, Bashkiri and Tartar of the period from second half of 1941 to June 1974).

589. Kireeva M.E. *et al*, Velikaia Pobeda. Rekomendatel'nyi ukazatel' literatury o Velikoi Otechestvennoi voine 1941-1945 gg. **The great victory. Recommended bibliography about the Great Patriotic War 1941-1945.** Moscow, Kniga, 1975. pp 223. Tirazh 250000. (Continuation of bibliography published by Kniga in 1965 and 1970, covering publications of the previous 4 to 5 years).

590. Diuzhev Iu.I. Velikaia Otechestvennaia voina na Severe v sovetskoi literature. Ukazatel' literatury za 1941-1972 gg. **The Great Patriotic War in the north in Soviet literature. Bibliography from 1941-1972.** Petrozavodsk, "Kareliia",

1976. pp. 105. Tirazh 10000. (Divided in three chronological parts. List of sources).

591. Gushchin N.Ia. Ed., Sibir' v gody Velikoi Otechestvennoi Voiny (iiun' 1941 - sentiabr' 1945 gg.) Bibliograficheskii ukazatel' **Siberia during the Great Patriotic War (June 1941 - September 1945) Bibliography** Novosibirsk, Sibirskoe Otdelenie Akademii nauk SSSR, 1976. pp. 250. Tirazh 800. (photo-offset).

592. Ezhakov V.I. et al O voine, o tovarishchakh, o sebe. Velikaia Otechestvennaia voina v vospominaniiakh uchastnikov boevykh deistvii. Annotirovannyi ukazatel' voenno-memuarnoi literatury (1941-1975 gg.). **About war, comrades, and oneself. The Great Patriotic War as remembered by the participants in the military actions. Annotated bibliography of military-memoir literature (1941-1975).** Moscow, Voenizdat, 1977. pp. 239. Tirazh 50000. 900 entries. See also under "Memoirs and biographies"). 2nd edn. Ogarev P.K., Sekirin M.K., Annotirovannyi ukazatel' voenno-memuarnoi literatury (1975-1981 gg.) **Annotated bibliography of military-memoir literature (1975-1981)**, Moscow, Voenizdat, 1982. 256 pp. Tirazh 35000. Appendix.

CHRONOLOGIES

593. Roginskii S.V. Lt. General, Ed., SSSR v Velikoi Otechestvennoi voine 1941-1945 gg. (Kratkaia khronika) **USSR in the Great Patriotic War 1941-1945. (A brief chronicle)** Moscow, Voenizdat, 1964. 867 pp. Tirazh 11000. Based on contemporary publications, archival material and documents.

594. Kliatskin S.M., Sinitsin A.M. Editors, SSSR v Velikoi Otechestvennoi voine 1941-1945. (Kratkaia khronika) Izdanie vtoroe, ispravlennoe i dopolnenoe **USSR in the Great Patriotic War 1941-1945. (Brief chronicle) Second edition, corrected and expanded**, Moscow, Voenizdat, 1979. 856 pp. Tirazh 35000.

595. Ivanov S.P. Army General, Ed. Osvobozhdenie gorodov. Spravochnik po osvobozhdeniiu gorodov v period Velikoi Otechestvennoi voiny 1941-1945 **Liberation of cities. Reference book on the liberation of cities in the Great Patriotic War 1941-1945** Moscow, Voenizdat, 1985. 598 pp. Tirazh 50000. Dates and details of the liberation of cities from German and Japanese forces by the Red Army in Europe, China and Korea.

596. Bukov K.I., Zarezina K.F. et al, Moskva i Moskovskaia oblast' v Velikoi Otechestvennoi voine 1941-1945: Kratkaia khronika **Moscow and Moscow region in the Great Patriotic War 1941-1945: Brief chronicle** Moscow, Moskovskii rabochii, 1986. 523 pp. Tirazh 25000. Based on documents, archival material and press.

ENCYCLOPEDIAS

597. Kozlov M.M., Editor, Army General, Velikaia Otechestvennaia voina 1941-1945. Entsiklopediia **The Great Patriotic War 1941-1945. Encyclopedia** Moscow, "Sovetskaia Entsiklopediia" 1985. 832 pp. Tirazh 500000. Biographical and operational data, maps, illustrations of weapons, medals, photographs, etc.

DOCUMENTS

598. Spravochnik k I-VIII tomam. Soobshchenii Sovetskogo Informbiuro **Guide to volumes I-VIII. Communiques of Sovinformbiuro**, Vol. I:22.6.1941-31.12.1941; Vol.II:1.1.1942-30.6.1942; Vol. III:1.7.1942-31.12.1942; Vol.IV: 1.1.1943-30.6.1943;   Vol.   V:1.7.1943-31.12.1943;   Vol.   VI:1.1.1944-21.6.1944; Vol. VII:22.6.1944-31.12.1944; Vol. VIII:1.1.1945-15.5.1945;

599. Vasilenko V.S., Orekhova E.D., Kommunisticheskaia partiia v period Velikoi Otechestvennoi voiny(iiun' 1941 goda-1945 god) Dokumenty i materialy **Communist Party during the Great Patriotic War (June 1941-1945) Documents and materials**, Moscow, Gospolitizdat, 1961. 704 pp. Tirazh 60000. Endnotes, subject index.

600. Zyrianov P.I. Ed., Pogranichnye voiska v gody Velikoi Otechestvennoi voiny 1941-1945. Sbornik dokumentov **Frontier troops during the Great Patriotic War 1941-1945. Collection of documents**, Moscow, Nauka, 1968. 707 pp. Tirazh 5001 - 20000. Photographs, 471 documents, extensive endnotes, list of documents.

601. Matrosov V.A. Ed., Pogranichnie voiska SSSR v Velikoi Otechestvennoi voine 1941. Sbornik dokumentov i materialov **Frontier troops of the USSR during the Great Patriotic War 1941. Collection of documents and materials**, Moscow, Nauka, 1976. 944 pp. Tirazh 25000. Photographs, 486 documents, extensive endnotes. Also Pogranichnie voiska SSSR v Velikoi Otechestvennoi voine 1942-1945. Sbornik dokumentov i materialov **Frontier troops of the USSR during the Great Patriotic War 1942-1945. Collection of documents and materials**, Moscow, Nauka, 1976. 975 pp. Tirazh 25000. Photographs, 494 documents, extensive endnotes.

Diplomatic Documents

602. Gromyko A.A. et al, Stalin's correspondance with Churchhill, Attlee, Roosevelt and Truman 1941-1945, London, Lawrence and Wishart, 1958. In two volumes. Vol. I 401 pp. Vol. II 302 pp. Endnotes. First published in the USSR in 1957. **Perepiska predsedatelia soveta ministrov SSSR s prezidentami SShA i prem'er-ministrami Velikobritanii vo vremia Velikoi Otechestvennoi Voiny 1941-1945 gg.** Reprinted in English by Progress publisher, Moscow.

603. Gromyko A.A. *et al*, Ed., Sovetsko-frantsuzskie otnosheniia vo vremia Velikoi Otechestvennoi voiny 1941-1945 gg. Dokumenty i materialy **Soviet-French relations during the Great Patriotic War 1941-1945. Documents and materials,** Moscow, Politizdat, 1959. 551 pp. 50000. Endnotes, appendixes.

604. Gromyko A.A. *et al* Ed., Sovetskii Soiuz na mezhdunarodnykh konferentsiiakh perioda Velikoi Otechestvennoi voiny 1941-1945 gg. **Soviet Union involvement in the international conferences during the Great Patriotic War,** Tom I Moskovskia konferentsiia ministrov inostrannykh del SSSR, SShA, i Velikobritanii (19-30 oktiabria 1943 g.) Sbornik documentov **Moscow conference of the USSR, USA, and Great Britain Foreign   Ministers (19-30 October 1943). Collection of documents,** Moscow, Politizdat, 1978. 422 pp. Tom II Tegeranskaia konferentsiia rukovoditelei trekhsoiuznykh derzhav-SSSR, SShA i Velikobritanii (28 noiabria-1 dekabria 1943 g.) Sbornik dokumentov Vol. II **Teheran conference of the leaders of the three allies' states-USSR, USA and Great Britain (28 November-1 December 1943),** Moscow, Politizdat, 1978. 198 pp. Tom III Konferentsiia predstavitelei SSSR, SShA i Velikobritanii v Dumbarton-Okse (21 avgusta-28 sentiabria 1944 g.) Sbornik dokumentov **Conference of the USSR, USA and Great Britain representatives in Dumbarton-Oaks (21 August-28 September 1944) Collection of documents.** Moscow, Politizdat, 1978. 294 pp. Tom IV Krymskaia konferentsiia rukovoditelei trekh soiuznykh derzhav - SSSR, SShA i Velikobritanii (4-11 fevralia 1945 g.) Sbornik dokumentov Vol. IV **Yalta conference of the leaders of the three allies' states - USSR, USA and Great Britain (4-11 February 1945) Collection of documents,** Moscow, Politizdat, 1979. 326 pp. Tom V. Konferentsiia Ob''edinennykh natsii v San-Frantsisko (25 aprelia-26 iiunia 1945 g.) Sbornik dokumentov **San-Francisco conference of the United Nations (25 April-26 June 1945) Collection of documents,** Moscow, Politizdat, 1980. 710 pp. Tom VI Berlinskaia (Potsdamskaia) konferentsiia rukovoditelei trekh soiuznykh derzhav - SSSR, SShA i Velikobritanii (17 iiulia-2 avgusta 1945 g.) Sbornik dokumentov **Potsdam conference of the leaders of the three allies's states - USSR, USA and Great Britain (17 July-2 August 1945) Collection of documents,** Moscow, Politizdat, 1980. 551 pp. All vols: Tirazh 50000. Photographs, endnotes, subject, names,index.

605. Gromyko A.A. *et al*, Sovetsko-angliskie otnosheniia vo vremia Velikoi Otechestvennoi voiny, 1941-1945: Dokumenty i materialy. V dvukh tomakh **Anglo-Soviet relations during the Great Patriotic War, 1941-1945: Documents and materials. In two volumes** Moscow, Politizdat, 1983. Tom I 1941-1943 Vol. I **1941-1943,** 542 pp. Endnotes. Tom II 1944-1945 Vol. II **1944-1945,** 494 pp. Tirazh (both) 100000. Endnotes, indexes: names, subject.

606. Gromyko A.A. *et al*, Sovetsko-frantsuzskie otnosheniia vo vremia Velikoi Otechestvennoi voiny 1941-1945: Dokumenty i materialy. V dvukh tomakh **Soviet-French relations during the Great Patriotic War, 1941-1945: Documents and materials. In two volumes** Moscow, Politizdat, 1983. Tom I 1941-1943 431 pp. Endnotes, 24 appendixes. Tom II 1944-1945 Vol. II **1944-1945,** 573 pp. Tirazh (both) 100000. Photographs, endnotes, indexes subject, names, 23 appendixes.

607. Gromyko A.A. *et al*, <u>Sovetsko-amerikanskie otnosheniia vo vremia Velikoi Ote-chestvennoi voiny 1941-1945: Dokumenty i materialy</u> V dvukh tomakh **Soviet-American relations during the Great Patriotic War 1941-1945: Documents and materials** In two volumes, Moscow, Politizdat, 1984. Tom I <u>1941-1943</u> Vol. I. **1941-1943**, 510 pp. Endnotes. Tom II <u>1944-1945</u> Vol. II **1944-1945**, Endnotes, index, names, subject, photographs. Tirazh 100000 (both vols).

OFFICIAL HISTORIES

608. Pospelov P.N. (Head Editorial Commission), Institute Marxism-Leninism, Section for History of GPW, <u>Istoriia Velikoi Otechestvennoi voiny Sovetskogo Soiuza 1941-1945</u> **History of the Great Patriotic War of the Soviet Union 1941-1945.** Collective authorship. In 6 volumes, Moscow, Voenizdat, 1960-1965. Tirazh 125000. Volume 1 was reprinted in 1963, with an additional print of 50000, but no further reprints appeared after a fall of Khrushchev.

609. Grechko A.A., Marshal, Chairman Main Editorial Commission, <u>Istoriia Vtoroi Mirovoi voiny 1939-1945.</u> **History of the Second World War 1939-1945.** Collective authorship. Moscow, Voenizdat, 1973-1982. In 12 volumes. Tirazh 330000.

ONE VOLUME HISTORIES

610. Stalin I.V. <u>O Velikoi Otechestvennoi voine Sovetskogo Soiuza</u> **The Great Patriotic War of the Soviet Union,** Moscow, Gospolitizdat, 1942. 51 pp. 2nd edn. 1943, 80 pp., 3rd edn. 1943, 159 pp. 4th edn. 1944 159 pp. 5th edn 1951, 208 pp.

611. Golikov S. <u>Vydaiushchiesia pobedy Sovetskoi Armii v Velikoi Otechestvennoi voine</u> **Outstanding victories of the Soviet Army in the Great Patriotic War,** 2nd edn. Leningrad, Gospolitizdat, 1954. 310 pp. Tirazh 150000. Photographs, maps, coloured map supplement.

612. Zhilin P.A., Ed., <u>Vazhneishie operatsii Velikoi Otechestvennoi voiny 1941-1945</u> **The most significant operations of the Great Patriotic War 1941-1945,** Moscow, Voenizdat, 1956. 624 pp. Map supplement; 38 individual authors' studies.

613. Tel'pukhovskii B.S. <u>Velikaia Otechestvennaia voina Sovetskogo Soiuza 1941-1945. Kratkii ocherk</u> **Great Patriotic War of the Soviet Union 1941-1945. Short study,** Moscow, Gospolitizdat, 1959. 575pp. Tirazh 50000. Footnotes with archival material, maps, 23 coloured maps supplement.

614. Vorob'ev F.D., Kravtsov V.M., <u>Velikaia Otechestvennaia voina Sovetskogo Soiuza 1941-1945. Kratkii voenno-istoricheskii ocherk</u> **The Great Patriotic War of the Soviet Union 1941-1945. Short military-historical study,** Moscow, Voenizdat, 1961. 456 pp. Tirazh 17000. For officers, generals, based on archives. General Staff maps, 10 maps supplement, footnotes.

615. Pospelov P.N. *et al*, Ed., Velikaia Otechestvennaia voina Sovetskogo Soiuza 1941-1945. Kratkaia istoriia **The Great Patriotic War of the Soviet Union 1941-1945. Brief history**, Moscow, Voenizdat, 1965. 618 pp. Tirazh 70000. Photographs, coloured maps, chronology. English edn. Great Patriotic War of the Soviet Union 1941-1945. A General Outline, Moscow, Progress Publishers, 1974.

616. Zhilin P.A., Lt. General, Ed., Velikaia Otechestvennaia voina. Kratkii nauchno-popularnyi ocherk **The Great Patriotic War. Brief scientific-popular study**, Moscow, Politizdat, 1970. 638 pp. Tirazh 200000. Maps, photographs, footnotes, index of names, appendix.

617. Samsonov A.M. Krakh fashistskoi agressii 1939-1945. Istoricheskii ocherk **Defeat of the fascist aggression 1939-1945. Historical study**, Moscow, Nauka, 1980. 2nd edn. 727 pp. Tirazh 50000. Chapter endnotes, maps.

618. Larionov V. *et al*, World War II. Decisive Battles of the Soviet Army **Vazhneishie bitvy Sovetskoi Armii vo vtoroi mirovoi voine**, Moscow, Progress Publishers, 1984. 527 pp. Chapter endnotes, maps.

619. Samsonov A.M. Vtoraia mirovaia voina 1939-1945. Ocherk vazhneishikh sobytii **Second World War 1939-1945. Study of the most significant events**, Moscow, Nauka, 1985. 584 pp. Tirazh 30000. Chapter endnotes, photographs, maps, index of names, places.

DOCUMENTARY MATERIAL

620. Bogdanov P.P., *et al*, Ed., Proryv podgotovlennoi oborony strelkovymi soedineniiami. Po opytu Velikoi Otechestvennoi voiny 1941-1945 gg. **Breakthrough of a prepared defence by rifle formations. According to the experience of the Great Patriotic War**, Moscow, Voenizdat, 1957. 376 pp. Based on MOD archives. Maps, illustrations, tables, footnotes with archival material, separate 41 maps booklet, 19 appendixes.

621. Sbornik takticheskikh primerov iz Velikoi Otechestvennoi voiny. Strelkovye podrazdeleniia i polk v razlichnykh vidakh boia **Collection of tactical examples from The Great Patriotic War. Rifle sub-units and the regiment in varying combat conditions**, Moscow, Voenizdat, 1957. 231 pp. Pt. I **Rifle companies** Pt. II **Rifle battalions** Pt. III **Rifle regiment**.

622. Kolganov K. Lt. General, Ed., Razvitie taktiki sovetskoi armii v gody Velikoi Otechestvennoi voiny **The development of Soviet Army tactics in the Great Patriotic War**, Moscow Voenizdat, 1958. 428 pp. Tables, 3 appendixes, album of coloured tactical diagrams.

623. Sychev K.V., Major General, Malakhov M.M., Ed., Nastuplenie strelkovogo korpusa. Sbornik takticheskikh primerov iz Velikoi Otechestvennoi voiny **rifle corps offensive. Collection of tactical examples from the Great Patriotic**

War, Moscow, Voenizdat, 1958. 504 pp. Tables, footnotes, separate book of 65 maps.

624. Platonov S.P., Lt. General, Ed., Sovetskoe voennoe iskusstvo v Velikoi Otechestvennoi voiny 1941-1945 gg. **Soviet military art in the Great Patriotic War 1941-1945**, Moscow, Voenizdat, 1962. Three volumes. Vol. I 752 pp. 73 tables. Vol. II 404 pp. 68 tables, maps. Vol. III 528 pp. 78 tables. Declassified, formerly secret.

625. Kalinin V.B., Nechipurenko V.I., Savel'ev V.M., Kommunisticheskaia partiia v Velikoi Otechestvennoi voine (Iun' 1941 g.-1945 g.) Dokumenty i materialy **Communist Party during the Great Patriotic War (June 1941-1945)**, Moscow, Politizdat, 1970. 494 pp. Tirazh 50000. Endnotes.

626. Soviet Documents on the Use of War Experience translated by Harold S. Orenstein, **Sbornik materialov po izucheniiu opyta voiny**, Moscow, Voenizdat, 26 vols. Vol. I The Initial Period of War 1991, 100 pp. Vol.II The Winter Campaign, 1941-1942, 1991, 280 pp. Vol. III Military Operations 1941-1942 1993, 280 pp. London, Frank Cass.

627. Kirshner L.A. Kanun i nachalo voiny: Dokumenty i materialy **The eve and the beginning of war: Documents and materials**, Leningrad, Lenizdat, 1991. 431 pp. Tirazh 50000. Footnotes, photographs, tables.

628. Zamlinskii V.A. et al, Leto 1941. Ukraina: Dokumenty i materialy. Khronika sobytii **Summer 1941. Ukraine: Documents and materials. The chronicle of events**, Kiev, Izd. Ukraina, 1991. 512 pp. Tirazh 10000. Based on TsAMO archives. Photographs, index of documents.

629. Knyshevskii P.N. et al, Skrytaia pravda voiny: 1941 god. Neizvestnye dokumenty **The hidden truth of the war: 1941. Unknown documents**, Moscow, Russkaia kniga, 1992. 384 pp. Tirazh 15000. Based on TsAMO archives. Photographs, index of names.

OPERATIONS

1941

630. Barbashin I.P., Kharitonov A.D. Boevye deistviia sovetskoi armii pod Tikhvinom v 1941 godu **Combat action of the Soviet army at Tikhvin during 1941**, Moscow, Voenizdat, 1958. 80 pp. Map appendix, footnotes with archival material.

631. Oreshkin A.K. Oboronitel'naia operatsiia 9-i armii (oktiabr'-noiabr' 1941 g.) **The defensive operation of the 9th Army (October-November 1941)**, Moscow, Voenizdat, 1960. 128 pp. Footnotes with archival material, photographs, maps, tables.

632. Klimov I.D. Geroicheskaia oborona Tuly. (Oboronitel'naia operatsiia voisk 50-i armii, oktiabr'-dekabr' 1941 goda) **The heroic defence of Tula. (Defensive operation of the 50th Army, October-December 1941)**, Moscow, Voenizdat, 1961. 136 pp. Tirazh 10500. Footnotes with archival material, maps, photographs, 6 appendixes.

633. Grigorovich D.F. Kiev gorod-geroi **Kiev hero-city**, Moscow, Voenizdat, 1962. 111 pp. Tirazh 30000. Photographs, maps, footnotes with archival material.

634. Rumiantsev N.M. Razgrom vraga v Zapoliar'e (1941-1944 gg) Voenno-istoricheskii ocherk **Defeat of the enemy in the Polar region (1941-1944). Military-historical study**, Moscow, Voenizdat, 1963. 288 pp. Tirazh 14000. For officers and generals. Footnotes with archival material, photographs, maps.

635. Platonov S.P. Lt. General, Ed., Bitva za Leningrad 1941-1944 **Battle for Leningrad,** Moscow, Voenizdat, 1964. 608 pp. Footnotes with archival material, maps, photographs, separate maps' appendix, index of names, places, front and fleet command.

636. Sokolovskii V.D. Marshal, Ed., Razgrom nemetsko-fashistskikh voisk pod Moskvoi **Destruction of German-fascist forces at Moscow**, Moscow, Voenizdat, 1964. Footnotes with archival material, coloured maps, photographs, index of names, separate appendix of 22 coloured maps.

637. Gurin G.A., Orlov K.L., Ed., Bor'ba za sovetskuiu Pribaltiku v Velikoi Otechestvennoi voine 1941-1945 v trekh tomakh. Tom I Pervye gody **The battle for the Soviet Baltic during the Great Patriotic war 1941-1945 in three volumes,** Bk. 1 **The initial years**, Riga, Liesma, 1966. 367 pp. Tirazh 7000. Fifteen maps.

638. Muriev D.Z. Proval operatsii "Taifun" **Failure of Operation "Typhoon"**, Moscow, Voenizdat, 1966. 272 pp. Tirazh 65000. Footnotes with archival material, photographs, maps, tables.

639. Samsonov A.M., Ed., Proval Gitlerovskogo nastupleniia na Moskvu **The failure of Hitler's attack on Moscow**, Moscow, Nauka, 1966. 352 pp. Tirazh 50000. Collection of distinguished authors' articles. Footnotes with archival material, coloured maps, photographs, index of names.

640. Zhilin P.A. Ed., Besprimernyi podvig **Unrivalled feat**, Moscow, Nauka, 1968. 463 pp. Tirazh 15000. Battle of Moscow. Footnotes with archival material, coloured maps, tables, index of names.

641. Zhilin P.A. Ed., Na severo-zapadnom fronte 1941-1943 **On the North-Western Front 1941-1943**, Moscow, Nauka, 1969. 448 pp. Tirazh 50000. Seventeen commanders' accounts. Coloured maps, footnotes with some archival material, photographs, index of names, short biographies of authors.

642. Anfilov V.A. Proval "blitskriga" **Collapse of the Blitzkrieg**, Moscow, Nauka, 1974. 614 pp. Tirazh 50000. Footnotes with archival material, coloured maps, photographs, index of names.

643. Samsonov A.M. Porazhenie vermakhta pod Moskvoi **Defeat of the Wermacht at Moscow**, Moscow, Mosk. rabochii, 1981. 336 pp. Tirazh 20000. Endnotes with archival material, coloured maps.

644. Babin A.I., Ed., Na Volkhovskom fronte 1941-1944 **On the Volkhov Front 1941-1944**, Moscow, Voenizdat, 1982. 399 pp. Tirazh 43000. Collective of distinguished authors. Coloured maps, 7 appendixes, photographs, index of names, places, endnotes with archival material, tables.

645. Babin A.I. Ed., Karel'skii front v Velikoi Otechestvennoi voine 1941-1945 gg. Voenno-istoricheskii ocherk **Karelian front during the Great Patriotic war 1941-1945. Military-historical study**, Moscow, Nauka, 1984. 360 pp. Tirazh 9600. Endnotes with archival material, coloured maps, photographs, 4 appendixes including command personnel.

646. Sokolov A.M. Ed., Bitva za Moskvu **The battle for Moscow**, Moscow, Moskovskii rabochii, 1985. 4th ed. 527 pp. Tirazh 75000. Collection of articles from distinguished commanders. Photographs, maps, some footnotes.

647. Basov A.V. Krym v Velikoi Otechestvennoi voine 1941-1945 **Crimea in the Great Patriotic war 1941-1945**, Moscow, Nauka, 1987. 336 pp. Tirazh 6500. Chapter endnotes with archival material, tables, 3 appendixes, 3 maps.

648. Shliapin I.M., Basovskii M.A. Ed., Nepokorennyi platsdarm. Vospominaniia uchastnikov oborony Oranienbaumskogo platsdarma 1941-1944 **Unsubdued bridgehead. Recollections of the defendants of Oranienbaum bridgehead 1941-1944**, Leningrad, Lenizdat, 1987. 301 pp. Tirazh 100000. Photographs, documents' extracts.

649. Anfilov V.A. Krushenie pokhoda Gitlera na Moskvu. 1941. **Collapse of Hitler's march on Moscow. 1941**, Moscow, Nauka, 1989. 350 pp. Tirazh 30000. Endnotes with archival material.

650. Gorshkov S.G. Admiral of the Fleet of the Soviet Union, Na iuzhnom primorskom flange osen' 1941 g - vesna 1944 g. Voenno-istoricheskii ocherk **On the southern coastal flank, autumn 1941-spring 1944. Military-historical study**, Moscow, Voenizdat, 1989. 286 pp. Tirazh 25000. For officers of USSR military. Footnotes with archival material, maps, photographs.

651. Khametov M.I. Ed., Bitva pod Moskvoi **Battle of Moscow,** Moscow, Voenizdat, 1989. 320 pp. Tirazh 50000. Footnotes with archival material, photographs, maps, 2 appendixes.

652. Parrish M. Ed., Battle for Moscow. The 1942 Soviet General Staff Study, Pergamon-Brassey's, 1989. 210 pp. Translation of unpublished manuscript: **Sbornik**

materialov po izucheniiu voiny. No. 2. Winter campaign 1941-42. Index of places, names, units, maps, 2 appendixes.

653. Sandalov L.M. Pervye dni voiny. Boevye deistviia 4-i armii 22 iiuna-10 iiula 1941 goda The first days of war. Combat actions of the 4th Army from 22 June to 10 July, Moscow, Voenizdat, 1989. 217 pp. Tirazh 15000. For military reader. Footnotes with archival material, maps, tables.

654. Vladimirskii A.V. Na kievskom napravlenii: Po opytu vedeniia boevykh deistvii voiskami 5-i armii Iugo-Zapadnogo fronta v iiune-sentiabre 1941 g. On the Kiev axis: The experience of the combat actions of the forces of the 5th Army on the South-Western Front during June-September 1941. Moscow, Voenizdat, 1989. 304 pp. Tirazh 10000. Footnotes with archival material, maps, tables.

655. Samsonov A.M. Moskva, 1941 god: Ot tragedii porazhenii - k velikoi pobede Moscow, 1941: From the tragedy of defeat to the great victory, Moscow, Moskovskii rabochii, 1991. 288 pp. Tirazh 10000. Footnotes, photographs, coloured maps, indexes of names, places, 23 appendixes.

1942

656. Derr. G. Pokhod na Stalingrad The march on Stalingrad, Moscow, Voenizdat, 1957. 140 pp. Supplement of 23 maps, footnotes, 4 appendixes; translation of: Doerr H. Major General, Der Feldzug nach Stalingrad Darmstadt, Mittler & Sohn, 1955.

657. Chuikov V.I. Nachalo puti Start of the journey, Moscow, Voenizdat, 1959. 359 pp.

658. Samsonov A.M. Stalingradskaia bitva. Ot oborony i otstuplenii k velikoi pobede na Volge. Istoricheskii ocherk. The battle of Stalingrad. From defence and retreat to the great victory on the Volga. Historical study, Moscow, Nauka, 1960. 606 pp. Tirazh 15000. Footnotes with archival material, coloured maps, photographs, index of names, places. 4th ed. 1989: 630 pp. Tirazh 30000. Chapter endnotes with archival material, maps, photographs, 26 appendixes, index of names, places.

659. Sandalov L.M. Col. General, Pogorelo-Gorodishchenskaia operatsiia. Nastupatel'naia operatsiia 20-i armii zapadnogo fronta v avguste 1942 goda The operation of Pogorelo Gorodishche. The offensive operation of the 20th Army of the Western Front during August 1942, Moscow, Voenizdat, 1960. 150 pp. For officers, generals and veterans. Footnotes with archival material, maps, photographs, 3 appendixes.

660. Rokossovskii K.K. Marshal, Ed., Velikaia Pobeda na Volge The great victory on the Volga, Moscow, Voenizdat, 1965. 528 pp. Tirazh 14000. In two parts. Footnotes with archival material, photographs, coloured maps suplement, index of names, places, commanders.

661. Samsonov A.M., Ed., <u>Stalingradskaia epopeia</u> **The Stalingrad epic**, Moscow, Nauka, 1968. 720 pp. Tirazh 50000. Twenty nine commanders' accounts. Footnotes with archival material, coloured maps, index of names.

662. Grechko A.A. Marshal, <u>Bitva za Kavkaz</u> **The battle for the Caucasus**, Moscow, Voenizdat, 1969. 496 pp. Tirazh 50000. 2nd ed. For officers, generals and historians. Footnotes with archival material, photographs, 24 coloured maps, 2 appendixes, index of names.

663. Chuikov V.I. Marshal, <u>Srazhenie veka,</u> **The battle of the century**, Moscow, Sovetskaia Rossiia, 1975. 400 pp. Tirazh 100000. Stalingrad battle. Photographs, footnotes, maps.

664. Chuikov V.I., Marshal, Ed., <u>Stalingrad: uroki istorii. Vospominaniia uchastnikov bitvy</u> **Stalingrad: lessons from history. The battle participants' recollections**, Moscow, Progress, 1976. 495 pp. Tirazh 50000. Senior Soviet commanders and Field-marshal Paulus, General Adam report and recall. Footnotes, photographs.

665. Rotundo L.C. Ed., <u>Battle for Stalingrad. The 1943 Soviet General Staff Study</u> Pergamon-Brassey's, 1989. 340 pp. Translation of unpublished manuscript: <u>Sbornik materialov po izucheniiu opyta voiny. No. 6.</u> Maps, editor's notes and appendix, index of names, subjects.

1943

666. Morozov V.P. <u>Zapadnee Voronezha. Kratkii voenno-istoricheskii ocherk nastupatel'nyikh operatsii sovetskikh voisk v ianvare-fevrale 1943 g.</u> **West of Voronezh. A short military-historical study of the offensive operations of Soviet forces during January-February 1943**, Moscow, Voenizdat, 1956. 200 pp. For military readers. Ten maps, 8 appendixes.

667. Iarkhunov V.M. <u>Cherez Nevu (67-ia armiia v boiakh po proryvu blokady Leningrada)</u> **Across Neva (67th Army in combat to break Leningrad blockade)**, Moscow, Voenizdat, 1960. 95 pp. Footnotes with archival material, maps, tables.

668. Lokshin V.S. <u>V bol'shom nastuplenii. Vospominaniia, ocherki i dokumenty ob osvobozhdenii Ukrainy v 1943-1944 gg.</u> **The great offensive. Recollections, studies and documents about the liberation of the Ukraine in 1943-1944**, Moscow, Voenizdat, 1964. 496 pp. Tirazh 22000. Photographs.

669. Utkin G.M. <u>Sturm "Vostochnogo vala" Osvobozhdenie levoberezhnoi Ukrainy i forsirovanie Dnepra</u> **The assault on the "Ostwall" Liberation of left-bank Ukraine and crossing of the Dnieper**, Moscow, Voenizdat, 1967. 464 pp. Tirazh 30000. Footnotes with archival material, maps, photographs, appendix includes command.

670. Koltunov G.A., Solov'ev B.G., <u>Kurskaia bitva</u> **The Kursk battle**, Moscow, Voenizdat, 1970. 400 pp. Tirazh 50000. For generals and officers of Soviet

armed forces. Footnotes with archival material, photographs, tables, coloured map supplement, command personnel in appendix.

671. Parot'kin I.V., Major General, Ed., Kurskaia bitva **The Kursk battle**, Moscow, Nauka, 1970. 544 pp. Tirazh 30000. Twenty five command accounts. Footnotes with archival material, coloured maps, tables, photographs, index of names, 36 appendixes include tables of strength, order of battle, operational orders. Translated in English The battle of Kursk Moscow, Progress publishers, 1974.

672. Solov'ev B.G. Vermakht na puti k gibeli. Krushenie planov nemetsko-fashistskogo komandovaniia letom i osen'iu 1943 g. **The Wehrmacht on the road to destruction. Collapse of the German command's plans in the summer and autumn of 1943**, Moscow, Nauka, 1973. 312 pp. Tirazh 50000. Footnotes with archival aterial, coloured maps, photographs, index of names, bibliography.

673. Istomin V.P. Smolenskaia nastupatel'naia operatsiia (1943) **The Smolensk offensive operation (1943)**, Moscow, Voenizdat, 1975. 215 pp. Tirazh 50000. Footnotes with archival material, photographs, tables, map, appendix includes command staff.

674. Moskalenko K.S., Marshal, Ed., Bitva na Kurskoi duge **Battle on the Kursk bulge**, Moscow, Nauka, 1975. 192 pp. Tirazh 200000. Footnotes with archival material, tables.

1944

675. Rumiantsev N.M. Pobeda Sovetskoi armii v Zapoliar'e (1944 god) Victory of the Soviet Army in the Polar Region (1944), Moscow, Voenizdat, 1955. 104 pp. Maps, photographs.

676. Mushnikov A.N. V boiakh za Vyborg i Petrozavodsk **In the battles for Vyborg and Petrozavodsk**, Moscow, Voenizdat, 1957. 104 pp. Maps, some footnotes, photographs.

677. Korotkov I.S., Koltunov G.A., Osvobozhdenie Kryma. Kratkii voenno-istoricheskii ocherk **Liberation of the Crimea. Short military-historical study**, Moscow, Voenizdat, 1959. 102 pp. Maps, photographs, footnotes with archival material.

678. Belkin I.M. 13 armiia v Lutsko-Rovenskoi operatsii 1944 g. **The 13th Army Lutsk-Rovno operation during 1944**, Moscow, Voenizdat, 1960. 159 pp. For generals and officers. Maps, tables, footnotes, 3 appendixes include battle orders, command staff.

679. Korovnikov I.T. Col.General, Novgorodskaia-Luzhskaia operatsiia. Nastuplenie voisk 59-i armii (ianvar'-fevral' 1944 g.) **Novgorod-Luga operation. The offensive of the 59th Army (January-February 1944)**, Moscow, Voenizdat, 1960. 178 pp. For officers and generals. Footnotes with archival material, photographs, illustrations, coloured maps supplement, appendix: battle orders.

680. Proektor D.M. Cherez Duklinskii pereval **Through the Dukla pass,** Moscow, Voenizdat, 1960. 216 pp. Maps, tables, photographs, footnotes with some archival material.

681. Kiriukhin S.P. 43-ia armiia v Vitebskoi operatsii **43rd Army in the Vitebsk operation,** Moscow, Voenizdat, 1961. 143 pp. Tirazh 11000. For officers and generals. Footnotes with archival material, maps, photographs.

682. Matsulenko V.A. Udar s Dnestrovskogo platsdarma. (Nastuplenie 37-i armii 3-go Ukrainskogo fronta v avguste 1944 goda) **Attack from the Dniester bridgehead. (The offensive of the 37th Army of the Ukranian Front during August 1944),** Moscow, Voenizdat, 1961. 182 pp. Tirazh 8000. For officers and generals. Footnotes with archival material, photographs, 13 maps supplement.

683. Liudnikov I.I. Col. General, Pod Vitebskom. (Vitebskaia operatsiia 39-i armii 23-27 iiunia 1944 goda) **At Vitebsk. (Vitebsk operation of the 39th Army from 23 to 27 June 1944),** Moscow, Voenizdat, 1962. 112 pp. For offcers and generals. Footnotes with archival material, maps, 5 appendixes.

684. Grylev A.N. Major General, Za Dneprom. (Osvobozhdenie pravoberezhnoi Ukrainy v ianvare-aprele 1944 g.) **Beyond the Dnieper. (Liberation of right-bank Ukraine during January-April 1944,** Moscow, Voenizdat, 1963. 228 pp. Tirazh 25000. For officers and generals. Footnotes with archival material, maps, photographs, chronology of events, command staffs, index of names, places.

685. Malinovskii R.Ia., Marshal, Ed., Iassko-Kishinevskie Kanny **Jassy-Kishinev Cannae,** Moscow, Nauka, 1964. 280 pp. Tirazh 20000. 2nd and 3rd Ukrainian Fronts 1944. Based on archives and commanders' recollections. Footnotes with archival references, photographs, coloured maps, appendix, index of names, places.

686. Terekhov P.V. Boevye deistviia tankov na severo-zapade v 1944 g. **Combat actions of the tanks in the north-west during 1944,** Moscow, Voenizdat, 1965. 176 pp. Tirazh 4300. For officers. Footnotes with archival material, maps, photographs, 3 appendixes, short bibliography.

687. Minasian M.M. Major General, Osvobozhdenie narodov Iugo-Vostochnoi Evropy. Boevye deistviia Krasnoi Armii na teritorii Rumynii, Bolgarii, Vengrii i Iugoslavii v 1944-1945 gg. **Liberation of the people of South-Eastern Europe. Red Army combat actions on the territories of Romania, Bulgaria Hungary and Yugoslavia during 1944-1945,** Moscow, Voenizdat, 1967. 504 pp. Tirazh 7600. For army, navy officers, generals. Footnotes with archival material, 16 coloured maps supplement.

688. Shtromberg A.I. Lt. General, Ed., Bor'ba za Sovetskuiu Pribaltiku v Velikoi Otechestvennoi Voine 1941-1945 V trekh knigakh K Baltiiskomu moriu Kniga vtoraia, **The battle for the Soviet Baltic during the Great Patriotic war 1941-1945 in three volumes Towards the Baltic Sea,** Vol II. Riga, Liesma, 1967. 373 pp. Tirazh 7000. Footnotes with archival material, coloured maps, index of names, places, subjects, chronology, photographs.

689.   Tolubko V.F. Col. General, Baryshev N.I., <u>Ot Vidina do Belgrada. Istoriko-memuarnyi ocherk o boevykh deistviiakh Sovetskikh tankistov v belgradskoi operatsii</u> **From Vidin to Belgrade. Historical-memoir study about combat actions of the Soviet tank troops in the Belgrade operation**, Moscow, Nauka, 1968. 240 pp. Tirazh 31000. Coloured maps, photographs, footnotes with some archival material, index of names, list of units.

690.   Polushkin M.A. <u>Na Sandomirskom napravlenii. L'vovsko-Sandomirskaia operatsiia (iiul'-avgust 1944 g.)</u> **On the Sandomir axis. Lvov-Sandomir operation (July-August 1944)**, Moscow, Voenizdat, 1969. 176 pp. Tirazh 30000. For officers and generals. Footnotes with archival material, photographs, tables, 2 appendixes, maps' suplement.

691.   Grechko A.A. Marshal, <u>Cherez Karpaty</u> **Through the Carpathians**, Moscow, Voenizdat, 1970. 432 pp. Tirazh 100000. Footnotes with archival material, photographs, 14 coloured maps supplement, index of names, command staff in appendix.

692.   Eronin N.V. <u>Osvobozhdenie Iugo-Vostochnoi i Tsentral'noi Evropy voiskami 2-go i 3-go Ukrainskikh frontov 1944-1945</u> **Liberation of the South-Eastern and Central Europe by the 2nd and 3rd Ukrainian Fronts 1944-1945,** Moscow, Nauka, 1970. 676 pp. Tirazh 30000. Footnotes with archival material, coloured maps, photographs, 4 appendixes, index of names.

693.   Grylev A.N., Major General, <u>Dnepr Karpty Krym. Osvobozhdenie Pravoberezhnoi Ukrainy i Kryma v 1944 godu</u> **Dnieper, Carpathians, Crimea. Liberation of right-bank Ukraine and the Crimea in 1944,** Moscow, Nauka, 1970. 352 pp. Tirazh 48000. Footnotes with archival material, coloured maps, 9 appendixes, bibliography, index of names, abbreviations.

694.   Eliseev E.P. <u>Na Belostokskom napravlenii</u> **On the Bialystok axis**, Moscow, Nauka, 1971. 230 pp. Tirazh 20000. Based on archives. Footnotes with archival material, photographs, coloured maps, tables, 4 appendixes, index of names, places.

695.   Antosiak A.V. <u>V boiakh za svobodu Rumynii</u> **In battles for the liberation of Romania**, Moscow, Voenizdat, 1974. 288 pp. Tirazh 25000. Footnotes with archival material, maps, photographs, appendix, bibliography.

696.   Samsonov A.M. Ed., <u>Osvobozhdenie Belorussii 1944</u> **Liberation of Belorussia 1944**, Moscow, Nauka, 1974. 2nd ed. 800 pp. Twenty-six command accounts. Footnotes with archival material, coloured maps, 2 appendixes, index of names.

1945

697.   Bagrov V.N. <u>Iuzhno-Sakhalinskaia i Kuril'skaia operatsii (Avgust 1945 goda)</u> **South Sakhalin and the Kuriles operations (August 1945)**, Moscow, Voenizdat, 1959. 112 pp. Footnotes with archival material, maps, photographs.

698. Kharitonov A.D. Gumbinnenskii proryv (Gumbinnenskaia operatsiia 28-i armii - ianvar' 1945 goda) **Gumbinnen breakthrough (28th Army's Gumbinnen operation, January 1945)**, Moscow, Voenizdat, 1960. 112 pp. For military reader. Based on archives and recollections. Maps, some footnotes, short bibliography.

699. Kir'ian M.M., Lt. General, S Sandomirskogo platsdarma. (Nastuplenie 5-i gvardeiskoi armii v ianvare 1945 goda) **From the Sandomir bridgehead. (The offensive of the 5th Guards Army during January 1945)**, Moscow, Voenizdat, 1960. 184 pp. Based on archives and documents. Maps, footnotes with archival material, tables.

700. Zav'ialov A.S., Kaliadin T.E., Vostochno-Pomeranskaia nastupatel'naia operatsiia Sovetskikh voisk. Fevral'-mart 1945g. Voenno-istoricheskii ocherk **East Pomeranian offensive of the Soviet forces. February-March 1945. Military-historical study**, Moscow, Voenizdat, 1960. 235 pp. For officers and generals. Based on archives. Supplement of 22 coloured maps, some footnotes with archival material, photogrpahs.

701. Blinov S.I. Ot Visly do Odera. Boevye deistviia 60-i armii v Sandomirsko-Silezskoi operatsii (Ianvar' 1945 g.) **From the Vistula to the Oder. Combat actions of the 60th Army in the Sandomir-Silesia operation (January 1945)**, Moscow, Voenizdat, 1962. 184 pp. Tirazh 16000. For officers and generals. Maps, tables, footnotes with some archival material, 4 appendixes.

702. Batov P.I. General, Operatsiia "Oder". Boevyie deistviia 65-i armii v Berlinskoi operatsii aprel'-mai 1945 goda **Operation "Oder". Combat actions of the 65th Army in the Berlin operation April-May 1945**, Moscow, Voenizdat, 1965. 144 pp. Tirazh 30000. Based on documents and personal recollections. Footnotes with archival material, maps, photographs.

703. Konev I.S. Marshal, Ed., Za osvobozhdenie Chekhoslovakii **For the liberation of Czechoslovakia**, Moscow, Voenizdat, 1965. 388 pp. Footnotes with archival material, coloured maps, tables, photographs, 6 appendixes, index of names, places.

704. Malinovskii R.Ia. Marshal, Ed., Budapest-Vena-Praga. Istoriko-memuarnyi trud **Budapest-Vienna-Prague. Historical memoir study**, Moscow, Nauka, 1965. 384 pp. Tirazh 18000. Footnotes with archival material, coloured maps, photographs.

705. Malinovskii R.Ia. Marshal, Final 3 sentiabria 1945. Istoriko-memuarnyi ocherk o razgrome imperialisticheskoi Iaponii v 1945 g. **The End 3 September 1945. Historical- memoir study on the destruction of Imperialist Japan in 1945**, Moscow, Nauka, 1966. 352 pp. Tirazh 35500. Footnotes with archival material, coloured maps, photographs, index of names. 2nd edn. Final Zakharov M.V. Marshal, Ed., 1969. English language translation Finale, Moscow, Progress Publishers, 1972.

706. Sharokhin M.N. Col. General, Petrukhin V.S., Put' k Balatonu **The Road to Balaton**, Moscow, Voenizdat, 1966. 144 pp. Tirazh 20000. Footnotes with archival material, photographs, maps.

707. Vnotchenko L.N. Pobeda na Dal'nem Vostoke. Voenno-istoricheskii ocherk o boevykh deistviiakh v avguste-sentiabre 1945 g **Victory in the Far East. Military-historical study about the combat actions during August-September 1945**, Moscow, Voenizdat, 1966. 328 pp. Tirazh 19000. For officers, generals, admirals. Footnotes with archival material, maps, tables, 7 appendixes, bibliography. 2nd edn. Voenizdat, 1971. 392 pp.

708. Samsonov A.A. Ed., 9 maia 1945 goda. Vospominaniia **9 May 1945. Recollections**, Moscow, Nauka, 1970. 760 pp. Tirazh 50000. Twenty three command recollections. Footnotes with archival material, coloured maps, photographs, index of names.

709. Vorob'ev F.D. *et al*, Poslednii shturm (Berlinskaia operatsiia 1945 g.) **The final assault (Berlin operation 1945)**, Moscow, Voenizdat, 1970. 461 pp. Tirazh 75000. For officers and generals. Footnotes with archival material, photographs, 1 appendix, 15 coloured maps supplement. 2nd edn. 1975. Tirazh 50000. 456 pp. 2 appendixes, 10 coloured maps supplement.

710. Pak V.P., Suslina S.S., Ed., Osvobozhdenie Korei. Vospominaniia i stat'i **The liberation of Korea. Recollections and articles**, Moscow, Nauka, 1976. 336 pp. Tirazh 6000. Footnotes, photographs.

711. Medvedev K.N., Petrikin A.I. Shturm Kenigsberga **Assault on Königsberg**, Kaliningrad, Kn. izd-vo, 1985. 440 pp. Tirazh 35000. 4th edn. Command accounts. Footnotes with archival material. Maps, photographs, 5 appendixes, index of names, places.

712. Akshinskii V.S. Kuril'skii desant. Dokumental'naia povest **The Kurile landing. Documentary story**, Petropavlovsk-Kamchatskii, Dal'nevostochnoe kn. izd-vo, 1984. 160 pp. Tirazh 5000. Footnotes, photographs.

ARMIES, CORPS, DIVISIONS

Armies

In the case of armies, corps, divisions and regiments given Guards designation, the original designation will be identified under: **OD**

713. Galitskii K.N. Army General, V boiakh za vostochnuiu Prussiu. Zapiski komanduiushchego 11-i gvardeiskoi armiei **In the battles for Eastern Prussia. Memoirs of the commander of the 11th Guards Army**, Moscow, Voenizdat, 1970. 499 pp. Tirazh 40000. Footnotes with archival material, coloured maps, photographs, appendixes. **OD: 16 Army (1918-1943).**

714. Krylov N.I, Marshal, Alekseev N.I. Major General, Dragan I.G., Na vstrechu pobede. Boevoi put' 5-i armii oktiabr' 1941 g -avgust 1945 g. **On the road to victory. Combat path of the 5th Army, October 1941-August 1945**, Moscow, Nauka, 1970. 462 pp. Tirazh 40000. Coloured maps, photographs, footnotes with archival material, index of names.

715. Domnikov V.M., Lt. General, et al, V nastuplenii gvardiia. Ocherk o boevom puti 2-i gvardeiskoi armii **Guards in the offensive. Study of the combat road of the 2nd Guards Army**, Moscow, Voenizdat, 1971. 312 pp. Tirazh 35000. Footnotes with archival material, maps, photographs, appendixes. **OD: 1st Reserve Army.**

716. Vorontsov T.F. Maj. General, Biriukov N.I. Lt. General, Smekalov A.F., Shinkarev I.I., Ot volzhskikh stepei do avstriiskikh Al'p (boevoi put' 4-i gvardeiskoi armii). **From the Volga steppes to the Austrian Alps (Combat path of the 4th Guards Army)**, Moscow, Voenizdat, 1971. 256 pp. Tirazh 30000. Maps, photographs, appendixes, footnotes with archival material. **OD: 9 Reserve Army, 24 Army**

717. Galitskii K.N. Army General, Gody surovykh ispitanii 1941-1944. Zapiski komandarma **Years of the severe ordeal 1941-1945. Memoirs of Army commander,** Moscow, Nauka, 1973. 600 pp. Tirazh 25000. Commanded 24th Samara-Ul'ianovsk Iron Division, 1st, 3rd and 11th Guards Armies. Footnotes with archival material, photographs, coloured maps, index of names.

718. Altukhov P.K. et al, Nezabyvaemye dorogi (boevoi put' 10-i gvardeiskoi armii). **Unforgettable roads (combat path of the 10th Guards Army),** Moscow, Voenizdat, 1974. 287 pp. Tirazh 50000. Footnotes with archival material, maps, photographs, appendixes. **OD:30th Army.**

719. Korovnikov I.T., Lebedev P.S., Poliakov Ia.G., Na trekh frontakh. Boevoi put' 59-i armii **On three fronts. Combat road of the 59th Army,** Moscow, Voenizdat, 1974. 327 pp. Tirazh 50000. Maps, photographs, footnotes with archival material, appendix.

720. Vyrodov I.Ia. et al, V srazheniiakh za pobedu. Boevoi put' 38-i armii v gody Velikoi Otechestvennoi voiny 1941-1945 **In the battles for victory. Combat path of the 38th Army during the Great Patriotic War 1941-1945,** Moscow, Nauka, 1974. 567 pp. Tirazh 50000. Coloured maps, photographs, footnotes with archival material, appendix.

721. Piatkov V.K. et al, Tret'ia udarnaia. Boevoi put' 3-i udarnoi armii. **Third Shock (Army). Combat path of the Third Shock Army,** Moscow, Voenizdat, 1976. 256 pp. Tirazh 30000. Based on documents. Footnotes with archival material, photographs, 4 appendixes, maps.

722. Ryzhov I.M. et al, Geroicheskaia shest'desiat chetvertaia **The heroic Sixty fourth (Army),** Volgograd, Nizhne-Volozhskoe knizhnoe izdatel'stvo, 1981. 318 pp. Tirazh 50000. Photographs, footnotes with archival material.

723. Povalii M.I. *et al*, <u>Vosemnadtsataia v srazheniiakh za rodinu. Boevoi put' 18-i armii</u> **The Eighteenth in the battles for fatherland. Combat road of the 18th Army,** Moscow, Voenizdat, 1982. 528 pp. Tirazh 65000. Coloured maps, footnotes with archival material, photographs.

724. Kuznetsov V.A. *et al*, Ed., <u>Vtoraia udarnaia v bitve za Leningrad. Vospominaniia i dokumenty</u> **Second Shock (Army) in the battle for Leningrad. Recollections, documents,** Leningrad, Lenizdat, 1983. 376 pp. Tirazh 65000. Personal accounts supported by archives. Photographs, appendix. Some footnotes with archival material.

725. Sarkis'ian S.M. <u>51ia Armiia (Boevoi Put')</u> **51st Army (Combat Road),** Moscow, Voenizdat, 1983. 285 pp. Tirazh 30000. Accent on Party-political work. Footnotes with archival material, photographs, maps.

726. Pankov F.D. <u>Ognennye rubezhi: Boevoi put' 50-i armii v Velikoi Otechestvennoi voine.</u> **Fiery lines: Combat road of the 50th Army in the Great Patriotic War,** Moscow, Voenizdat, 1984. 248 pp. Tirazh 35000. Extensive footnotes based on archives, maps, photographs, appendix: names of all war time commanders.

727. Sviridov I.K., Marchuk Iu.A., <u>Oni osvobozhdali Moldaviiu, oni shturmovali Berlin.:(Vospominaniia i ocherki o 5-i udarnoi armii)</u> **They liberated Moldavia, they stormed Berlin.:(Recollections and studies about the 5th Shock Army),** Kishinev, Kartia Moldoveniaske, 1984. 195 pp. Tirazh 15000. Collection of personal accounts of the veterans. Photographs.

728. Berdnikov G.I. <u>Pervaia udarnaia: Boevoi put' 1-i udarnoi armii v Velikoi Otechestvennoi voine.</u> **First Shock Army: Combat road of the First Shock Army in the Great Patriotic War,** Moscow, Voenizdat, 1985. 255 pp. Tirazh 30000. Extensive footnotes based on archive; photographs, maps.

729. Grigorenko M.G. *et al*, <u>Skvoz' ognennye vikhri</u> **Through vortex of fire,** Moscow, Voenizdat, 1987. 287 pp. Tirazh 30000. War experience of the 11th Guards Army. Footnotes with archival material, photographs, maps. **OD: 16th Army.**

Tank Armies

730. Vysotskii F.I., Makukhin M.E., Sarychev F.M., Shaposhnikov M.K., <u>Gvardeiskaia tankovaia</u> **Guards Tank (Army),** Moscow, Voenizdat, 1963. 244 pp. Tirazh 28000. Combat road of the 2nd Guards Tank Army. Maps, photographs, appendix. **OD: 2 Tank Army 1942.**

731. Zavizion G.T., Korniushin P.A., <u>I na Tikhom Okeane...</u>**And on the Pacific Ocean,** Moscow, Voenizdat, 1967. 256 pp. Tirazh 35000. Combat road of 6th Guards Tank Army. Photographs, footnotes with archival material, maps, schematic drawing. **Raised originally as 6th Tank Army (1944).**

732. Babadzhanian A.Kh., Popel' N.K., Shalin M.A., Kravchenko I.M., Liuki ot-kryli v Berline. Boevoi put' 1-i gvardeiskoi tankovoi armii. **Hatches opened in Berlin**, Moscow, Voenizdat, 1973. 357 pp. Tirazh 50000. Footnotes with archival material, maps, photographs, appendixes. **OD: 1st Tank Army (1st formation: 1942; reformed: 1943).**

733. Zvartsev A.M. Lt. General, Ed., 3-ia gvardeiskaia tankovaia: Boevoi put' 3-i gvardeiskoi tankovoi armii **3rd Guards Tank (Army): Combat road of the 3rd Guards Tank Army,** Moscow, Voenizdat, 1982. 288 pp. Tirazh 35000. Based on archives and vetrans' recollections. Footnotes, mostly archival, photographs, maps. **OD: 3 Tank Army, May 1943.**

Tank/Mechanized Corps

734. Samsonov A.M. Ot Volgi do Baltiki. Ocherk istorii 3-go gvardeiskogo mekhani-zirovannogo korpusa, 1942-1945 gg., **From the Volga to the Baltic. Historical study of the 3rd Guards Mechanized Corps, 1942-1945,** Moscow, Nauka, 1963. 450 pp. Tirazh 18000. Coloured maps, footnotes with archival material, photographs, index of persons. **OD: 4th Mechanized Corps.** 2nd edition, corrected and suplemmented, Moscow, Nauka, 1973.

735. Solomatin M.D. Lt. General (Tank Troops), Krasnogradtsy **Men of Krasnograd,** Moscow, Voenizdat, 1963. 189 pp. Tirazh 27500. Military-historical study about the 1st Mechanized Corps during the GPW. Maps, photographs, footnotes with archival material.

736. Kuz'min A.V., Krasnov I.I., Kantemirovtsy. Voenno-istoricheskii ocherk o boe-vom puti 4-go gvardeiskogo tankogo korpusa **The Kantemirovtsy. Military-historical study of the combat path of the 4th Guards Tank Corps,** Moscow, Voenizdat, 1971. 319 pp. Tirazh 30000. (Formed in 1942, the Corps fought on the Volga, Donbas, Kursk, Dniepr, Poland, Czechoslovakia, Germany. Photographs, footnotes with archival material, maps, appendixes. Battle honors: Order of Lenin, Order of the Red Banner. **OD: 17 Tank Corps 1942.**

737. Reznik Ia.L. Dobrovol'tsy Urala. Vospominaniia, ocherki **Volunteers of the Urals. Recollections, studies,** Sverdlovsk, Sredne-Ural'skoe Knizhnoe Izdatel'stvo, 1972. 255 pp. Tirazh 22000. Combat road of the 10th Guards Urals-Lwow Red Banner Orders of Suvorov and Kutuzov Volunteer Tank Corps. Maps, photographs. **OD: Urals Volunteer Tank Corps 1943.**

738. Getman A.L., Army General, Tanki idut na Berlin (1941-1945) **Tanks are advancing on Berlin (1941-1945),** Moscow, Nauka, 1973. 389 pp. Tirazh 30000. History of the battles of the 11th Guards Tank Corps. Maps, footnotes with archival material, photographs, index of names, places, appendixes. **OD: 6 Tank Corps 1942.**

739. Tolubko V.F. Army General, Baryshev N.I. Na Iuzhnom flange. Boevoi put' 4-go gvardeiskogo mekhanizirovannogo korpusa (1942-1945 gg.) **On the southern flank. Combat road of the 4th Guards Mechanised Corps (1942-1945),** Mos-

cow, Nauka, 1973. 400 pp. Tirazh 30000. Footnotes with archival material, photographs, maps, appendixes, index of names. **OD: 13 Tank Corps.**

740. Riazanskii A.P., Major General, V ogne tankovykh srazheniia **In the fire of the tank battles,** Moscow, Nauka, 1975. 239 pp. Tirazh 50000. Combat road of the 5th Guards Mechanized Ziminovskii Corps. Footnotes with archival material, photographs, coloured maps, appendixes giving the command posts, index of persons. **OD: 14 Tank Corps, then 6th Mechanized Corps.**

741. Kravchenko I.M., Burkov V.V., Desiatyi tankovyi Dneprovskii. Boevoi put' 10-go tankogo Dneprovskogo ordena Suvorova korpusa. **Tenth Tank Dneprov (Corps). Combat path of the Tenth Tank Dnieper, Order of Suvorov, Corps,** Moscow, Voenizdat, 1986. 191 pp. Tirazh 30000. Footnotes with archival material, photographs, maps.

742. Demin V.A., Portugal'skii R.M. Tanki vkhodiat v proryv. Boevoi put' 25-go tankogo korpusa **Tanks go for the breakthrough. Combat road of the 25th Tank Corps,** Moscow, Voenizdat, 1988. 208 pp. Tirazh 10000. Based on archives and recollections. Footnotes with archival material, photographs.

Divisions

743. Savchenko V.I. Gvardeiskaia Latyshskaia **Latvian Guards (Division),** Riga, Akademiia Nauk Latviiskoi SSR, 1961. 166 pp. Tirazh 3000. War history of 43rd Latvian Rifle Division. Footnotes with archival material, maps, photographs. **OD: 201st Latvian Rifle Division.**

744. Sazonov I.F. Pervaia gvardeiskaia. Boevoi put' 1-i gvardeiskoi ordena Lenina strelkovoi divizii **The First Guards. Combat battle of the 1st Order of Lenin Rifle Division,** Moscow, Voenizdat, 1961. 231 pp. Tirazh 10500. Footnotes with archival material, photographs, maps. **OD: 100th Rifle Division (1941).**

745. Kuznetsov P.G., Lt. General, Gvardeitsy - Moskvichi **The Guards - Moscovites,** Moscow, Voenizdat, 1962. Tirazh 28000. History of the Moscow Proletarian Rifle Division; awarded Orders of Lenin, Suvorov, Kutuzov, Red Banner. Photographs, maps, footnotes with some archival material.

746. Smakotin M.P. Ot Dona do Berlina **From the Don to Berlin,** Moscow, Voenizdat, 1962. 198 pp. Tirazh 21500. Combat history of the 57th Guards Rifle Division. Based on documents and veterans' accounts. Maps, photographs. **OD: 153rd Rifle Division.**

747. Samchuk I.A. Gvardeiskaia Poltavskaia. Kratkii ocherk o boevom puti 97-i gvardeiskoi Poltavskoi Krasnoznamennoi ordenov Suvorova i Bogdana Khmel'nitskogo strelkovoi divizii **Poltava Guards (Division). A brief study about the combat path of the 97th Poltava Guards Red Banner, Order of Suvorov and Bogdan Khmel'nitskii Rifle Division,** Moscow, Voenizdat, 1965. 151 pp. Tirazh 20000. Photographs, maps. **OD: 343 Rifle Division.**

748. Mal'kov D.K., Lt. General (Rear Services), <u>Skvoz' dym i plamia.</u> <u>Boevoi put'</u> <u>12-i gvardeiskoi Pinskoi Krasnoznamennoi ordena Suvorova strelkovoi divizii</u> **Through smoke and flames. Combat road of the 12th Guards Pinsk Red Banner Order of Suvorov Rifle Division,** Moscow, Voenizdat, 1966. 192 pp. Tirazh 22000. Maps, photographs, footnotes with archival material, 2 appendixes. **OD: 258 Rifle Division**

749. Kondaurov I.A. <u>Ordena Lenina strelkovaia.</u> <u>Sbornik</u> **Order of Lenin Rifle (Division),** Perm', Permskoe kniznoe izdatel'stvo, 1967. 208 pp. Tirazh 10000. Photographs, footnotes with archival material. **OD: 359th Rifle Division.**

750. Zeinalov R.E., Borodetskii L.S. <u>416 Taganrogskaia (Voenno-istoricheskii</u> <u>ocherk)</u> **416th Taganrog (Division) (Military-historical study),** Baku, Azerbaidzhanskoe Gosudarstvennoe Izdatel'stvo, 1969. 256 pp. Tirazh 16000. Division's war record. Photographs, maps footnotes with some archival material.

751. Shevchenko I.N., Kalinovskii P.N., <u>Deviataia plastunskaia.</u> <u>Ocherk o boevom</u> <u>puti 9-i strelkovoi divizii</u> **Ninth "Plastunskaia" Cossack scout (Division). Study of combat road of the 9th Rifle Division,** Moscow, Voenizdat, 1970. 192 pp. Tirazh 30000. Footnotes with archival material, photographs.

752. Tuzov A.V. <u>V ogne voiny.</u> <u>Boevoi put' 50-i gvardeiskoi dvazhdy Krasoznamennoi ordenov Suvorova i Kutuzova strelkovoi divizii</u> **In the heat of the battle. Combat road of the 50th Guards twice Red Banner Order of Suvorov and Kutuzov Rifle Division,** Moscow, Voenizdat, 1970. 165 pp. Tirazh 30000. Photographs, maps, footnotes with archival material. **OD: 124 Rifle Division.**

753. Andreev A.A. <u>Po voennym dorogam.</u> <u>Boevoi put' 69-i strelkovoi Sevskoi dvazhdi Krasnoznamennoi ordenov Suvorova i Kutuzova divizii</u> **On military roads. Combat path of the 69th Rifle Sevsk, twice Red Banner, Order of Suvorov and Kutuzov, Division,** Moscow, Voenizdat, 1971. 264 pp. Tirazh 30000. Photographs, maps, footnotes with archival material, 3 appendixes, including war commanders.

754. Iatsynov P.S. Ed.,<u>123 shla vpered</u> **123rd advanced,** Leningrad, Lenizdat, 1971. 216 pp. Tirazh 52000. Fourteen authors. War history of 123rd Rifle Division. Photographs, footnotes.

755. Khatukaev A.T. <u>Slavoi oveiannye.</u> <u>Boevoi put' 115-i Kabardino-Balkarskoi kavaleriiskoi divizii</u> **Covered with glory. Combat road of the 115th Kabardino-Balkarii Division,** Nal'chik, El'brus, 1971. 236 pp. Tirazh 10000. Footnotes with archival material, photographs, maps.

756. Krapivin V.I. <u>313-ia Petrozavodskaia</u> **313th Petrograd (Division)** 2nd edition, Petrozavodsk, Kareliia, 1971. 199 pp. Tirazh 10000. Based on archival material and veterans' accounts. Photographs.

757. Popov S.E. Lt. General, Artillery, <u>Na ognevykh rubezhakh.</u> <u>Boevoi put' 3-i gvardeiskoi artilleriiskoi Vitebskoi, Khinganskoi Krasnoznamennoi, ordenov Suvorova i Kutuzova divizii propva rezerva Verkhovnogo Glavnokomandovaniia</u>

On the firing lines. Combat road of the 3rd Guards artillery Vitebsk, Khingan Red Banner, Orders of Suvorov and Kutuzov breakthrough Division, Supreme Commander's Reserve. Moscow, Voenizdat, 1971. 192 pp. Tirazh 30000. Photographs, footnotes with archival material, maps. **OD: 8 Artillery Division 1942.**

758.   Samchuk I.A. Trinadtsataia gvardeiskaia. Boevoi put' Trinadtsatoi gvardeiskoi Poltavskoi ordena Lenina dvazhdy Krasnoznamennoi ordenov Suvorova i Kutuzova strelkovoi divizii (1941-1945) 2nd Ed., **Thirteenth Guards (Division). Combat road of the Thirteenth Guards Poltava, Order of Lenin, twice Red Banner, Order of Suvorov and Kutuzov Rifle Division (1941-1945),** Moscow, Voenizdat, 1971. 280 pp. Tirazh 30000. Photographs, maps. **OD: 87 Rifle Division 1941.**

759.   Avramov I.F. 82-ia Iartsevskaia. Boevoi put' 82-i Iartsevskoi Krasnoznamennoi, ordenov Suvorova i Kutuzova strelkovoi divizii **82nd Iartsevo (Division). Combat road of the Iartsevo Red Banner, Orders of Suvorov and Kutuzov Rifle Division,** Moscow, Voenizdat, 1973. 216 pp. Tirazh 50000. Footnotes with archival material, photographs, maps, appendix of command personnel.

760.   Nikolaev A.N., Dudinkov A.G., 139-i Roslavl'skaia Krasnoznamennaia **139th Roslavl' Red Banner (Rifle Division),** Cheboksary, Chuvashskoe knizhnoe izdatel'stvo, 1975. 112 pp. Tirazh 30000. Photographs.

761.   Napalkov F.M., Vecher M.N., Medvedev E.V. Ot Tiumeni do Kirkenesa. O boevom puti 368-i Pechengskoi Krasnoznamennoi strelkovoi divizii **From Tiumen' to Kirkenes. About combat road of the 368th Pechenga Red Banner Rifle Division,** Sverdlovsk, Sredne-Ural'skoe knizhnoe izdatel'stvo, 1976. 176 pp. Tirazh 10000. Photographs.

762.   Bezuglyi I.S. *et al* Dvazhdy Krasnoznamennaia. Kniga o podvigakh voinov 5-i Moskovskoi (158-i Lioznensko-Vitebskoi) strelkovoi divizii v 1941-1945 gg. **Twice Red Banner (Division). Book about the feats of the soldiers of the 5th Moscow (158th Vitebsk) Rifle Division during 1941-1945 period.** Moscow, Moskovskii rabochii, 1977. 191 pp. Tirazh 30000. Based on documents and recollections of veterans. Photographs, footnotes with some archival material, map.

763.   Dragan I.G. Vilenskaia Krasnoznamennaia. Boevoi put' 144-i strelkovoi Vilenskoi Krasnoznamennoi, ordenov Suvorova, Kutuzova, Aleksandra Nevskogo divizii. **Vilnius Red Banner (Division). Combat road of the 144th Vilnius Red Banner, Orders of Suvorov, Kutuzov, Aleksandr Nevski Rifle Division.** Moscow, Voenizdat, 1977. 151 pp. Tirazh 30000. Footnotes with archival material, photographs, maps.

764.   Belan P.S., Timoshenko A.D., Barkov N.S., Frontovye dorogi **Roads of the fronts,** Alma-Ata, Kazakhstan, 1978. 136 pp. Tirazh 38500. Combat history of the 391st Rifle Division. Photographs, footnotes with some archival material.

765. Zakurenkov N.K. 32-ia gvardeiskaia: Boevoi put' 32-i gvardeiskoi strelkovoi Tamanskoi Krasnoznamennoi, ordena Suvorova divizii. **32nd Guards Division: Combat road of the 32nd Guards Rifle Taman Red Banner, Order of Suvorov Division.** Moscow, Voenizdat, 1978. 207 pp. Tirazh 30000. Footnotes with archival material, photographs, maps, appendixes. **OD: 2nd Airborne Corps.**

766. Bogoiavlenskii A.V. Division's Commander, *et al*, S boiami do El'by. 1-ia diviziia narodnogo opolcheniia Moskvy (60-ia strelkovaia Sevsko-Varshavskaia) na frontakh Velikoi Otechestvennoi voiny. **Fighting to the Elbe. The First Moscow People's Militia Division (60th Sevsk-Warsaw Rifle Division) on the fronts of the Great Patriotic War.** Moscow, Moskovskii Rabochii, 1979. 224 pp. Tirazh 40000. Photographs, footnotes with archival material, map.

767. Gurkin V.V., Ivashchenko A.E., 5-ia gvardeiskaia Kalinkovichskaia. Boevoi put' 5-i gvardeiskoi minometnoi Kalinkovicheskoi Krasnoznamennoi, ordena Suvorova divizii. **5th Kalinkovichi Guards (Division). Combat road of the 5th Guards Mortar Kalinovichi Red Banner, Order of Suvorov Division.** Moscow, Voenizdat, 1979. 173 pp. Tirazh 50000. Photographs, footnotes, mostly archival, maps. **(Formed as Guards January 1943)**

768. Venkov B.S., Dudinov P.P., Gvardeiskaia doblest'. Boevoi put' 70-i gvardeiskoi strelkovoi glukhovskoi ordena Lenina, dvazhdy Krasnoznamennoi, ordenov Suvorova, Kutuzova i Bogdana Khmel'nitskogo divizii **Guards' prowess. Combat road of the 70th Glukhov Guard Rifle Order of Lenin, twice Red Banner, Orders of Suvorov, Kutuzov and Bogdan Khmel'nitskii Division**, Moscow, Voenizdat, 1979. 181 pp. Tirazh 50000. Footnotes, mostly archival, photographs, maps. **OD: 138th Rifle Division (1939)**

769. Vylitok V.S., Leskin S.F., Novomoskovskaia Krasnoznamennaia. Boevoi put' 195-i Novomoskovskoi Krasnoznamennoi divizii **Novomoskovski Red Banner (Division). Combat path of the 195th Novomoskovski Red Banner Division**, Moscow, Voenizdat, 1979. 200 pp. Tirazh 35000. Footnotes with archival material, photographs, maps.

770. Kartashev L.S. Ot Podmoskov'ia do Keningsberga: Boevoi put' 83-i gvardeiskoi strelkovoi Gorodoskoi Krasnoznamennoi, ordena Suvorova divizii. **From Moscow environs to Königsberg: Combat road of the 82rd Guards Rifle Gorodok Red Banner, Order of Suvorov Division**, Moscow, Voenizdat, 1980. 128 pp. Tirazh 65000. Footnotes with archival material, photographs. **OD: 97 Rifle Division.**

771. Oleinikov A.I., Guards Major General Rt. Rozhdennaia na zemliakh zaporozhskikh. Literaturnaia zapis' M.M. Gilelakha **Born on the Zaporozhe. Literary notes by M.M. Gilelakh,** 2nd edn. Kiev, Politizdat Ukrainy, 1980. 178 pp. Tirazh 11500 Combat road of 95th Guards Rifle Division. Photographs, footnotes. **OD: 226 Rifle Division.**

772. Vylitok V.S., Leskin S.F., Podvigi ne merknut **Heroic deeds do not fade**, Kishinev, Kartia Moldoveniaske, 1980. 236 pp. Tirazh 30000. War experience of the 195th Rifle Division. Footnotes, mostly archival, photographs.

773. Bagirov N.T., *et al*, 77-ia Simferopol'skaia. Kratkaia istoriia. **77th Simferopol (Division). Short history**, 2nd ed. supplemented. (First ed. 1974) Baku, Azerneshr, 1981. 133 pp. Tirazh 8000. Combat road of the 77th Simferopol' Red Banner, Order of Suvorov 2nd class, in the name of Sergo Ordzhonikidze, Rifle Division. Footnotes with archival material, photograps.

774. Terekhov A.F. *et al,* Gvardeiskaia Tamanskaia **Taman Guards (Division)**, 3rd edn., Moscow, Voenizdat, 1981. 271 pp. Tirazh 35000. Photographs, footnotes with archival material, appendix. **OD:127 Rifle Division**

775. Karsanov K.D., Major General Artillery, Ogon' vedut gvardeiskie minomety: Boevoi put' 7-i gvardeiskoi minometnoi divizii. **Guards mortars are firing: Combat road of the 7th Guards Mortar Division**, Moscow, Voenizdat, 1982. 152 pp. Tirazh 35000. Division was armed with "Katiusha" multiple-rocket launchers (MRLs). Photographs, footnotes with archival material.

776. Sinkliner A.A. Na severnykh bastionakh. Raskaz o podvigakh voinov 104-i strelkovoi divizii na Karel'skom fronte **On the northern bastions. Story about soldiers' deeds of the 104th Rifle Division on the Karelia Front**, Petrozavodsk, Kareliia, 1982. 78 pp. Tirazh 10000. Based on archives. Photographs.

777. Smol'nyi M.K. 7000 kilometrov v boiakh i pokhodakh. Boevoi put' 161-i strelkovoi Stanislavskoi Krasnoznamennoi, ordena Bogdana Khmel'nitskogo divizii 1941-1945 gg. **7000 kilometres in battles and marches. Combat road of the 161 Rifle Stanislav Red Banner Order of Boris Khmel'nitskii Division 1941-1945**, 2nd ed., Moscow, Voenizdat, 1982. 192 pp. Tirazh 39000. Footnotes with archival material, photographs, maps.

778. Anisimov I.G. *et al*, Nash 252-ia. Veterany divizii vspominaiut **Our 252nd (252 RD). The veterans of the division remember**, Perm', Permskoe knizhnoe izdatel'stvo, 1983. 231 pp. Tirazh 10000. Photographs.

779. Kniazev V.N. Gvardeitsi 4-i strelkovoi **Guards of the 4th Rifle (Division)**, Kishinev, Kartia Moldoveniaske, 1983. 132 pp. Tirazh 20000. Photographs. **OD: 161 Rifle Division**

780. Lavrent'ev K.G. Gvardeiskaia zenitnaia: Boevoi put' 2-i gvardeiskoi zenitnoi artilleriiskoi Baranovichskoi Krasnoznamennoi, ordena Aleksandra Nevskogo divizii RVGK. **Guards Anti-Aircraft (Division): Combat road of the 2nd Guards Anti-Aircraft Artillery, Baranovichi, Red Banner, Order of Aleksandr Nevski Division Supreme Commander's Reserve**, Moscow, Voenizdat, 1984. 160 pp. Tirazh 35000. Footnotes, mostly archival, photographs, maps. **OD: 1st Anti-Aircraft Artillery Division Supreme Commander's Reserve.**

781. Oshambaev K.A. Gvardeiskaia trizhdy ordenonosnaia **Three times decorated Guards (Division)**, Alma-Ata, Kazakhstan, 1984. 144 pp. Tirazh 32000. War experience of the 62nd Guards Rifle Division. Footnotes with archival material, photographs. **OD: 127 Rifle Division.**

782. Sergeev N.S. Major General, *et al*, Diviziia pervogo saliuta **Division of the first salute**, Moscow, Moskovskii Rabochii, 1984. 191 pp. Tirazh 39000. Combat

experience of the 2nd Moscow - 129th Orlov Red Banner, Order of Kutuzov Rifle Division. Based on recollections of veterans. Photographs.

783. Shilov K.K. Rechitskaia Krasnoznamennaia: Boevoi put' 194-i strelkovoi Rechitskoi Krasnoznamennoi divizii **Rechitsa Red Banner (Divison): Combat road of the 194th Rifle Rechitsa Red Banner Division,** Moscow, Voenizdat, 1984. 160 pp. Tirazh 30000. Footnotes, mostly archival, photographs.

784. Ivanov K., Kurbanov B., Mitrofanov V., V boiakh i pokhodakh **In battles and campaigns,** 2nd edn. Kazan', Tatarskoe knizhnoe izdatel'stvo, 1985. 286 pp. Tirazh 22000. Combat experience of the 334th Vitebsk Rifle Division. Photographs.

785. Kadyrov N.Z. Ot Minska do Veny. Boevoi put' 4-i gvardeiskoi strelkovoi Apostolovsko-Venskoi Krasnoznamennoi divizii **From Minsk to Vienna. Combat road of the 4th Guards Rifle Apostolovsko-Vienna Red Banner Division,** Moscow, Voenizdat, 1985. 176 pp. Tirazh 30000. Footnotes, mostly archival, photographs. **OD: 161 Rifle Divison**

786. Kupriianov N.V. S veroi v pobedu. Boevoi put' 38-i gvardeiskoi strelkovoi Lozovskoi Krasnoznamennoi divizii **With faith in victory. Combat road of the 38th Guards Rifle Lozovaia Red Banner Division,** Moscow, Voenizdat, 1985. 173 pp. Tirazh 30000. Extensive archival footnotes, photographs. **OD: 4th Airborne Corps**

787. Sekretov A..N. Gvardeiskaia postup' (Boevoi put' 17-i Mozyrskoi Krasnoznamennoi ordenov Lenina, Suvorova i Kutuzova kavaleriiskoi divizii, podshefnoi Tadzhikistanu, v gody Velikoi Otechestvennoi voiny, 1941-1945 gg. **Step of the Guards (Combat road of the 17th Mozir Red Banner Orders of Lenin, Suvorov and Kutuzov Cavalry Division, sponsored by Tadzhikistan, during the Great Patriotic War, 1941-1945),** Dushanbe, Donish, 1985. Extensive archival footnotes, five appendixes, photographs. **OD: 20th Mountain Cavalry Division**

788. Shatilov V.M. Col. General, V boiakh rozhdennoe znamia **In battles the banner was born,** Moscow, Sovetskaia Rossiia, 1985. 128 pp. Tirazh 100000. Feats of the soldiers of the 150th Rifle Division, which took part in the storming of the Reichstag. Photographs.

789. Dudinov P.P. Varshavskaia Krasnoznamennaia. Boevoi put' 328-i strelkovoi Varshavskoi Krasnoznamennoi divizii **Warsaw Red Banner (Division). Combat road of the Warsaw Red Banner 328th Rifle Division,** Moscow, Voenizdat, 1986. 150 pp. Tirazh 30000. Footnotes with archival material, photographs, maps.

790. Egorov V.F. et al, Rozhdenaia v boiakh: Boevoi put' 71-i gvardeiskoi strelkovoi Vitebskoi ordena Lenina, Krasnoznamennoi divizii **Born in battles: Combat road of the 71st Guards Vitebsk Rifle Order of Lenin, Red Banner Division,** Moscow, Voenizdat, 1986. 168 pp. Tirazh 30000. Footnotes, mostly archival, photographs. **OD: 23rd Rifle Division (1920s)**

791. Lysukhin I.F., Kukovenko S.E., Gorlovskaia dvazhdy Krasnoznamennaia. Bo-evoi put' 126-i strelkovoi Gorlovskoi dvazhdy Krasnoznamennoi ordena Suvo-rova II stepeni divizii **Gorlovka Twice Red Banner (Division). Combat path of the Gorlovka, Twice Red Banner, Order of Suvorov II class 126th Rifle Division,** Moscow, Voenizdat, 1986. 199 pp. Tirazh 20000. Authors claim to have used extensively archives of the Ministry of Defence and veterans' material. Photographs, footnotes with archival material.

792. Panasenko P.S. Gvardeiskaia Irkutsko-Pinskaia: Boevoi put' gvardeiskoi moto-strelkovoi Irkutsko-Pinskoi ordenov Lenina, Oktiabr'skoi Revoliutsii, trizhdy Krasnoznamennoi, ordena Suvorova divizii imeni Verkhovnogo Soveta RSFSR **Guards Irkuts-Pinsk (Division): Combat road of the Guards Motor-rifle Irkutsk-Pinsk, Order of Lenin, October Revolution, three times Red Ban-ner, Order of Suvorov Division, in the name of the Supreme Soviet of the RSFSR,** Moscow, Voenizdat, 1986. 174 pp. Tirazh 30000. Footnotes, mostly archival, photographs, maps on covers. **OD: 30th Rifle Division**.

793. Stankevskii D.I., Major General Rt., Vernost' pamiati **Faithful to the memory,** Kiev, Politizdat Ukrainy, 1986. 221 pp. Tirazh 65000. Author's wartime recol-lections commanding the 346th Rifle Division.

794. Borovinskikh A.Z. Valginskaia Krasnoznamennaia: Voenno-istoricheskii ocherk boevogo puti 377-i strelkovoi Valginskoi Krasnoznamennoi divizii **Valga Red Banner: Military-historical study of the combat road of the 377th Rifle Val-ga Red Banner Division,** Moscow, Voenizdat, 1987. 120 pp. Tirazh 25000. Footnotes, mostly archival, photographs.

795. Domank A.S., Lazutkin S.P., Rezerva Verkhovnogo Glavnokomandovaniia. Boevoi put' 1-i gvardeiskoi artilleriiskoi Glukhovskoi ordena Lenina, Krasnoznamennoi, ordenov Suvorova, Kutuzova i Bogdana Khmel'nitskogo di-vizii proryva rezerva Verkhovnogo glavnokomandovaniia **Reserve of the Su-preme High Command. Combat path of Glukhov, Order of Lenin, Red Banner, Order of Suvorov, Kutuzov and Bogdan Khmel'nitskii, 1st Guards Artillery Breakthrough Division, Reserve of the Supreme High Command,** Moscow, Voenizdat, 1987. 190 pp. Tirazh 10000. Footnotes with archival ma-terial, photographs. **OD: 1 Artillery Division**

796. Naumenko K.E. 266-ia Artemovsko-Berlinskaia. Voenno-istoricheskii ocherk boevogo puti 266-i strelkovoi Artemovsko-Berlinskoi Krasnoznamennoi, ordena Suvorova II stepeni divizii **266th Artemovsk-Berlin (Division). Military-his-torical study of the combat path of Artemovsk-Berlin Red Banner, Order of Suvorov II class 266th Rifle Division,** Moscow, Voenizdat, 1987. 144 pp. Ti-razh 10000. Footnotes with archival material, photographs.

797. Pavlov I.N. Legendarnaia Zheleznaia: Boevoi put' motostrelkovoi Samaro-Ul'ianovskoi, Berdichevskoi Zheleznoi ordena Oktiabr'skoi Revoliutsii, trizhdy Krasnoznamennoi, ordenov Suvorova i Bogdana Khmel'nitskogo divizii **The Legendary Iron (Division): Combat road of the Motor-rifle Samara-Ul-ianovsk, Berdichev, Iron, Order of October Revolution, three times Red Banner, Orders of Suvorov and Bogdan Khmel'nitskii Division,** Moscow,

Voenizdat, 1987. 224 pp. Tirazh 20000. Footnotes, archival and others, photographs, 2 appendixes. **OD: 1st Simbirsk Infantry Division 1918. "Iron" Division 1921. 24 Rifle Division 1922. Deactivated in disgrace 1941. Reformed 1942.**

798. Kachur V.P., Nikol'skii V.V., Pod znamenem Sivashtsev. Boevoi put' 169-i strelkovoi Rogachevskoi Krasnoznamennoi, ordenov Suvorova II stepeni i Kutuzova II stepeni divizii (1941-1945) **Under the banner of the men from Sivash. Combat path of the Rogachev Red Banner, Order of Suvorov II class and Kutuzov II class, 169th Rifle Division (1941-1945)**, Moscow, Voenizdat, 1989. 192 pp. Tirazh 10000. Footnotes with archival material, photographs.

799. Maslenikov P.V., Kartsev K.E., Sagaidak P.T., Zhertvuia soboi: Ocherk o boevom puti 92-i strelkovoi divizii **I sacrifice myself: Study about the combat road of the 92nd Rifle Division,** Moscow, Voenizdat, 1989. 216 pp. Tirazh 30000. Footnotes, mostly archival, photographs, maps.

Airborne Corps

800. Gromov I.I., Pigunov V.N., Chetvertyi vozdushno-desantnyi: Boevoi put' korpusa. **The Fourth Airborne Assault (corps): combat road of the corps**, Moscow, Voenizdat, 1990. pp. 272. Tirazh 25000. Based on documents and some personal and family archives. Photographs, footnotes with archival material, maps.

Regiments

801. Isaev I.P. Ot Tuly do Kenigsberga. Vospominaniia o boevykh podvigakhvoinov Tul'skogo rabochego polka From Tula to Königsberg. Recollections about combat feats of the Tula Workers Regiment, 2nd ed. corrected and supplemented, Tula, Priokskoe knizhnoe izdatel'stvo, 1972. pp. 237. Tirazh 30000. Footnotes with Tula Oblast Party Archive material, photographs.

802. Belykh V.T. Motory zaglushili na El'be **Engines shut down on the Elbe**, Kiev, Politizdat Ukrainy, 1986. pp. 224. Tirazh 115000. Recollection of the commander of the 1205th Self-propelled Artillery Regiment operating with the 77th Guards Rifle Division. Photographs from private collections.

AIR FORCE

803. Rudenko S.I., Air Marshal, *et al*, Ed., Sovetskie voenno-vozdushnye sily v Velikoi Otechestvennoi voine 1941-1945 gg. **The Soviet Air Force during the Great Patriotic War 1941-1945**, Moscow, Voenizdat, 1968. 452 pp. Tirazh 32700. Footnotes with archival material, maps, photographs. English translation The Soviet Air Force in the World War II, translated by Leland Fetzer, Ed., Ray Wagner, Garden City, N.Y., Doubleday, 1973.

Air Armies

804. Komarov G.O. *et al*, 16-ia vozdushnaia. Voenno-istoricheskii ocherk o boevom puti 16-i vozdushnoi armii (1942-1945), **16th Air (Army). Military-historical study about the combat road of the 16th Air Army (1942-1945)**, Moscow, Voenizdat, 1973. 392 pp. Tirazh 40000. Based on archival material and veterans' recollections. Photographs, footnotes with archival material.

805. Skomorokhov N.M., Air Marshal, *et al*, 17-ia vozdushnaia armiia v boiakh ot Stalingrada do Veny. Voenno-istoricheskii ocherk o boevom puti 17-i vozdushnoi armii v gody VOV **17th Air Army in battles from Stalingrad to Vienna. Military-historical study about combat road of the 17th Air Army during the GPW**, Moscow, Voenizdat, 1977. 261 pp. Tirazh 30000. Authors used MOD archives, historical memoirs and articles from military journals. Photographs, footnotes with archival material.

806. Inozemtsev I.G. Pod krylom - Leningrad. Boevoi put' VVS Leningradskogo voennogo okruga, Leningradskogo fronta i 13-i vozdushnoi armii v gody Velikoi Otechestvennoi voiny **Under the wings - Leningrad. Combat road of the Leningrad District Air Force, Leningrad Front and the 13th Air Army during the Great Patriotic War**, Moscow, Voenizdat, 1978. 272 pp. Tirazh 65000. Based on central and local archives, recollections of veterans. Endnotes mostly archival material, photographs.

807. Anishchenkov P.S., Shirinov V.E., Tret'ia Vozdushnaia: Voenno-istoricheskii ocherk o boevom puti VVS Kalinskogo fronta i 3-i vozdushnoi armii v gody Velikoi Otechestvennoi Voiny **Third Air (Army): Military-historical study about the combat road of the Kalinin Front Air Force and the 3rd Air Army during the Great Patriotic War**, Moscow, Voenizdat, 1984. 191 pp. Tirazh 30000. Photographs, footnotes with archival material.

808. Gubin B.A., Kisilev V.A., Vos'maia vozdushnaia: Voenno-istoricheskii ocherk boevogo puti 8-i vozdushnoi armii v gody Velikoi Otechestvnnoi voiny **Eighth Air (Army): Military-historical study of combat road of the 8th Air Army during the Great Patriotic War**, Moscow, Voenizdat, 1986. 239 pp. Tirazh 30000. Photographs donated by the veterans, footnotes with archival material.

809. Davtian S.M. Piataia vozdushnaia: Voenno-istoricheskii ocherk boevogo puti 5-i vozdushnoi armii v gody Velikoi Otechestvennoi voiny **5th Air (Army). Military-historical study of combat road of the 5th Air Army during the GPW**, Moscow, Voenizdat, 1990. 256 pp. Tirazh 20000. Based on archival material and veterans' recollections. Footnotes with archival material, photographs.

Air Divisions

810. Boikov P.M. Na glavnykh napravleniiakh. Boevoi put' 10-i gvardeiskoi istrebitel'noi aviatsionnoi Stalingradskoi Krasnoznamennoi, ordena Suvorova II stepeni divizii **On the main axis. Combat path of the 10th Guards Stalingrad Red Banner, Order of Suvorov II class Fighter Aviation Division**, Moscow,

Voenizdat, 1984. 172 pp. Tirazh 35000. Footnotes with archival material, photographs.

FLEETS AND FLOTILLAS

811. Mankevich A.I. Krasnoznamennaia Ladozhskaia flotiliia v Velikoi Otechestvennoi voine **The Red Banner Ladoga flotilla during the Great Patriotic War,** Moscow, Voenizdat, 1955. 104 pp. Photographs, maps.

812. V'iunenko N.P., Mordvinov R.N., Voennye flotiilii v Velikoi Otechestvennoi voine (Kratkii voenno-istoricheskii ocherk) **Flotillas in the Great Patriotic War (Brief military-historical study),** Moscow, Voenizdat, 1957. 272 pp. For military reader. Maps, photographs, footnotes.

813. Kirin I.D. Chernomorskii flot v bitve za Kavkaz **The Black Sea Fleet in the battle for the Caucasus,** Moscow, Voenizdat, 1958. 200 pp. Based on archival material and veterans' recollections. Maps, photographs, footnotes.

814. Loktionov I.I. Dunaiskaia flotiliia v Velikoi Otechestvennoi voine (1941-1945 gg.) **The Danube flotilla in the Great Patriotic War,** Moscow, Voenizdat, 1962. 319 pp. Tirazh 5500. For officers and historians. Footnotes with archival material, maps, photographs, bibliography.

815. Kolyshkin I., Rear-Admiral, Submarines in Artic Waters (Memoirs) **V glubinakh poliarnykh morei,** Moscow, Progress Publishers, 1966. 253 pp.

816. Achkasov V.I. Ed., Krasnoznamennyi Baltiiskii flot v bitve za Leningrad 1941-1944 gg. **The Red Banner Baltic Fleet in the battle for Leningrad 1941-1944,** Moscow, Nauka, 1973. 448 pp. Tirazh 20000. Footnotes with archival material, tables, coloured maps.

817. Solov'ev A.G., Ed., V nebe letchiki Baltiki. Iz boevoi istorii aviatsii dvazdy Krasnoznamennogo Baltiiskogo flota v gody Velikoi Otechestvennoi voiny. Vospominaiia, ocherki **Baltic pilots in the sky. From combat aviation history of the twice Red Banner Baltic Fleet during the Great Patriotic War. Recollections, essays,** Tallin, Eesti raamat, 1974. 294 pp. Tirazh 20000. Photographs.

818. Achkasov V.I. Ed., Krasnoznamennyi Baltiiskii flot v zavershaiushchii period Velikoi Otechestvennoi voiny 1944-1945 gg. **The Red Banner Baltic Fleet in the closing period of the Great Patriotic War 1944-1945,** Moscow, Nauka, 1975. 488 pp. For military historians. Footnotes with archival material, coloured maps, tables.

819. Kozlov I.A., Shlomin V.S., Krasnoznamennyi Baltiiskii flot v geroicheskoi oborone Leningrada **The Red Banner Baltic Fleet during the heroic defence of Leningrad,** Leningrad, Lenizdat, 1976. 398 pp. Tirazh 50000. Based on archives. Endnotes with archival material, photographs, maps, index of names.

820. Basov A.V. Flot v Velikoi Otechestvennoi voine 1941-1945. Opyt operativno-strategicheskogo primeneniia **The Fleet in the Great Patriotic War 1941-1945. Experience of its operational-strategic application**, Moscow, Nauka, 1980. 304 pp. Footnotes with archival material, coloured maps, tables, appendix.

821. Samsonov A.M., Ed., Krasnoznamennyi Baltiiskii flot v Velikoi Otechestvennoi voine 1941-1945. Stat'i i ocherki **The Red Banner Baltic Fleet in the Great Patriotic War 1941-1945. Articles and studies**, Moscow, Nauka, 1981. 504 pp. Tirazh 15000. Footnotes with archival material, tables, map.

822. Kamalov Kh.Kh. Morskaia pekhota v boiakh za Rodinu **Naval infantry in battles for the Fatherland**, 2nd ed. Moscow, Voenizdat, 1983. 221 pp. Tirazh 39000. Based on archives, monographs, veterans' recollections. Footnotes with archival material, photographs, 2 appendixes.

823. Samsonov A.M., Ed., Moriaki-Baltiitsy na zashchite Rodiny 1941-1945. (Ocherki dokumenty illiustratsii) **Baltic sailors defending the Fatherland 1941-1945. (Studies, documents, illustrations)**, Moscow, Nauka, 1986. 480 pp. Tirazh 21000. Footnotes with archival material, photographs, tables, appendix, index of names.

824. Kasatonov V.A., Admiral, Ed., Oborona Pribaltiki i Leningrada 1941-1944 gg. Kniga pervaia **The defence of the Baltic and Leningrad 1941-1944**. Vol. I. Moscow, Nauka, 1990. 512 pp. Tirazh 6500. Footnotes with archival material, tables, index of names. First vol. of proposed 4 vol. series.

REPUBLICS, REGIONS, CITIES

825. Karasev A.V. Leningradtsy v gody blokady 1941-1943 **Leningraders during the blockade 1941-1943**, Moscow, Nauka, 1959. 316 pp. Tirazh 5000. Footnotes with archival material, maps, bibliography.

826. Pokrovskii S.N. *et al*, Ed., Kazakhstan v period Velikoi Otechestvennoi voiny Sovetskogo Soiuza 1941-1945. Sbornik dokumentov i materialov. Tom pervyi Iiun' 1941-1943 gg. **Kazakhstan during the Great Patriotic War of USSR 1941-1945. Collection of documents and materials, Vol. I, June 1941-1943**, Alma-Ata, Nauka, 1964. 596 pp. Tirazh 2465. Based on archives, footnotes, endnotes, illustrations, list of sources. Tom vtoroi 1944-1945 gg. **Vol. II 1944-1945**, Alma-Ata, Nauka, 1967. 528 pp. Tirazh 4050. Footnotes, endnotes, lists of sources, published documents.

827. Tsaplin F.S. Sovetsko-Mongol'skoe sotrudnichestvo v gody vtoroi mirovoi voiny **Soviet-Mongolian co-operation during the Second World War**, Moscow, Nauka, 1964. 84 pp. Tirazh 1500. Footnotes.

828. Koval'chuk V.M. *et al*, Ed., Ocherki istorii Leningrada. Period Velikoi Otechestvennoi voiny Sovetskogo Soiuza 1941-1945 gg. **Essays on history of Leningrad. Period of the Great Patriotic War of the Soviet Union 1941-1945**, Leningrad, Nauka, 1967. 748 pp. Tirazh 6000. Footnotes with archival

material, coloured maps, photographs, indexes of names, places, organisations, enterprises.

829. Samsonov A.M., Ed., Oborona Leningrada, 1941-1944. Vospominaniia i dnevnik uchastnikov **The defence of Leningrad, 1941-1944. Recollections and diaries of the participants**, Leningrad, Nauka, 1968. 791 pp. Tirazh 14500. Endnotes with archival material, photogrphs, maps.

830. Tskitishvili K.V. Zakavkaz'e v gody Velikoi Otechestvennoi voiny 1941-1945 gg. **The Transcaucasus during the Great Patriotic War 1941-1945**, Tbilisi, Izdatel'stvo TsKKP Gruzii, 1969. 488 pp. Tirazh 3000. Footnotes with archival material, tables.

831. Drizul A.A. *et al*, Ed., Bor'ba latyshskogo naroda v gody Velikoi Otechestvennoi voiny 1941-1945 **The struggle of Latvian people during the Great Patriotic War 1941-1945**, Riga, Zinatne, 1970. 932 pp. Tirazh 3000. Footnotes with archival material, photographs, maps.

832. Kozybaev M.K. Kazakhstan - arsenal fronta **Kazakhstan - arsenal of the front**, Alma-Ata, Kazakhstan, 1970. 476 pp. Tirazh 3500. Footnotes with archival material, tables.

833. Lentsman L.N. *et al*, Ed., Estonskii narod v Velikoi Otechestvennoi voine Sovetskogo Soiuza 1941-1945 **Estonian people during the Great Patriotic War of the Soviet Union 1941-1945**, in two volumes, Tallin, Eesti raamat, 1973. Vol. I. 615 pp. Tirazh 4000. Footnotes with archival material, photographs, maps, tables, indexes of names, places, chronology. Vol. II 1980, 800 pp. Tirazh 5000. Footnotes with archival material, coloured maps, photographs, indexes of names, places, chronology.

834. Kuznetsov I.I. Vostochnaia Sibir' v gody Velikoi Otechestvennoi voiny 1941-1945 **Eastern Siberia during the Great Patriotic War 1941-1945**, Irkutsk, Vostochno-Sibirskoe knizhnoe izdatel'stvo, 1974. 511 pp. Tirazh 2000. Footnotes with regional archival material, appendixes with statistical data.

835. Afteniuk S.Ia. *et al*, Ed., Moldavskaia SSR v Velikoi Otechestvennoi voine Sovetskogo Soiuza. Sbornik documentov i materialov v dvukh tomakh. Na frontakh voiny i v Sovetskom tylu, Tom pervyi **Moldavian SSR during the Great Patriotic War of the Soviet Union. Collection of documents and materials in two volumes. On the war fronts and in the Soviet rear, Vol. I**, Kishinev, Shtiintsa, 1975. 656 pp Tirazh 3300. Based on archives, endnotes, list of utilised newspapers, index of names, places, documents. V tylu vraga, Tom vtoroi **In the rear of the enemy, Vol. II**, Kishinev, Shtiintsa, 1976. 676 pp. Tirazh 3800. Endnotes, index of names, places, documents.

836. Akhazov T.A. *et al*, Ed., Chuvashskia ASSR v period Velikoi Otechestvennoi voiny. (Iiun' 1941-1945 gg). Sbornik dokumentov i materialov **Chuvash Autonomous Soviet Socialist Republic during the Great Patriotic War. June 1941-1945). Collection of documents and materials**, Cheboksary Chuvashskoe

knizhnoe izdatel'stvo, 1975. 528 pp. Tirazh 3000. Footnotes, endnotes, index of places, 4 appendixes.

837. Arutiunian A.O. *et al*, Ed., Sovetskaia Armeniia v gody Velikoi Otechestvennoi voiny (1941-1945). Sbornik dokumentov i materialov **Sovet Armenia during the Great Patriotic War (1941-1945). Collection of documents and materials,** Erevan, Akademiia Nauk Armianskoi SSR, 1975. 839 pp. Tirazh 3000. Based on archives, endnotes, index of names, places, documents.

838. Madatov G.A. Azerbaidzhan v Velikoi Otechestvennoi voine **Azerbaidzhan in the Great Patriotic War,** Baku, Elm, 1975. 406 pp. Tirazh 3000. Footnotes with archival material, bibliography.

839. Morozov K.A., Aleksandrov D.S. Ed., Kareliia v gody Velikoi Otechestvennoi voiny 1941-1945. Dokumenty. Materialy **Karelia during the Great Patriotic War 1941-1945. Documents, materials,** Petrozavodsk, Kareliia, 1975. 448 pp. Tirazh 3000. Endnotes, footnotes, index of names, places, regular and partisan units, utilized sources.

840. Tron'ko P.T. *et al*, Ed., Ukrainskaia SSR v Velikoi Otechestvennoi voine Sovetskogo Soiuza 1941-1945 gg. V trekh tomakh **Ukrainian Soviet Socialist Republic during the Great Patriotic War. In three volumes,** Kiev, Politizdat, 1975. Tirazh 33000. Photographs, coloured maps, footnotes, index of names, maps, dates. 2nd. edn. Iurchuk V.I. *et al*, Ed. Sovetskaia Ukraina v gody Velikoi Otechestvennoi voiny 1941-1945. Dokumenty i materialy v trekh tomakh **Soviet Ukraine during the Great Patriotic War 1941-1945. Documents and materials,** Kiev, Naukova dumka, 1980. Tirazh 8000. Based on archives. Photographs, endnotes, index of names, places, documents. 3rd edn. Iurchuk V.I. *et al*, Ed., 1985. Tirazh 35000. Vol. I Ukrainskaia SSR v pervyi period Velikoi Otechestvennoi voiny (22 iiunia 1941 g. - 18 noiabria 1942g.) **Ukrainian SSR during the first period of the Great Patriotic War (22 June-18 November 1942)** 518 pp., Vol. II Ukrainskaia SSR v periode korennogo pereloma v khode Velikoi Otechestvennoi voiny (19 noiabria 1942 g. - konets 1943 g.) **Ukrainian SSR during the fundamental turning point of the Great Patriotic War (19 November 1942 - end of 1943),** 511 pp., Vol. III Ukrainskaia SSR v zavershaiushchii period Velikoi Otechestvennoi voiny (1944-1945 gg.) **Ukrainian SSR during the concluding period of the Great Patriotic War (1944-1945),** 510 pp.

841. Babalashvili I.P. Gruzinskaia SSR v gody Velikoi Otechestvennoi voiny 1941-1945 **Georgian Soviet Socialist Republic during the Great Patriotic War 1941-1945,** Tbilisi, Sabchota Sakartvelo, 1977. 328 pp. Tirazh 3000. Footnotes with mainly archival material, photographs, tables, appendix.

842. Shushkin N.N., Ulitin S.D., Soiuz rabochikh i krest'ian v Velikoi Otechestvennoi voine (na materialakh respublik i oblastei Severo-Zapada RSFSR) **Union of workers and peasants during the Great Patriotic War (using the material from the north-western republics and regions of the RSFSR),** Leningrad, Leningradskii universitet, 1977. 182 pp. Tirazh 1785. Footnotes with archival material, tables.

843. Volkov B.N., Major-General *et al*, Ed., <u>Sibir' v Velikoi Otechestvennoi voine</u> <u>(Materialy konferentsii, posviashchennoi tridtsatiletiiu pobedy v Velikoi</u> <u>Otechestvennoi voine)</u> **Siberia during the Great Patriotic War (Materials from the conference devoted to the thirtieth anniversary of victory in the Great Patriotic War**, Novosibirsk, Nauka, 1977. 334 pp. Tirazh 8400. Footnotes with archival material, statistical tables.

844. Burov A.V. *et al*, Ed., <u>Blokada den' za dnem. 22 iiunia 1941 goda, 27 ianvaria</u> <u>1944</u> **Blockade day after day. 22 June 1941, 27 January 1944**, Leningrad, Lenizdat, 1979. 480 pp. Tirazh 50000. Diary of blockade. Footnotes, photographs, index of names, bibliography.

845. Kerimbaev S.K. <u>Sovetskii Kirgizstan v Velikoi Otechestvennoi voine 1941-1945</u> <u>gg.</u> **Soviet Kirghizstan during the Great Patriotic War 1941-1945**, Frunze, Ilim, 1980. 302 pp. Tirazh 1000. Footnotes with archival material, statistics, bibliography, list of archives. 2nd edn. 1985, 316 pp. Tirazh 1000.

846. Akhunova M.A. *et al*, Ed., <u>Uzbekskaia SSR v gody Velikoi Otechestvennoi</u> <u>voiny (1941-1945 gg.) V trekh tomakh. Tom I Uzbekistan v pervyi period</u> <u>Velikoi Otechestvennoi voiny (1941-Noiabr'1942 gg.)</u> **Uzbekistan SSR during the Great Patriotic War (1941-1945) In three volumes. Vol. I Uzbekistan SSR during the initial period of the Great Patriotic War (1941-November 1942)**, Tashkent, Fan, 1981. 408 pp. Tirazh 2000. Footnotes with archival material, photographs, index of names, places.

847. Bazarzhapov V.B. <u>Natsional'nye raiony Sibiri i Dal'nego Vostoka v gody</u> <u>Velikoi Otechestvennoi voiny</u> **National regions of Siberia and the Far East during the Great Patriotic War**, Novosibirsk, Nauka, 1981. 257 pp. Tirazh 2200. Footnotes with archival material, statistical tables, appendix.

848. Kolesnik A.D. <u>RSFSR v gody Velikoi Otechestvennoi voiny. Problemy tyla i</u> <u>vsenarodnoi pomoshchi frontu</u> **RSFSR during the Great Patriotic War. Problems of the rear and nationwide aid for the front**, Moscow, Nauka, 1982. 328 pp. Tirazh 5450. Endnotes with archival material, tables.

849. Dudarenko M.L. *et al*, <u>Osvobozhdenie gorodov: Spravochnik po osvobozhdeniiu</u> <u>gorodov v period Velikoi Otechestvennoi voiny 1941-1945</u> **Liberation of the cities: Handbook on liberation of the cities during the Great Patriotic War 1941-1945**, Moscow, Voenizdat, 1985. 598 pp. Tirazh 50000. Six appendixes.

850. Bukov K.I., Zarezina K.F., *et al*, <u>Moskva i Moskovskaia oblast' v Velikoi</u> <u>Otechestvennoi voine 1941-1945. Kratkaia khronika</u> **Moscow and Moscow region during the Great Patriotic War 1941-1945. Short chronicle**, Moscow, Moskovskii rabochii, 1986. 523 pp. Tirazh 25000. Based on archives and contemporary publications. Index of military formations, organisations, businesses, places.

851. Vavilov F.I. <u>Ferganskaia oblast' v Velikoi Otechestvennoi voine</u> **The Fergana region during the Great Patriotic War**, Tashkent, Izdatel'stvo "Fan" Uzbekskoi SSR, 1988. 127 pp. Tirazh 1000. Endnotes with archival material.

852. Natmeladze M.V., Ed., Uchastie Gruzinskoi SSR v Velikoi Otechestvennoi voine (1941-1945 g.g.) (Sbornik trudov) **The participation of Georgian SSR during the Great Patriotic War (1941-1945) (Collection of studies)**, Tbilisi, Metsniereba, 1989. 174 pp. Tirazh 1000. Footnotes with archival material.

WAR ECONOMY

853. Voznesenskii N.A. Voennaia ekonomika SSSR v period Otechestvennoi voiny **War economy of the USSR during the Great Patriotic War**, Moscow, Gospolitizdat, 1947. 192 pp. English translation War Economy of the USSR in the Period of the Patriotic War, Moscow, Foreign Languages Publishing House, 1948.

854. Shigalin G.I. Narodnoe khoziaistvo SSSR v period Velikoi Otechestvennoi voiny **National economy of the USSR during the Great Patriotic War**, Moscow, Izdatel'stvo sotsial'no-ekonomicheskoi literatury, 1960. 279 pp. Tirazh 10000. Footnotes with archival material, tables.

855. Kravchenko G.S. Voennaia ekonomika SSSR 1941-1945 **War economy of the USSR 1941-1945**, Moscow, Voenizdat, 1963. 399 pp. Tirazh 9000. Footnotes with archival material, 40 tables.

856. Chadaev Ia.E. Ekonomika SSSR v period Velikoi Otechestvennoi voiny (1941-1945 gg.) **USSR economy during the Great Patriotic War (1941-1945)**, Moscow, Mysl', 1965. 390 pp. Tirazh 11000. Tables, footnotes. 2nd edn. 1985, includes bibliography.

857. Gladkov I.A. Ed., Sovetskaia ekonomika v period Velikoi Otechestvennoi voiny 1941-1945 gg. **Soviet economy during the Great Patriotic War 1941-1945**, Moscow, Nauka, 1970. 504 pp. Tirazh 4000. Tables, statistics, footnotes with archival material, index of names.

WAR EFFORT

858. Cherniavskii U.G. Voina i prodovol'stvie. Snabzhenie gorodskogo naseleniia v Velikuiu Otechestvennuiu voinu (1941-1945) **War and food supply. Supplying the cities' population during the Great Patriotic War**, Moscow, Nauka, 1964. 208 pp. Tirazh 3800. Footnotes with archival material, tables, bibliography.

859. Arutiunian Iu.V. Sovetskoe krest'ianstvo v gody Velikoi Otechestvennoi voiny **Soviet peasantry during the Great Patriotic War**, 2nd edn. Moscow, Nauka, 1970. 467 pp. Tirazh 6000. Based on documents. Footnotes with archival material, statistics, photographs, index of places, names, bibliography, 7 appendixes.

860. Mitrofanova A.V. Rabochii klass SSSR v gody Velikoi Otechestvennoi voiny **The working class of the USSR during the Great Patriotic War**, Moscow, Nauka, 1971. 483 pp.

861. Dokuchaev G.A. Rabochii klass Sibiri i Dal'nego Vostoka v gody Velikoi Otechestvennoi voiny **Working class of Siberia and the Far East during the Great Patriotic War**, Moscow, Nauka, 1973. 420 pp. Tirazh 3650. Footnotes with archival material, tables, appendixes, index of names, places, subjects, enterprises.

862. Kirsanov N.A. Po zovu Rodiny. Dobrovol'cheskie formirovaniia Krasnoi Armii v period Velikoi Otechestvennoi voiny **At the call of the motherland. Volunteer formations of the Red Army during the Great Patriotic War**, Moscow, Mysl', 1974. 277 pp. Tirazh 40000. Based on central and local archives. Footnotes with archival material, photographs, tables.

863. Kolesnik A.D. Narodnoe opolchenie gorodov-geroev **People's militia of the hero-cities**, Moscow, Nauka, 1974. 368 pp. Tirazh 11000. Footnotes with archival material, photographs, tables, index of names, army units, 6 appendixes.

864. Pospelov P.N. Ed., Sovetskii tyl v Velikoi Otechestvennoi voine Kniga pervaia Obshchie problemy **Soviet rear during the Great Patriotic War Vol. I General problems**, Moscow, Mysl', 1974. 300 pp. Tirazh 30000. Footnotes with archival material, tables, photographs, index of names, 70 pp. bibliography. Kniga vtoraia Trudovoi podvig naroda **Working feat of the people**, Moscow, Mysl', 1974. 367 pp. Tirazh 30000. Footnotes with archival material, tables, photographs, index of names.

865. Kotliar E.S. Gosudarstvennyie trudovye rezervy SSSR v gody Velikoi Otechestvennoi voiny **USSR state labour reserves during the Great Patriotic War**, Moscow, Vysshaia shkola, 1975. 240 pp. Tirazh 13000. Footnotes with archival material, statistics, 85 tables, bibliography.

866. Shekhtsov N.I. *et al*, Ed., Velikaia Pobeda Sovetskogo naroda 1941-1945. Materialy nauchnoi konferentsii, posviashchennoi 30-letiiu Pobedy sovetskogo naroda v Velikoi Otechestvennoi voine 1941-1945 godov **The great victory of the Soviet people 1941-1945. Materials presented at the scientific conference devoted to the 30th anniversary of the victory by the Soviet people in the Great Patriotic War 1941-1945**, Moscow, Nauka, 1976. 648 pp. Tirazh 45500. Footnotes with archival material, photographs, index of names.

867. Smirnov V.I. Podvig sovetskogo krest'ianstva **Feat of the Soviet peasantry**, Moscow, Mosk. rabochii, 1976. 312 pp. Tirazh 10000. Footnotes with archival material, tables.

868. Zagorul'ko M.M., Iudenkov A.F., Krakh plana "Ol'denburg". (O sryve ekonomicheskikh planov fashistskoi Germanii na vremenno okkupirovannoi teritorii SSSR) 3rd edn. **Collapse of the "Plan Oldenburg". (Breakdown of the economic plans of the fascist Germany in the temporarily occupied territory of the USSR)**, Moscow, Ekonomika, 1980. Uses German archives. Footnotes with archival material, photographs, tables, index of names, places.

869. Stishova L.I. Ed., V tylu i na fronte: Zhenshchiny-kommunistki v gody Velikoi Otechestvennoi voiny **In the rear and at the front: Women-communists dur-**

ing the Great Patriotic War, Moscow, Politizdat, 1984. 319 pp. Tirazh 20000. Photographs.

870. Zinich M.S. Trudovoi podvig rabochego klassa v 1941-1945 gg.(po materialam otraslei mashinostroeniia) **Labour feat by the working class during 1941-1945 (based on data from heavy engineering/machine-tool industry)**, Moscow, Nauka, 1984. 232 pp. Tirazh 1800. Based on archives. Endnotes with archival material, tables.

871. Sinitsin A.M. Vsenarodnaia pomoshch frontu **Nationwide aid for the front**, Moscow, Voenizdat, 1985. 2nd edn. 319 pp. Tirazh 35000. Footnotes with archival material, index of names, subjects.

872. Galagan V.Ia. Ratnyi podvig zhenshchin v gody Velikoi Otechestvennoi voiny **The war feat of women during the Great Patriotic War**, Kiev, Vishcha shkola, 1986. 304 pp. Tirazh 7000. Factual. Index of names, 15 pp bibliography, appendix.

873. Morekhina G.G. Partiinoe stroitel'stvo v period Velikoi Otechestvennoi voiny Sovetskogo Soiuza 1941-1945 **Party structure during the Great Patriotic War 1941-1945**, Moscow, Politizdat, 1986. 392 pp. Tirazh 28000. Footnotes with archival material, tables.

874. Poliakov Iu.A. Ed., Vozrozhdenie prifrontovykh i osvobozhdennykh raionov SSSR v gody Velikoi Otechestvennoi voiny 1941-1945 **Revival of the front-line and liberated regions of the USSR during the Great Patriotic War 1941-1945**, Moscow, Nauka, 1986. 216 pp. Tirazh 2750. Chapter endnotes with archival material, photographs, appendix of 27 documents.

875. Brodskii E.A. Oni ne propali bez vesti. Ne slomlennye fashistskoi nevolei **They did not perish without trace. No bowing to fascist bondage**, Moscow, Mysl', 1987. 461 pp. Tirazh 100000. Based on archives and recollections. Photographs, bibliography, appendix.

876. Kolesnik A.D. *et al* Ed., RSFSR - frontu 1941-1945. Dokumenty i materialy **RSFSR aid to the front 1941-1945**, Moscow, Sov. Rossiia, 1987. 384 pp. Tirazh 5000. Based on archives. Endnotes with archival material, photographs, index of places.

877. Bilenko S.V. Na okhrane tyla strany: Istrebitel'nye batal'ony i polki v Velikoi Otechestvennoi voine 1941-1945 gg. **Protecting the rear: "Destruction battalions" and regiments during the Great Patriotic War 1941-1945**, Moscow, Nauka, 1988. 256 pp. Tirazh 8800. For historians. Combatting black marketeering, desertion. Chapter endnotes with archival material, appendix.

878. D'iakov Iu.L. Kapital'noe stroitel'stvo v SSSR 1941-1945 **Major construction work in the USSR 1941-1945**, Moscow, Nauka, 1988. 256 pp. Tirazh 1250. For historians. Endnotes with archival material, indexes of names, places, enterprises, organisations.

879. Kolesnik A.D. Opolchenskie formirovaniia Rossiiskoi Federatsii v gody Velikoi Otechestvennoi voiny **Militia formations of the Russian Federation during the Great Patriotic War**, Moscow, Nauka, 1988. 266 pp. Tirazh 3500. Endnotes with archival material, indexes of names, places, units.

880. Mizin V.M. Snaiper Petrova **Sniper Petrova**, Leningrad, Ienizdat, 1988. Biography of highly decorated woman sniper. Photographs.

881. Nurbekova G.D. Zhenshchiny Kazakhstana - frontu. Trudovoi podvig zhenshchin Kazakhstana v promyshlennosti i sel'skom khoziaistve respubliki v gody Velikoi Otechesvennoi voiny **Kazakhstan women - to the front. Labour feat of the Kazakhstan women in industry and agriculture of the republic during the Great Patriotic War**, Alma-Ata, Kazakhstan, 1988. 2nd edn. 168 pp. Tirazh 7500. Footnotes with archival material.

882. Iablochkin Iu.N., Iun' 1941-mai 1945: O podvige Leningrada strokami khroniki **June 1941-May 1945: Chronicle of the feat of Leningrad**, Leningrad, Lenizdat, 1989. 720 pp. Tirazh 5000. Based on previously unpublished archives. Endnotes with archival material.

883. Zhavoronkov N.M. Ed., Stranitsy geroicheskogo truda khimikov v gody Velikoi Otechestvennoi voiny 1941-1945 **Pages of chemists' heroic labour during the Great Patriotic War 1941-1945**, Moscow, Nauka, 1989. 287 pp. Tirazh 8600. Collection of articles. Chapter endnotes, footnotes, photographs.

884. Khazanov B.A., Major General, Podvig odnogo zavoda **The feat of one factory**, Moscow, Voenizdat, 1990. 272 pp. Tirazh 30000. Artillery munition factory - director's account. Photographs.

REAR SERVICES, TRANSPORT, MILITARY/MEDICAL

885. Edlinskii S.F. Kaspiiskii transportnyi flot v Velikoi Otechestvennoi voine Sovetskogo Soiuza 1941-1945 gg. **Caspian transport fleet during the Great Patriotic War of the Soviet Union 1941-1945**, Moscow, Morskoi transport, 1963. 228 pp. Tirazh 5600. Footnotes with archival material, photographs, maps, tables, index of names, bibliography.

886. Edlinskii S.F. Severnyi transportnyi flot v Velikoi Otechestvennoi voine Sovetskogo soiuza 1941-1945 gg. **The Northern transport fleet during the Great Patriotic War 1941-1945**, Moscow, Morskoi transport, 1963. 251 pp. Tirazh 3000. Footnotes with archival material, photographs, maps, tables, index of names, ports, bibliography.

887. Kumanev G.A. Sovetskie zheleznodorozhniki v gody Velikoi Otechestvennoi voiny (1941-1945) **Soviet railwaymen during the Great Patriotic War (1941-1945)**, Moscow, Nauka, 1965. 324 pp. Tirazh 1700. Footnotes with archival material, photographs, index of names, places, railway lines and junctions, bibliography.

888.   Poliakov Iu.A. Ed., Eshelony idut na vostok. Sbornik statei i vospominanii iz istorii perebazirovaniia proizvoditel'nykh sil SSSR v 1941-1942 gg. **The echelons go east. Collection of articles and recollections from the history of the relocation of industrial power of the USSR during 1941-1942**, Moscow, Nauka, 1966. 264 pp. Tirazh 7200. Footnotes with archival material, photographs.

889.   Tamarchenko M.L. Sovetskie finansy v period Velikoi Otechestvennoi voiny **Soviet Finance during the Great Patrotic War**, Moscow, Finansy, 1967, 144 pp.

890.   Vishnevskii A.A. Dnevnik khirurga. Velikaia Otechestvennaia voina 1941-1945 gg **Diary of a surgeon. The Great Patriotic War 1941-1945**, Moscow, Meditsina, 1970. 2nd edn. 424 pp. Tirazh 10000. Coloured maps, photographs, footnotes.

891.   Antipenko N.A., General, Rear Services, Na glavnom napravlenii **On the main axis**, Moscow, Nauka, 1971. 392 pp. Tirazh 40000. Photographs, maps, index of names, footnotes.

892.   Kumanev G.A. Na sluzhbe fronta i tyla. Zheleznodorozhnyi transport SSSR nakanune i v gody Velikoi Otechestvennoi voiny 1938-1945 **On service of the front and the rear. USSR railway transport on the eve and during the Great Patriotic War 1938-1945**, Moscow, Nauka, 1976. 456 pp. Tirazh 6800. Endnotes with archival material, photographs, graphs, maps, bibliography, appendix, index of names, places.

893.   Kurkotkin S.K., General, Ed., Tyl Sovetskikh Vooruzhennykh Sil v Velikoi Otechestvennoi voine 1941-1945 gg. **Soviet Armed Forces' Rear during the Great Patriotic War 1941-1945**, Moscow, Voenizdat, 1977. 559 pp. Tirazh 50000. For officers and generals. Footnotes with archival material, photographs, tables, 2 coloured maps.

894.   Smirnov E.I. Wartime Head of Red Army Military-Medical Administration Voina i voennaia meditsina. 1939-1945 gody **The war and military medicine 1939-1945**, Moscow, Meditsina, 1979. 528 pp. Tirazh 11000. Tables, illustrations, maps, photographs, footnotes with archival material.

895.   Likhomanov M.I. et al, Organizatorskaia i massovo-politicheskaia rabota partiinykh organizatsii RSFSR v tylu 1941-1945 gg. **Organisational and large-scale political work of the RSFSR Party organisations in the rear during 1941-1945**, Leningrad, Leningradskii universitet, 1980. 287 pp. Tirazh 2409. Footnotes with archival material.

896.   Chebotarev M.N. et al, Sovetskii rechnoi transport v Velikoi Otechestvennoi voine **Soviet river transport during the Great Patriotic War**, Moscow, Voenizdat, 1981. 328 pp. Tirazh 25000. Footnotes with archival material, photographs, tables.

897. Kovalev I.V., Lt. General, Transport v Velikoi Otechestvennoi voine (1941-1945 gg.) **Transport during the Great Patriotic War (1941-1945)**, Moscow, Nauka, 1981. 480 pp. Tirazh 7650. Endnotes with archival material, photographs, tables. Wartime Head Central Administration Military Communication (VOSO).

898. Koval'chuk V.M. Doroga pobedy osazhdennogo Leningrada. Zheleznodorozhnaia magistral' Shlissel'burg - Poliany v 1943 g **The victory road of besieged Leningrad. The main railway line Schlusselburg - Poliany in 1943**, Leningrad, Nauka, 1984. 214 pp. Tirazh 9400. Footnotes with archival material, photographs, maps, appendix.

899. Kumanev G.A. Ed., Sovetskii tyl v pervyi period Velikoi Otechestvennoi voiny **Soviet Rear during the first period of the Great Patriotic War**, Moscow, Nauka, 1988. 422 pp. Tirazh 3600. Endnotes with archival material.

900. Kumanev G.A. Voina i zheleznodorozhnyi transport SSSR 1941-1945 **The war and the railway transport in the USSR 1941-1945**, Moscow, Nauka, 1988. 368pp. Tirazh 2600. Endnotes with archival material, photographs, maps, tables, index of names.

901. Mikhel'son V.I., Ial'gin M.I., Vozdushnyi most **Air bridge**, 2nd edn. Moscow, Politizdat, 1988. 336 pp. Tirazh 20000. Air lift into Leningrad. Uses personal and local archives. Photographs.

902. Mitrofanova A.V., Ed., Sovetskii tyl v period korennogo pereloma v Velikoi Otechestvennoi voine, noiabr' 1942-1943 **Soviet Rear in the period of the fundamental turning point of the Great Patriotic War, November 1942-1943**, Moscow, Nauka, 1989. 392 pp. Tirazh 4400. Endnotes with archival material, tables.

903. Aleksanian I.V., Knopov M.Sh., Rukovoditeli meditsinskoi sluzhby frontov i flotov v Velikoi Otechestvennoi voine 1941-1945 gg. **Directors of the medical service on the fronts and in the fleets during the Great Patriotic War**, Moscow, Meditsina, 1992. 288 pp. Tirazh 1291. Footnotes with archival material, photographs.

PARTISANS, RESISTANCE MOVEMENTS

904. Zalesskii A.I. V partizanskikh kraiakh i zonakh. Patrioticheskii podvig sovetskogo krest'ianstva v tylu vraga (1941-1944 gg.) **In partisan country and zones of operation. Patriotic feat of the Soviet peasantry in the rear of the enemy (1941-1944)**, Moscow, Izdatel'stvo sotsial'no-ekonomicheskoi literatury, 1962. 397 pp. Tirazh 20000. Footnotes with archival material, photographs, illustrations, coloured map.

905. Bychkov L.N. Partizanskoe dvizhenie v gody Velikoi Otechestvennoi voiny 1941-1945 (Kratkii ocherk) **Partisan movement during the Great Patriotic**

War 1941-1945 (Short study), Moscow, Mysl', 1965. 454 pp. Tirazh 14000. Footnotes with archival material, photographs, chronology.

906. Kalinin P. Partizanskaia respublika **The partisan republic**, Minsk, Belarus', 1968. 2nd edn. 384 pp. Tirazh 10000. Author: former Chief of Staff of partisan movement in Belorussia. Photographs.

907. Bogatyr' Z.A. Bor'ba v tylu vraga **Struggle in the rear of the enemy**, Moscow, Mysl', 1969. 2nd edn. 470 pp. Tirazh 60000. Footnotes with archival material, photographs, tables, map.

908. Samukhin V.P. Volkhovskie partizany. Rasskaz o bor'be leningradskikh partizan v polose Volkhovskogo fronta **Partisans of Volkhov. Story about the fight of Leningrad partisans in the zone of the Volkhov Front**, Leningrad, Lenizdat, 1969. 269 pp. Tirazh 54000. Footnotes with archival material, photographs, maps, illustrations.

909. Petrova Z.A. et al, Partizany Brianshchiny. Sbornik dokumentov i materialov o Brianskom partizanskom krae v gody Velikoi Otechestvennoi voiny **Partisans of Bryansk district. Collection of documents and material from Bryansk partisan area during the Great Patriotic War**,   Tula, Priokskoe knizhnoe izdatel'stvo, 1970. 2nd edn. 488 pp. Tirazh 15000. Based on Bryansk Party archives. Index of names, places.

910. Logunova T.A. Partiinoe podpol'e i partizanskoe dvizhenie v tsentral'nykh oblastiakh RSFSR iiul' 1941-1943 gg. **The Party underground and the partisan movement in the central regions of the RSFSR July 1941-1943**, Moscow, Izdatel'stvo Moskovskogo Universiteta, 1973. 228 pp. Tirazh 8300. Footnotes with archival material, photographs, tables, maps.

911. Petrov Iu.P. Partizanskoe dvizhenie v Leningradskoi oblasti 1941-1944 **Partisan movement in Leningrad region,** Leningrad, Lenizdat, 1973. 454 pp. Tirazh 25000. Footnotes with archival material including East German, photographs, maps, index of names.

912. Tskitishvili K. Zakavkaz'e v partizanskoi voine 1941-1945 g.g. **Transcaucasus in the partisan war 1941-1945**, Tbilisi, Izdatel'stvo TsKKP Gruzii, 1973. 302 pp. Tirazh 4000.

913. Bystrov V.E. et al, Voina v tylu vraga. O nekotorykh problemakh istorii sovetskogo partizanskogo dvizheniia v gody Velikoi Otechestvennoi voiny **War in the enemy rear. About some historical problems of the Soviet partisan movement during the Great Patriotic War**, Moscow, Politizdat, 1974. 447 pp. Tirazh 30000. Footnotes with archival material, photographs.

914. Dzhuraev T.D. Uzbekistantsy - uchastniki partizanskoi voiny **The Uzbeks - participants in the partizan war**, Tashkent, Izdatel'stvo Uzbekistan, 1975. 176 pp. Tirazh 7000. Footnotes with archival material, photographs, appendix.

915. Gridnev V.M. Bor'ba krest'ianstva okkupirovannykh oblastei RSFSR protiv ne-metsko-fashistskoi okkupatsionnoi politiki 1941-1944 **Peasants' struggle in the occupied regions of the RSFSR against the German-fascist occupation policy 1941-1944**, Moscow, Nauka, 1976. Footnotes with archival material, tables, illustrations, bibliography.

916. Iudenkova A.F., Ed., Partiia vo glave narodnoi bor'by v tylu vraga (1941-1944 gg) **The Party at the head of people's struggle in the enemy rear (1941-1944)**, Moscow, Mysl', 1976. 325 pp. Tirazh 15000. Footnotes with archival material. See important contribution by P.K. Ponomarenko pp. 191-215 *"Tsentralizatsiia rukovodstva partizanskim dvizheniem"*.

917. Makarov V.A. Nepokorennaia zemlia Rossiiskaia **The unsubdued Russian land**, Moscow, Politizdat, 1976. 319 pp. Tirazh 100000. Footnotes with archival material.

918. Kasatkin M.A. V tylu nemetsko-fashistskikh armii "Tsentr". Vsenarodnaia bor'-ba na okkupirovannoi teritorii zapadnykh oblastei RSFSR 1941-1943 gg. **In the rear of the German Army Group "Centre". Nationwide battle on the occupied territory of the western regions of the RSFSR 1941-1943**, Moscow, Mysl', 1980. 318 pp. Tirazh 20000. Endnotes with archival material, bibliography.

919. Khatskevich A.F., Kriuchok R.R., Stanovlenie partizanskogo dvizheniia v Belo-russii i druzhba narodov SSSR **Creation of partisan movement in Belorussia and the friendship of the peoples of USSR**, Minsk, Nauka i tekhnika, 1980. 320 pp. Tirazh 4000. Endnotes comprise bibliography; archival material.

920. Koval'chuk V.M., Ed., V tylu vraga. Bor'ba partizan i podpol'shchikov na ok-kupirovannoi territorii Leningradskoi oblasti 1942 g. Sbornik dokumentov **In the rear of the enemy. The struggle of the partisans and the underground workers on the territory of Leningrad region. Collection of documents 1942**, Leningrad, Lenizdat, 1981. 360 pp. Tirazh 10000. Endnotes, index of places, tables, maps, photographs.

921. Kuz'min A.T. *et al*, Ed., Vsenarodnaia bor'ba v Belorussii protiv nemetsko-fa-shistskikh zakhvatchikov v gody Velikoi Otechestvennoi voiny: V 3-kh tomakh. Tom pervyi **Nationwide struggle against the German-fascist occupiers during the Great Patriotic War: In three volumes. Vol. I**, Minsk, Belarus', 1983. 591 pp. Photographs from the government archives. Endnotes contain archival material. Tom vtoroi **Vol. II**, 1984. 551 pp. Tom tretii **Vol. III**, 1985. 531 pp. All vols. Tirazh 25000.

922. Makarov N.I., Ed., Partiinoe podpol'e. Deiatel'nost' podpol'nykh part. organov i organizatsii na okkupirovannoi sov. territorii v gody Velikoi Otechestvennoi voiny **The Party underground. Activities of the Party underground organs and organisations on the occupied Soviet territory during the Great Patriotic War**, Moscow, Politizdat, 1983. 352 pp. Tirazh 50000. Footnotes with archival material, photographs, index of names.

923. Manaenkov A.L. *et al*, Partizanskie formirovaniia Belorussii v gody Velikoi Otechestvennoi voiny (iun' 1941-iul' 1944) Kratkie svedeniia ob organizatsionnoi strukture partizanskikh soedinenii, brigad (polkov), otriadov (batal'onov) i ikh lichnom sostave **Partisan formations in Belorussia during the Great Patriotic War (June 1941-July 1944). Short reports on organisational structure of partisan formations, brigades (regiments), detachments (battalions) and their personnel**, Minsk, Belarus', 1983. 765 pp. Tirazh 20000. Index of formations, names, tables.

924. Starozhilov N.V. Partizanskie soedineniia Ukrainy v Velikoi Otechestvennoi voine **Partisan formations in the Ukraine during the Great Patriotic War**, Kiev, Vishcha shkola, 1983. 240 pp. Tirazh 5000. Endnotes with archival material, tables.

925. Klokov V.I. Deistviia partizan Ukrainy na zheleznodorozhnykh kommunikatsiiakh v tylu fashistskikh voisk 1941-1944 **Ukranian partisans' actions concerning railway communications in the rear of the Fascist forces 1941-1944**, Kiev, Naukova dumka, 1984. 168 pp. Tirazh 2000. Endnotes comprising bibliography with archival material.

926. Logunova T.A. Sovetskaia istoriographiia narodnoi bor'by v tyly nemetsko-fashistskikh voisk 1941-1945 **Soviet historiography of the people's struggle in the rear of the German-Fascist forces 1941-1945**, Moscow, Moskovskii universitet, 1985. 128 pp. Tirazh 1630. For specialist historians. Footnotes, bibliography.

927. Lemeshchuk N.M. Ne skloniv golovy. (O deiatel'nosti antifashistskogo podpol'ia v gitlerovskikh zastenkakh) **We did not yield. (Activities of the anti-fascist resistance in Hitler's torture-chambers)**, 2nd edn. Kiev, Politizdat Ukrainy, 1986. 155 pp. Tirazh 25000. Endnotes with archival material, photographs.

928. Lobanok V.E., Ed., Partinoe podpol'e v Belorussii 1941-1944. Stranitsy vospominanii. Vileiskaia, Baranovichskaia, Pinskaia, Brestskaia, Belostokskaia oblasti **The Party underground in Belorussia 1941-1944. Pages of recollections. Vileisk, Baranovich, Pinsk, Brest, Belostok regions**, Minsk, Belarus', 1986. 415 pp. Tirazh 13000. Photographs, index of names.

929. Petliak F.A. Partiinoe rukovodstvo sovetami na Ukraine v gody Velikoi Otechestvennoi voiny (1941-1945) **Party leadership of the Soviets in the Ukraine during the Great Patriotic War (1941-1945)**, Kiev, Vishcha shkola, 1986. 182 pp. Tirazh 1000. For lecturers, scientific workers. Endnotes with archival material.

930. Ponomarenko P.K. Vsenarodnaia bor'ba v tylu nemetsko-fashistskikh zakhvatchikov 1941-1944 **Nationwide struggle on the rear of the German-fascist occupiers 1941-1944**, Moscow, Nauka, 1986. 440 pp. Tirazh 50000. Endnotes with archival material, appendix, bibliography, index of utilised archives.

931. Galleni M. Sovetskie partizany v ital'ianskom dvizhenii soprotivleniia **Soviet partisans in the Italian Resistance movement**, 2nd edn. translation from Italian

I partigiani sovietici nella Resistenza italiana, Moscow, Progress 1988. 229 pp. Tirazh 25000. Footnotes, appendix with archival photographs.

932. Shomodi V.E. Major General, Marshrutami narodnoi slavy **On the itinerary of national glory**, Minsk, Polymia, 1988. 2nd edn. 352 pp. Tirazh 15000. Ten appendixes, maps, bibliography.

933. Zevelev A.I. *et al*, Nenavist' spressovannaia v tol **Hatred compressed into TNT**, Moscow, Mysl', 1991. 331 pp. Tirazh 100000. OMSBON NKVD Special Forces brigade. Footnotes with archival material, appendix.

LOSSES

934. Poliakov L.E. Tsena voiny: Demograficheskii aspekt **The price of the war: Demographic aspect**, Moscow, Finansy i statistika, 1985. 136 pp. Tirazh 50000. Footnotes, tables, graphs.

935. Krivosheev G.F. Col. General, Ed., Grif Sekretnosti sniat. Poteri Vooruzhennykh Sil SSSR v voinakh, boevykh deistviiakh i voennykh konfliktakh. Statisticheskoe issledovanie **The stamp of secrecy removed. Losses of the USSR Armed Forces in wars, combat actions and military conflicts. Statistical analysis**, Moscow, Voenizdat, 1993. 416 pp. Tirazh 30000. Footnotes with archival material, 111 tables. Manuscript finished in 1991. Soviet-German losses, Great Patriotic War Chapter 3 pp. 128-393.

OTHER THEATRES OF WAR

936. Kulish V.M. Vtoroi front. Operatsii v Zapadnoi Evrope v 1944-1945 gg. **Second Front. Operations in Western Europe 1944-1945**, Moscow, Voenizdat, 1960. 476 pp. Footnotes, tables, index of names, subjects, bibliography, separate book of 45 maps.

937. Sevost'ianov G.N. Podgotovka voiny na Tikhom Okeane (Sentiabr' 1939 g. - dekabr' 1941 g.) **The preparation of war in the Pacific (September 1939 - December 1941)**, Moscow, Nauka, 1962. Includes Pearl Harbour. Footnotes with archival material, coloured map, 11 pp. bibliography, index of names, places.

938. Proektor D.M. Voina v Evrope 1939-1941 **War in Europe 1939-1941**, Moscow, Voenizdat, 1963. 437 pp. Tirazh 12000. For generals and officers.

939. Nekrich A. *et al*, Ed., Protiv fal'sifikatsii istorii vtoroi mirovoi voiny. Sbornik sta-tei **Against the falsification of the history of the Second World War. Collection of articles**, Moscow, Nauka, 1964. 399 pp. Tirazh 4500. Footnotes.

940. Strel'nikov V.S., Cherepanov N.M., Voina bez riska. (Deistviia anglo-amerikanskikh voisk v Italii v 1943-1945 godakh) **War with no risk. (Anglo-**

American operations in Italy), Moscow, Voenizdat, 1965. 279 pp. Tirazh 7000. Primarily for officers, generals, admirals. Footnotes, bibliography.

941. Belli V.A., Penzin K.V., Boevye deistviia v Atlantike i na Sredizemnom more. 1939-1945 **Combat actions in the Atlantic and the Mediterranean. 1939-1945**, Moscow, Voenizdat, 1967. 479 pp. Tirazh 5000. For officers, generals, admirals. Footnotes, 9 appendixes, index of operations, bibliography.

942. Sekistov V.A. Voina i politika (voenno-politicheskii ocherk voennykh deistvii v Zapadnoi Evrope i basseine Sredizemnogo moria, 1939-1945) **War and politics (military-political study of military actions in Western Europe and the Mediterranean basin 1939-1945)**, Moscow, Voenizdat, 1970. 496 pp. Tirazh 22000. Footnotes, tables.

943. Kulish V.M. Istoriia vtorogo fronta **History of the Second Front**, Moscow, Nauka, 1971. 659 pp. Tirazh 25000. Footnotes, coloured maps, index of names, bibliography.

944. Ivanov S.P., General, Ed., Nachal'nyi period voiny. (Po opytu pervykh kampanii i operatsii mirovoi voiny) **The initial period of war. (According to the experience of the first campaigns and operations of the Second World War)**, Moscow, Voenizdat, 1974. 357 pp. Tirazh 50000. Covers Western, Soviet and Far Eastern theatres. Coloured maps supplement, tables, footnotes. Also USAF translation.

945. Sapozhnikov B.G. Kitai v ogne voiny (1931-1950) **China in the blaze of war (1931-1950)**, Moscow, Nauka, 1977. 351 pp. Tirazh 10000. Endnotes.

946. Rzheshevsky O.A. Operation Overlord, from the History of the Second Front **Operatsiia "Overlord". Iz istorii vtorogo fronta**, Moscow, Novosti, 1984. 46 pp. Footnotes.

947. Rzheshevsky O.A. World war II: Myths and Realities **Vtoraia mirovaia voina: Mify i deistvitel'nost'**, Moscow, Progress Publishers, 1984. 279 pp. Tirazh 9990. Footnotes, photographs, index of names.

948. Sapozhnikov B. The China Theatre in World War II 1939-1945 **Kitaiski front vo vtoroi mirovoi voine 1939-1945**, Moscow, Progress Publishers, 1985. 256 pp. Tirazh 4515. Footnotes, bibliographical endnotes, tables.

949. Bezymenskii L. Tainyi front protiv vtorogo fronta **Secret front against the Second Front**, Moscow, Novosti, 1987. 277 pp. Tirazh 200000. States book based on little known US documents. Footnotes, photographs.

950. Rzheshevsky O.A., Ed., Pravda i lozh' o vtoroi mirovoi voine **The truth and the lies about the Second World War**, Moscow, Voenizdat, 1988. 296 pp. Tirazh 30000. Footnotes.

MISCELLANY

951. Dubovikov A.N., Trifonov N.A., Ed., <u>Sovetskie pisateli na frontakh Velikoi Otechestvennoi voiny</u> in the series <u>Literaturnoe nasledstvo</u>, **Soviet writers on the front during the Great Patriotic War**, in the series **Literary Inheritance**, <u>Kniga pervaia</u> **Book one**, 639 pp. <u>Kniga vtoraia</u> **Book two**, 732 pp. Moscow, Nauka, 1966. Tirazh 8500. Photographs, illustrations.

952. Levshin B.V. <u>Akademiia nauk SSSR v gody Velikoi Otechestvennoi voiny. Arkhiv AN SSSR</u> **The Academy of Sciences during the Great Patriotic War. The Archive of the Academy of Sciences USSR**, Moscow, Nauka, 1966. 188 pp. Tirazh 3000. Footnotes with archival material, photographs.

953. Iurov Iu., Ed., <u>Reportazh s frontov voiny</u> **Reports from the war fronts**, Moscow, Politizdat, 1970. 286 pp. Tirazh 100000. Photographs.

954. Kim M.P. *et al*, Ed., <u>Istoriografiia Velikoi Otechestvennoi voiny. Sbornik statei</u> **The historiography of the Great Patriotic War. Collection of articles**, Moscow, Nauka, 1980. 285 pp. Tirazh 6000. Footnotes, appendix.

955. Krasil'shchik S. <u>Ot sovetskogo informbiuro 1941-1945. Publitsistika i ocherki voennykh let</u> **From the Soviet Informbureau 1941-1945. Wartime journalism**, Moscow, Novosti, 1982. Vol. I 317 pp. Vol.II 473 pp. Tirazh 400000. Photographs.

956. Levin Iu., Loshak V., Ed., <u>Zhivye stroki voiny...</u> **Living lines of the war**, Sverdlovsk, Sredne-Ural'skoe knizhnoe izdatel'stvo, 1984. 352 pp. Tirazh 25000. Letters from soldiers to families.

PART THREE

THE NUCLEAR AGE

This chapter is divided into four sections: **Arms and Services, Military Districts, NATO and WTO (Warsaw Pact), Armament and Disarmament.**

SOVIET ARMS AND SERVICES

The arrangement under **SOVIET ARMS AND SERVICES** (post 1945) follows the ordering presented in 50 let Vooruzhennykh Sil SSSR, Moscow, Voenizdat, 1968.
1) Strategic Rocket Forces/SRF (Raketnye voiska strategicheskogo naznacheniia),
2) Ground Forces (Sukhoputnye voiska),
3) Air Defence Troops/PVO (Voiska PVO strany),
4) Air Force (Voenno-vozdushnye sily),
5) Navy (Voenno-Morskoi Flot),
6) Rear Services (Tyl vooruzhennykh sil)

Strategic Rocket Forces/SRF

957. Vermishev Iu.Kh Osnovy upravleniia raketami **The principles of rocket guidance systems**, Moscow, Voenizdat, 1968. 320 pp. Tirazh 17000. For military academies and engineering staff, 245 illustrations, math.

958. Varfolomeev V.I., Kopytov M.I., Ed., Proektirovanie i ispytaniia ballisticheskikh raket **Design and testing of ballistic rockets**, Moscow, Voenizdat, 1970. 392 pp. Tirazh 6400. For specialists in rocket technology, math, illustrations, appendixes, bibliography.

959. Collective authorship, Fizicheskie osnovy raketnogo oruzhiia **Physical bases of rocket weaponry**, Moscow, Voenizdat, 1972. 312 pp. Tirazh 11000. Bibliography.

960. Siniukov A.M. Ed., <u>Ballisticheskaia raketa na tverdom toplive</u> **Solid fuel ballistic rockets**, Moscow, Voenizdat, 1972. 512 pp. A manual for rocket engineers, math, illustrations.

961. Supakov N.K. <u>Bezopasnost' ekspluatatsii raketnogo oruzhiia</u> **Security in exploiting rocket armaments**, Moscow, Voenizdat, 1972. 77 pp. Tirazh 9000. For soldiers, sergeants and military students. Tables, illustrations, schematic drawings, bibliography.

962. Fridenson E.S. <u>Osnovy raketnoi tekhniki</u> **Basic rocket technology**, Moscow, Voenizdat, 1973. 204 pp. Tirazh 20000. For sergeants and officers. Illustrations, tables, photographs.

963. Moshkin E.K. <u>Razvitie otechestvennogo raketnogo dvigatelestroeniia</u> **The development of native (Soviet) rocket engine construction**, Moscow, Mashinostroenie, 1973. 255 pp. For those concerned with space and rocket technology. Illustrations, schematic drawings, photographs.

964. Morozov N.I. <u>Ballisticheskie rakety strategicheskogo naznacheniia</u> **ICBMs**, Moscow, Voenizdat, 1974. 206 pp. Tirazh 10000. For military rocket technology readers. Diagrams, math, photographs, tables, 4 appendixes, bibliography.

965. Anureev I.I. <u>Rakety mnogokratnogo ispol'zovaniia</u> **Multiple use rockets**, Moscow, Voenizdat, 1975. 214 pp. Tirazh 11000. Studies of "shuttle" technology. Diagrams, illustrations, short bibliography.

966. Golovkov L.G. <u>Gibridnye raketnye dvigateli</u> **Hybrid rocket engines,** Moscow, Voenizdat, 1976. 168 pp. Tirazh 6000. For specialists in rocket engines. Math, illustrations, tables, bibliography.

967. Panov V.V. <u>Nadezhnost' raket</u> **Reliability of rockets**, Moscow, Voenizdat, 1978. 117 pp. Tirazh 3950. For officers and military students. Math, illustrations, tables, photographs, appendix, short bibliography.

968. Aleksandrov V.A. *et al*, <u>Rakety-nositeli</u> **Carrier rockets**, Moscow, Voenizdat, 1981. 315 pp. Tirazh 17000. For engineering-technical workers. Math, illustrations, tables, short bibliography.

969. Feoktistov K.P., Ed., <u>Kosmicheskie apparaty</u> **Space vehicles**, Moscow, Voenizdat, 1983. 319 pp. Tirazh 10000. For rocket engineers. Math, diagrams, tables, photographs, bibliography.

970. Volkov E.B. *et al*, <u>Tekhnicheskie osnovy effektivnosti raketnykh sistem</u> **Technical basis of the effectiveness of missile systems,** Moscow, Mashinostroenie, 1989. 253 pp. Tirazh 31000. For specialists in military rocket technology. Illustrations, math, tables, appendix, bibliography.

971. Burdakov V.P., Danilov Iu.I., <u>Rakety budushchego</u> **Future rockets**, Moscow, Energoatomizdat, 1991. 2nd edn. 174 pp. Tirazh 24000. Math, photographs, table.

972. Maksimov Iu.P., General, Ed., Raketnye Voiska Strategicheskogo Naznacheniia. Voenno-istoricheskii trud **Strategic Rocket Forces. Military-historical work**, TsIPK, copyright RVSN (Strategic Rocket Forces), 1992. 186 pp. Based on material prepared by the scientific-research establishments of the Rocket Forces, leading construction organisation developing missiles, test ranges, Dzerzhinskii Military Academy, official publications and the archives of the Museum of the History of the Strategic Rocket Forces. Important photographic collections, listing of command staff, commanders of Missile Armies and Divisions, heads of military-educational institutions, chiefs of test ranges, cosmodromes, chief of weapon depots. Coloured charts comparing US and Soviet missile developments 1945-1991.

Ground Forces

973. Bogdanov P.P., Al'tgovzen M.L., Vnotchenko L.N. Ed., Proryv podgotovlennoi oborony strelkovymi soedineniiami (po opytu Velikoi Otechestvennoi voiny 1941-1945 gg.) **Breakthrough of the prepared defence by rifle formations (as experienced in the Great Patriotic war 1941-1945)**, Moscow, Voenizdat, 1957. 376 pp. To assist Soviet Army generals and officers. Tables, footnotes and 45 schematic illustrations.

974. Golubovich V.S., Presniakov M.V., Deistviia vzvoda noch'iu. Sbornik boevykh primerov po opytu Velikoi Otechestvennoi voiny **Platoon night actions. Collection of combat examples as experienced during the Great Patriotic War**, Moscow, Voenizdat, 1957. 168 pp. Based on archival material. For officers and sergeants. Illustrations, maps.

975. Prozorov V.G. Takticheskaia vnezapnost' **Tactical surprise**, Moscow, Voenizdat, 1958. 130 pp.

976. Sychev K.V., Major-General, Malakhov M.M., Ed., Nastuplenie strelkogo korpusa. Sbornik takticheskikh primerov iz Velikoi Otechestvennoi voiny **The rifle corps in the offensive. Collection of tactical examples in the Great Patriotic War**, Moscow 1958, Voenizdat. 504 pp. Tables, footnotes, 65 illustrations in a separate volume depicting combat actions.

977. Iamanov A.A. Vstrechnyi boi. Operativno-takticheskoe issledovanie na voenno-istoricheskoi osnove (kniga pervaia) **The meeting engagement. Operational-tactical research on a military-historical basis (book one)**, Moscow, Voenizdat 1959. 265 pp. For officers and generals; 45 illustrations, footnotes.

978. Varvarzhovskii L. Manevrennost' (avtorizovannyi perevod s cheshskogo) **Manoeuvrability,** (authorised translation from Czech). Moscow, Voenizdat, 1963 175 pp. Tirazh 3500. For officers and generals; some footnotes.

979. Razvitie taktiki Sovetskoi Armii v gody Velikoi Otechesvennoi voiny (1941-1945) **The development of Soviet Army tactics in the Great Patriotic War (1941-1945)**, Moscow, Voenizdat, 1958. 430 pp. Coloured diagrams, tables.

980. Kurochkin P.A., Army General, Ed., Obschevoiskovaia armiia v nastuplenii; Po opytu Velikoi Otechestvennoi voiny 1941-1945 gg. **All-arms army in the offensive; as experienced in the Great Patriotic War 1941-1945**, Moscow, Voenizdat, 1966. 244 pp. Tirazh 6000. Tables, 5 appendixes, 30 coloured illustrations, footnotes.

981. Reznichenko V.G., Major-General, Ed., Taktika **Tactics,** Moscow, Voenizdat 1966. 408 pp. Tirazh 40000. For officers, students of military schools and reserve officers. Drawings, index, bibliography, tables, footnotes.

982. Petrus' P.M., Shemanskii P.V., Chul'skii N.K., Iadernoe oruzhie i razvitie taktiki **The nuclear weapon and the development of tactics**, Moscow, Voenizdat, 1967. 224 pp. Tactical diagrams.

983. Pombrik I.D., Shevchenko N.A., Rabochaia karta komandira 2nd edition **Commander's operational map**, Moscow, Voenizdat, 1967. 96 pp. Tirazh 55000. A manual for all-arms officers, in particular of the Ground Forces. Coloured illustration, appendix of a sample map.

984. Collective authorship, "Dnepr" **"Dnieper"**, Moscow, Voenizdat, 1968. 128 pp. Tirazh 65000. Military exercise. Photographs.

985. Loza D.F. Marsh i vstrechnyi boi **March and the meeting engagement**, Moscow, Voenizdat 1968. 208 pp. Tirazh 15000. For officers and generals of land forces and students of military schools. Bibliography, some footnotes.

986. Simonian R.G., Major-General, Eremenko F.I., Nikolaev N.S., Tumas V.A., Takticheskaia razvedka **Tactical reconnaissance**, Moscow, Voenizdat, 1968. 276 pp. Twenty drawings, short bibliography.

987. Skachko P.G., Volkov G.T., Kulikov V.M., Planirovanie boevykh deistvii i upravlenie voiskami s pomoshch'iu setevykh grafikov **Planning combat operations and troop control with the help of network planning**, Moscow, Voenizdat, 1968. 144 pp. Tirazh 13500. For all arms generals and officers. Tables, illustration, appendix, short bibliography.

988. Perminov S.I. Voiskovye razvedchiki v boiu **Troop reconnaissance patrols in combat**, Moscow, Voenizdat 1969. 152 pp. Tirazh 25000. Illustrations, footnotes with archival material.

989. Prokof'ev A.V. Sredstva mekhanizatsii i avtomatizatsii v shtabakh **Means of mechanization and automation in staffs**, Moscow, Voenizdat, 1969. 247 pp. Tirazh 6500. 2nd edn. 1976. 252 pp. tirazh 8350. For service personnel working on technical improvements in staff work. Footnotes, many illustrations.

990. Chuev Iu.V. Issledovanie operatsii v voennom dele **Operational research in military affairs**, Moscow, Voenizdat 1970. 256 pp. Tirazh 11000. For officers, staffs, military schools. Bibliography, illustrations, math.

991. Govorukhin A.M., Kuprin A.M., Nazemnaia navigatsiia **Ground navigation**, Moscow, Voenizdat, 1970. 104 pp. Tirazh 11000. Military-topographical aid for Ground Forces officers, military school students. Thirty-nine illustrations.

992. Kolgushkin A.N. Lingvistika v voennom dele (Razrabotka i ispol'zovanie chastotnykh slovarei voennoy leksiki). **Linguistics in military affairs (Exploitation and utilization of frequency dictionaries in military lexicons)**, Moscow, Voenizdat, 1970. 180 pp. For scientists and students of mathematical linguistics. Alphabetic-frequency dictionary of 3000 words, tables, illustrations, bibliography.

993. Lutskov V.N. Metody obucheniia Sovetskikh voinov (Voenno-pedagogicheskie ocherki) **Methods of training the Soviet soldiers (Military-pedagogical studies)**, Moscow, Voenizdat, 1970. 176 pp. Tirazh 35000. For commanders of platoons, companies and their equivalents; useful for sergeants and warrant officers. Photographs, illustrations, tables, footnotes, bibliography.

994. Riabov V.S., Major General, Ed., "Dvina". Voiskovye manevry, provedennye na territorii Belorussii v marte 1970 goda **"Dvina". Military manoeuvres performed on the territory of Belorussia in March 1970**, Moscow, Voenizdat, 1970. 192 pp. Tirazh 20000. Photographs.

995. Sidorenko A.A. Nastuplenie **The offensive**, Moscow, Voenizdat 1970. 232 pp. Tirazh 13000. For officers, military schools, reserve officers. Bibliography, tables, footnotes. Translated into English in the series Soviet Military Thought No.1 **The Offensive**, published by US Air Force.

996. Fendrikov N.M., Iakovlev V.I., Metody raschetov boevoi effektivnosti vooruzheniia **Methods of calculating weapon effectiveness**, Moscow, Voenizdat, 1971. 224 pp. Tirazh 7000. Ground Forces weapons. Tables, math, short bibliography.

997. Shovkolovich A.K., Konasov F.I., Tkach S.I., Boevye deistviia motostrelkogo batal'ona v gorode **Combat operations of the motor rifle battalion in the city**, Moscow, Voenizdat, 1971. 192 pp. Tirazh 8000. For officers of motor rifle troops. Illustrations.

998. Biriukov G., Major-General Artillery, Melnikov G., Antitank warfare **Bor'ba s tankami**, Moscow, Progress Publishers, 1972. 156 pp. Tables, illustrations. Translated from Russian.

999. Garbuz G.I. *et al*, Motostrelkovyi batal'on v boiu **Motor-rifle battalion in combat**, Moscow, Voenizdat, 1972. 2nd edn. 366 pp. Tirazh 19000.

1000. Kukushkin P.V. Batal'on v morskom desante **Battalion in sea-borne assault landing**, Moscow, Voenizdat, 1972. 175 pp. Tirazh 6000. For Ground Forces and navy officers. Illustrations, photographs, footnotes.

1001. Novikov Y., Sverdlov F., Manoeuvre in modern land warfare **Manevr v obshchevoiskovom boiu**, Moscow, Progress Publishers 1972. 139 pp. Illustrations, translated from Russian.

1002. Savkin V.E. Osnovnye printsipy operativnogo iskusstva i taktiki **The basic principles of operational art and tactics**, Moscow, Voenizdat, 1972. pp. 376. Tirazh 13000. For officers and generals. Tables, illustrations, footnotes. See No.4 in the series Soviet Military Thought. Translated and published under the auspices of The United States Air Force. U.S. Government Printing Office, 1974.

1003. Simonian R.G., Major General, *et al*, Razvedka v boevykh primerakh (Velikaia Otechestvennaia voina 1941-1945 gg. i poslevoennyi period) **Reconnaissance within the combat examples (The Great Patriotic War 1941-1945 and the post-war period)**, Moscow, Voenizdat, 1972. 312 pp. Tirazh 43000. Illustration, maps.

1004. Latukhin A.N. Protivotankovoe vooruzhenie **Anti-tank weaponry**, Moscow, Voenizdat, 1973. 270 pp. Tirazh 15500.

1005. Rodionov P.F., Major-General, Ed., Posobie dlia ofitserov zapasa motostrelkovikh i tankovykh voisk **Handbook for reserve officers of motor rifle and tank troops**, Moscow, Voenizdat, 1973. 352 pp. Tirazh 55000. For officers and students of higher military schools. Illustrations, tables, footnotes, 4 appendixes.

1006. Shramchenko A.F. Voprosy psikhologii v upravlenii voiskami **Questions of psychology in troop control**, Moscow, Voenizdat, 1973. pp. 196. Tirazh 25000. For generals, officers and students. Bibliography, footnotes.

1007. Popel' N.N., Savel'ev V.P., Shemanskii P.V., Upravlenie voiskami v gody Velikoi Otechestvennoi voiny **Troop control during the Great Patriotic War**, Moscow, Voenizdat, 1974. 176 pp. Tirazh 21000. Footnotes with archival material, tables, 10 appendixes.

1008. Shemakin Iu.I. Tezaurus v avtomatizirovannykh sistemakh upravleniia i obrabotki informatsii **Thesaurus in automated control and information processing systems**, Moscow, Voenizdat, 1974. 192 pp. Tirazh 10000. For organizations and personnel dealing with automated systems controls and information processing. Tables, bibliography, illustrations.

1009. Taktika v boevykh primerakh **Tactics in combat examples**, 5 volumes. Rota **Company**, Ed. E.T. Marchenko, Moscow, Voenizdat, 1974. 184 pp. For officers of motor rifle and tank subunits; Vzvod **Platoon**, A.M. Adgamov, A.F. Demin, A.I. Smetanin, Moscow, Voenizdat 1974. 164 pp. Batal'on **Battalion**, Ed. E.T. Marchenko, Voenizdat, 1974. 254 pp. Tirazh 24000. Polk **Regiment**, Ed. A.I. Radzievskii, Army General, Voenizdat, 1974. 286 pp. Tirazh 20000 Diviziia **Division** Ed A.I. Radzievskii, Voenizdat, 1976. 295 pp. Tirazh 15000.

1010. Chuev Iu.V., Mikhailov Iu.B., Prognozirovanie v voennom dele **Forecasting in military affairs**, Moscow, Voenizdat, 1975. 280 pp. Tirazh 12000. Illustrations, tables, bibliography. Translated in English in the series Soviet Military Thought under the auspices of the United States Air Force.

1011. Ivanov S.P. O nauchnykh osnovakh upravleniia voiskami **Concerning scientific foundations of troop control**, Moscow, Voenizdat, 1975. 112 pp. Tirazh 25000. For officers, generals and admirals. Footnotes.

1012. Matsulenko V.A. Operativnaia maskirovka voisk (Po opytu Velikoi Otechestvennoi voiny) **Operational camouflage of troops (As experienced during the Great Patriotic War)**, Moscow, Voenizdat, 1975. 200 pp. Tirazh 20500. Illustrations, archival references, 7 appendixes.

1013. Beketov A.A., Belokon' A.P., Chermashentsev S.G., Maskirovka deistvii podrazdelenii sukhoputnykh voisk **Camouflage operations of subunits in the ground forces**, Moscow, Voenizdat, 1976. 140 pp. Tirazh 26000. For Ground Forces officers and students. Illustrations, tables, photographs.

1014. Shramchenko A.F. Takticheskie ucheniia **Tactical training**, Moscow, Voenizdat, 1976. 254 pp. Tirazh 25000. Second edition. For Ground Forces officers, lecturers and military academy students. Bibliography, illustrations, some footnotes, 3 appendixes.

1015. Gareev M.A. Takticheskie ucheniia i manevry. (Istoricheskii ocherk) **Tactical training and manoeuvres. (Historical study)**, Moscow, Voenizdat, 1977. 279 pp. Tirazh 17000. For generals and officers and students of higher military schools. Coloured illustrations, footnotes with archival material, bibliography.

1016. Ivanov D.A., Savel'ev V.P., Shemanskii P.V., Osnovy upravleniia voiskami v boiu 2nd edition. Translated into English in the series Soviet Military Thought No. 18 as **Fundamentals of Tactical Command and Control. A Soviet View**, Moscow, Voenizdat, 1977. 389 pp. For Ground Forces officers and generals. Illustrations, tables, footnotes, bibliography.

1017. Kuprin A.M. Orientirovanie na marshe i v boiu **Orientation on march and in combat**, Moscow, Voenizdat, 1977. 80 pp. Tirazh 40000. For commanders of subunits. Illustrations.

1018. Radzievskii A.I. Army General, Ed., Armeiskie operatsii (Primery iz opyta Velikoi Otechestvennoi voiny) **Army operations (Examples from the Great Patriotic War)**, Moscow, Voenizdat, 1977. 254 pp. Tirazh 20000. For officers, generals, students. Footnotes with archival material, illustrations, maps, tables.

1019. Vainer A.Ia. Takticheskie raschety **Tactical calculations,** Moscow, Voenizdat, 1977. 112 pp. Tirazh 22000. For Ground Forces officers, students of military establishments. Tables, illustrations, short bibliography. 2nd enlarged edition published 1982, 176 pp. Tirazh 30000.

1020. Veshchunov S.S. Motostrelkovoe otdelenie v razvedke **The motor rifle unit in reconnaissance**, Moscow, Voenizdat, 1977. 93 pp. Tirazh 30000. For officers, warrant officers and sergeants of motor rifle units. Six appendixes, tables, illustrations.

1021. Kriat V.M. Metodika otsenki vodnykh pregrad **Methodology of assessing water barriers**, Moscow, Voenizdat, 1978. 160 pp. Tirazh 12000. For sergeants, officers of combat engineering, all-arms subunits and units. Illustrations, aerial photographs, tables, nomograms, short bibliography.

1022. Tonkikh A.V. Preodolenie protivotankovoi oborony **Overcoming the antitank defence**, 2nd edn., Moscow, Voenizdat, 1978. 143 pp. Tirazh 10000. For Ground Forces and navy officers. Photographs, illustrations, tables.

1023. Radzievskii A.I. Army General, Proryv (Po opytu Velikoi Otechestvennoi voiny 1941-1945) **The Breakthrough (Experience of the Great Patriotic War)**, Moscow, Voenizdat, 1979. 191 pp. Tirazh 17000. Sixteen coloured illustrations, tables, footnotes with archival material. For officers, generals, students of higher military schools.

1024. Zakharov V.N. Ed., Kibernetika v sistemakh voennogo naznacheniia **Cybernetics in systems for military applications**, Moscow, Voenizdat, 1979. 263 pp. Tirazh 7500. Application to automated command and control. Diagrams, math, short bibliography.

1025. Simonian R.G., Grishin S.V., Razvedka v boiu **Reconnaissance in combat**, Moscow, Voenizdat, 1980. 208 pp. Tirazh 30000. For sergeants, officers. Illustrations. Translated in English in the series Soviet Military Thought No. 23 as **Tactical Reconnaissance**.

1026. Tovstukha P.P., Lt. General, Portugal'skii R.M., Upravlenie voiskami v nastuplenii: Po opytu Velikoi Otechestvennoi voiny **Troop control in an offensive: As experienced in the Great Patriotic War**, Moscow, Voenizdat, 1981. 222 pp. Tirazh 12000. For generals and officers. Illustrations, tables, footnotes with archival material, bibliography.

1027. Kir'ian M.M., Lt. General, Ed., Voenno-tekhnicheskii progress i Vooruzhennye Sily SSSR (Analiz razvitiia vooruzheniia, organizatsii i sposobov deistvii) **Military-technical progress and the armed forces of the USSR (Analysis of the development of armaments, organization and modes of operations)**, Moscow, Voenizdat, 1982. 335 pp. Tirazh 35000. Footnotes with archival material.

1028. Skryl'nik A.I., Major General, Ed., "Zapad - 81" Ucheniia voisk i sil flota 4-12 sentiabria 1981 goda **Troop and naval exercise 4-12 September 1981**, Moscow, Voenizdat, 1982. 173 pp. Tirazh 30000. Photographs.

1029. Sverdlov F.D. Takticheskii manevr **Tactical manoeuvre**, Moscow, Voenizdat, 1982. 192 pp. Tirazh 25000. For army officers. Illustrations.

1030. Gareev M.A., General, Obshchevoiskovye ucheniia **All-arms training**, Moscow, Voenizdat, 1983. 256 pp. Tirazh 15000. For generals, officers, students of higher military schools. Coloured maps, footnotes, bibliography.

1031. Matsulenko V.A. Operatsii i boi na okruzhenie: Po opytu Velikoi Otechestvennoi voiny **Operations and combat in encirclement: In the experience of the Great Patriotic War**, Moscow, Voenizdat, 1983. 231 pp. Tirazh 13000. For officers and students of higher military schools. Sixteen coloured maps, footnotes, some based on archival material, tables.

1032. Altukhov P.K., Lt. General, Ed., Osnovy teorii upravleniia voiskami **The fundamentals of the theory of troop control**, Moscow, Voenizdat, 1984. 221 pp. Tirazh 18000. For officers. Subject index, bibliography.

1033. Kovalenko A.N. Topograficheskaia podgotovka podrazdeleniia **Sub-unit training in topography**, Moscow, Voenizdat, 1984. 176 pp. Tirazh 39000. Text book approved by the General Staff. Illustrations, 4 appendixes include bibliography.

1034. Merimskii V.A. Takticheskaia podgotovka motostrelkovykh i tankovykh podrazdelenii. **Tactical training of motor rifle and tank subunits**, Moscow, Voenizdat, 1984. 216 pp. Tirazh 30000. For commanders of subunits. Fifteen coloured illustrations, tables.

1035. Rybian A.A. Podrazdeleniia v nochnom boiu **Subunits in night combat**, Moscow, Voenizdat, 1984. 208 pp. Tirazh 25000. For commanders of subunits. Tables, illustrations.

1036. Tonkikh F.P., Fokin Iu.G., Kak vy upravliaete?: Psikhologicheskiye aspekty povsednevnoi upravlencheskoi deiatel'nosti ofitsera **How do you control?: Psychological aspects of everyday managerial activities of an officer**, Moscow, Voenizdat, 1984. 190 pp. Tirazh 27000. For commanders and political workers of army and fleet. Three appendixes, tables, illustrations, footnotes.

1037. Pavlovskii I.G., Army General, Sukhoputnye voiska SSSR: Zarozhdenie, razvitie, sovremennost' **Ground Forces of the USSR: Origin, development, now**, Moscow, Voenizdat, 1985. 320 pp. Tirazh 27000. Photographs, footnotes, maps.

1038. Dragunskii D.A., Ed., Motostrelkovyi (tankovyi) batal'on v boiu **Motor rifle (tank) battalion in combat**, Moscow, Voenizdat, 1986. 304 pp. Tirazh 35000. Handbook for Ground Forces officers. Eleven coloured illustrations.

1039. Kir'ian M.M., Lt. General, Ed., Vnezapnost' v nastupatel'nykh operatsiiakh Velikoi Otechestvennoi voiny **Surprise in offensive operations of the Great Patriotic War**, Moscow, Nauka, 1986. 208 pp. Tirazh 8200. End notes with archival material.

1040. Babakov A.A. Vooruzhennye Sily SSSR posle voiny (1945-1986 gg.). Istoriia stroitel'stva **Armed forces of the USSR after the war (1945-1986) History of development**, Moscow, Voenizdat, 1987. 288 pp. Tirazh 15000. For generals and officers, lecturers and students at military academies. Footnotes, tables.

1041. Gaivoronskii F.F., Lt. General, Ed., Evoliutsiia voennogo iskusstva: etapy, tendentsii, printsipy **Evolution of military art: stages, tendencies and principles**, Moscow, Voenizdat, 1987. 248 pp. Tirazh 15000. For officers, generals and historians. Footnotes.

1042. Krivda F.F., Army General, Komandirami ne rozhdaiutsia: Opyt. Prakticheskie rekomendatsii **Commanders are not born: Experience. Practical recommendations**, Moscow, Voenizdat, 1987. 232 pp. Tirazh 15000. For commanders of subunits. Coloured maps, photographs.

1043. Merimskii V.A., Lt. General, Takticheskaia podgotovka motostrelkovykh i tankovykh podrazdelenii **Tactical preparation of rifle and tank subunits**, Moscow, Voenizdat, 1987. 352 pp. Tirazh 25000. For commanders of subunits, students of military schools. Layouts of training targets, illustrations of protective works.

1044. Reznichenko V.G. Ed., Taktika 2nd edn. **Tactics**, Moscow, Voenizdat, 1987. 496 pp. Tirazh 100000. Series "Biblioteka ofitsera". For officers. Footnotes, coloured illustrations. 1st edn. 1984. Also Tactics   A Soviet View English translation in the series Soviet Military Thought No. 21, under the auspices of US Air Force.

1045. Moiseenko N.P. *et al* Motostrelkovaia (tankovaia) rota v boiu **Motor rifle (tank) company in combat**, Moscow, Voenizdat, 1988. 287 pp. Tirazh 30000. Handbook for Ground Forces officers, students of military schools. Coloured tactical illustrations.

1046. Andrusenko I.M., Dukov R.G., Fomin Iu.R., Motostrelkovyi (tankovyi) vzvod v boiu **Motor rifle (tank) platoon in combat**, Moscow, Voenizdat, 1989. 363 pp. Tirazh 70000. Handbook for commanders of Ground Forces subunits, students. Coloured illustrations, tables.

1047. Kirillov A.I., Kuznetsov V.P., Agafonov V.I. *et al*, Podgotovka ofitserov zapasa Sukhoputnykh voisk: Uchebnoe posobie **Training Ground Forces reserve officers: training manual**, Moscow, Voenizdat, 1989. 448 pp. Tirazh 90000. For reserve officers. Two appendixes, illustrations.

1048. Kuznetsov Iu.K., Lt. General, Peredvizhenie i vstrechnyi boi **Troop movement and meeting engagement**, Moscow, Voenizdat, 1989. 287 pp. Tirazh 40000. For Ground Forces officers, students. Illustrations, appendix.

1049. Psarev A.A., Kovalenko A.N., Topograficheskaia podgotovka komandira **Topographic training of a commander**, Moscow, Voenizdat, 1989. 224 pp. Tirazh 65000. For officers and students of military schools. Two appendixes, coloured illustrations, tables.

1050. Byzov B.E., Kovalenko A.N., Voennaia topografiia dlia kursantov uchebnykh podrazdelenii **Military topography for students in training subunits**, Moscow, Voenizdat, 1990. 224 pp. Tirazh 50000. For students and sergeants of Ground Forces. Illustrations, aerial photographs, tables, 6 appendixes, short bibliography.

1051. Welzer W. <u>Aerosnimki v voennom dele</u> translation from German *Luftbilder im Militärwesen* (**Aerial photographs in military affairs**), Moscow, Voenizdat, 1990. 288 pp. For photo-interpreters. Coloured photographs, diagrams, tables, 2 appendixes.

1052. Apakidze V.V., Dukov R.G., Poloz P.P., <u>Stroevaia podgotovka</u> **Drill training**, 2nd edn., Moscow, Voenizdat, 1991. 350 pp. Tirazh 65000. 1st edn. 1988. For officers, sergeants, students. Nine appendixes, illustrations.

Artillery and Missiles

1053. Glav. uprav. komanduiushchego artillerii Krasnoi Armii <u>Nastavlenie artillerii Krasnoi Armii. Pravila strel'by nazemnoi artillerii 1945 g.</u> **Instruction for Red Army artillery. Rules for artillery firing 1945**, Moscow, Voenizdat, 1946. 288 pp.

1054. Belugin D.A., Zverov V.Ia., Danilin V.N., <u>Artilleriiskaia instrumental'naia razvedka</u> **Artillery reconnaissance with instrumentation (accoustic, optical)**, Moscow, Voenizdat, 1956. 482 pp. Text book for artillery schools; 17 appendixes.

1055. Prochko I.S. <u>Artilleriia v boiakh za rodinu</u> **Artillery in battles for the motherland**, Moscow, Voenizdat, 1957. 328 pp. Historical outline of Russian and Soviet artillery; photographs, illustrations.

1056. Kazakov K.P., Marshal of Artillery, Ed., <u>Artilleriia i rakety</u> **Artillery and rockets**, Moscow, Voenizdat, 1968. 416 pp. Tirazh 17000. Photographs, illustrations; short bibliography.

1057. Dudarev S.N., Shipov B.V., <u>Artilleriia v osobykh usloviiakh</u> **Artillery in special conditions**. Moscow, Voenizdat, 1970. 191 pp. Tirazh 8500. Photographs, illustrations, short glossary, short bibiliography.

1058. Gordon Iu.A., Khorenkov A.V., <u>Artilleriiskaia razvedka</u> **Artillery reconnaissance**, Moscow, Voenizdat, 1971. 216 pp. Tirazh 7700. For artillery officers, sergeants and soldiers; photographs, illustrations.

1059. Malikov V.G., Komisarik S.F., Korotkov A.M., <u>Nazemnoe oborudovanie raket</u> **Ground equipment of rockets**, Moscow, Voenizdat, 1971. 304 pp. Tirazh 10000. For command, rocket forces engineers, officers, military academies; illustrations, short bibliography.

1060. Razuvaev A.P. <u>Metodika takticheskoi podgotovki artilleriiskikh podrazdelenii</u> **Methodology of tactical training of artillery subunits**, Moscow, Voenizdat, 1972. 175 pp. Tirazh 10000. For artillery officers, sergeants, artillery schools; short bibliography, appendix.

1061. Mikhailov V.P., Nazarov G.A., <u>Razvitie tekhniki puska raket</u> **Development of missile launch technology**, Moscow, Voenizdat, 1976. 196 pp. Tirazh 9000. For specialists in rocket technology; illustrations, photographs, tables.

1062. Nevskii N.A., Sergeev Iu.D., Deistviia orudiia (vzvoda) v boiu **Operations of guns (artillery platoon) in combat**, Moscow, Voenizdat, 1976. 84 pp. Tirazh 15000. For sergeants, officers of ground artillery, military schools.

1063. Perechnev Iu.G. Sovetskaia beregovaia artilleriia. Istoriia razvitiia i boevogo primeneniia. 1921-1945 gg. **Soviet coastal artillery. History of its development and combat employment, 1921-1945**, Moscow, Nauka, 1976. 336 pp. Tirazh 9600. Footnotes with archival material, maps, charts of commands, illustrations, appendix giving the complement of the coastal artillery deployed with fleet and flotilla commands, 22.6.41-9.5.45.

1064. Anashkin I.N. *et al*, Trenirovochnye i imitatsionnye sredstva nazemnoi artillerii **Trainers and simulation devices of surface-to-surface artillery**, Moscow, Voenizdat, 1977. 240 pp. Tirazh 10000. For artillery units officers, military academy lecturers; nine appendixes, short bibliography.

1065. Braginskii R.B., Popel'nitskii N.S., Usenkov M.G., Taktika artillerii v boevykh primerakh (podrazdeleniia i chasti) **Artillery tactics in combat examples (subunits and units)**, Moscow, Voenizdat, 1977. 264 pp. Tirazh 15000. For rocket forces, artillery officers, other officers. Illustrations, short bibliography.

1066. Konofeev N.T. Transportirovka raket **Transportation of rockets**, Moscow, Voenizdat, 1978. 151 pp. Tirazh 3400. For missile technology specialist; illustrations, short bibliography.

1067. Malakhovskii E.K. Strel'ba na porazhenie opornykh punktov **Fire for the destruction of strong points**, Moscow, Voenizdat, 1978. 112 pp. Tirazh 10000. For ground artillery officers. Three appendixes, tables, illustrations.

1068. Surikov B.T. Boevoe primenenie raket sukhoputnykh voisk **Combat application of rockets in the ground forces**, Moscow, Voenizdat, 1979. 199 pp. Tirazh 10000. For readers interested in missiles; 4 appendixes, short bibliography.

1069. Peredel'skii G.E., Tokmakov A.I., Khoroshilov G.T., Artilleriia v boiu i operatsii (Po opytu Velikoi Otechestvennoi voiny) **Artillery in battle and operations (As experienced in the Great Patriotic War)**, Moscow, Voenizdat, 1980. 136 pp. Tirazh 15000. For rocket forces and artillery staff officers, military academies. Coloured illustrations, tables, graphs.

1070. Kuznetsov P.I. Ogon' vedet batareia **Battery firing**, Moscow, Voenizdat, 1982. 224 pp. Tirazh 10000. For students of higher artillery schools, artillery subunits commanders, reserve artillery officers. Ten firing tables and recommended literature: "Rukovodstvo po primeneniiu priborov dlia razvedki i strel'by nazemnoi artillerii **Direction for the use of instruments for reconnaissance and firing by ground force artillery**, Moscow, Voenizdat, 1972. Pravila strel'by i upravleniia ognem nazemnoi artillerii (divizion, batareia, vzvod, orudie) **Firing rules and control of land forces' artillery fire (battalion, battery, platoon, gun)**. Voenizdat, Moscow 1975. Ukazaniia po rabote meteorologicheskogo posta artilleriiskogo diviziona **Regulations for the work of the meteorological post of an artillery battalion**, Moscow, Voenizdat, 1975. Posobie po izucheniiu pravil strel'by i upravleniia ognem nazemnoi artillerii (divizion, bateria, vzvod, orudie). **Manual for studying Firing Rules and the control of land forces artillery (battalion, battery, platoon, gun)**, Moscow, Voenizdat, 1976. Ukazaniia po ballisticheskoi podgotovke strel'by nazemnoi artillerii (divizion, bateria). **Regulations for ballistic preparation of ground force artillery firing (battalion, battery)**, Moscow, Voenizdat, 1977. Rukovodstvo po boevoi rabote ognevykh podrazdelenii artillerii. **The direction of combat work of artillery fire subunits**, Moscow, Voenizdat, 1978. Ukazaniia po rabote grupp samopriviazki artilleriiskikh podrazdelenii **Regulations for the work of groups of self-surveying artillery subunits**, Moscow, Voenizdat, 1978."

1071. Peredel'skii G.E., Marshal of Artillery, Artilleriiskii divizion v boiu **Artillery battalion in battle**, Moscow, Voenizdat, 1984. 216 pp. Tirazh 16000. For ground forces officers, military schools; maps, tables, illustrations.

1072. Peredel'skii G.E., Marshal of Artillery, Ed., Otechestvennaia artilleriia 600 let **600 years of our nation's artillery,** Moscow, Voenizdat, 1986. 368 pp. Tirazh 35000. Photographs, illustrations and bibliography.

Armour

1073. Antonov A., Artamonov V., Korobkov V., Magidovich E., Tank **The tank,** Moscow, Voenizdat, 1954. 607 pp. Diagrams, illustrations, graphs, tables.

1074. Andronikov N.G., *et al*, Bronetankovye i mekhanizirovannye voiska Sovetskoi Armii (Kratkii ocherk razvitiia i boevogo puti) **Armoured and mechanised troops of the Soviet Army (Short outline of their development and combat path)**, Moscow, Voenizdat, 1958. 267 pp. Maps, photographs and illustrations.

1075. Mostovenko V.D. Tanki (Ocherk iz istorii zarozhdeniia i razvitiia bronetankovoi tekhniki) **Tanks (essays from the history of the birth and development of tank technology)**, 2nd edition, corrected and enlarged. Moscow, Voenizdat, 1958. 207 pp. Illustrations of tanks.

1076. Nikulin V.Ia. Osnovy strel'by iz tanka. Uchebnik. **Basis of tank gunnery. Text book**, Moscow, Voenizdat, 1958. 324 pp. Bibliography.

1077. Got G. Tankovye operatsii **Tank operations**, (Translated from original German *Panzer-operationen* by Hermann Hoth). Moscow, Voenizdat, 1961. 208 pp. Tirazh 11000. For generals and officers.

1078. Stetsiuk L.S. Tankovye podrazdeleniia v boiu **Tank subunits in combat**, Moscow, Voenizdat, 1961. 256 pp. Tirazh 12000. For tank troops officers; illustrations.

1079. Musienko V.A., Pechenezhskii K.S., Tankovyi vzvod v boiu **Tank platoon in combat**, Moscow, Voenizdat, 1967. 152 pp. Tirazh 13000. For tank and motor-rifle subunits officers, military academies; illustrations.

1080. Petrov M.M., Sotnikov V.F. Metodika izucheniia osnov iz pravil strel'by iz tanka **Methodology of teaching the basis and the rules of tank gunnery**, Moscow, Voenizdat, 1968. 159 pp. Tirazh 10000. Tank gunnery for officers and sergeants; illustrations.

1081. Babadzhanian A.Kh., Marshal of Tank Troops, Ed., Tanki i tankovye voiska **Tanks and tank troops**, Moscow, Voenizdat, 1970. 336 pp. Tirazh 9000. Photographs, illustrations, tactical diagrams.

1082. Konoplia P.I., Maikov N.A. Tankovyi batal'on v boiu. **The tank battalion in combat**, 2nd edition. Moscow, Voenizdat, 1972. 296 pp. Tirazh 21000. Illustrations, bibliography.

1083. Rotmistrov P.A., Chief Marshal of Tank Troops, Vremia i tanki **Time and tanks**, Moscow, Voenizdat, 1972. 336 pp. Tirazh 30000. Photographs, illustrations.

1084. Zelenski V.D., Chistov A.A., Chulkov G.S., Tekhnicheskoe obespechenie tankovykh i motostrelkovykh podrazdelenii v sovremenom boiu **Technical support for tank and motor-rifle sub-units in contemporary combat**, Moscow, Voenizdat, 1972. 184 pp. Tirazh 15000. For tanks and motor-rifle troops officers; short bibliography.

1085. Sovetskie tankovye voiska 1941-1945, Voenno-istoricheskii ocherk, Collective authorship. **Soviet tank troops, Military-historical outline**, Moscow, Voenizdat, 1973. 334 pp. Map supplement, photographs.

1086. Belonovskii A.S. Ed., Elektroobrudovanie bronetankovoi tekhniki **Electrics in tank technology**, Moscow, Voenizdat, 1976. 224 pp. Tirazh 11000. Photographs of electrical equipment, wiring diagrams, engineering illustrations of equipment and tables of types/performance of electric motors.

1087. Katunskii A.M. Vozhdenie tankov **Driving tanks**, Moscow, Voenizdat, 1976. 176 pp. Tirazh 27000. Illustrations; for existing and future members of tank crews.

1088. Radzievskii A.I. Tankovyi udar (tankovaia armiia v nastupatel'noi operatsii fronta po opytu Velikoi Otechestvenoi voiny **Tank attack (tank army in the Front offensive operation as experienced in the Great Patriotic War**, Moscow, Voenizdat, 1977. 272 pp. Tirazh 20000. Illustrations, map supplement, footnotes with archival material.

1089. Kuznetsov M.I., Presnov V.K., Surat L.I., Tankovye navigatsionnye sistemy **Navigational systems in tanks**, Moscow, Voenizdat, 1978. 120 pp. Tirazh 14000. Approved and recommended instruction manual. Photographs, illustrations.

1090. Losik O.A., Marshal of Tank Troops, Ed., Stroitel'stvo i boevoe primenenie sovetskikh tankovykh voisk v gody Velikoi Otechestvennoi voiny **Structure and combat employment of the Soviet tank troops during the Great Patriotic**

War, Moscow, Voenizdat, 1979. 414 pp. Tirazh 15000. Footnotes, with some archival material. Photographs, appendixes.

1091. Babadzhanyan A.Kh. Ed., Tanki i tankovye voiska **Tanks and tank troops,** 2nd enlarged edition, Moscow, Voenizdat, 1980. 432 pp. Tirazh 25000. Photographs, illustrations.

1092. Anan'ev I.M. Tankovye armii v nastuplenii: Po opytu Velikoi Otechestvennoi voiny 1941-1945 **Tank armies in the offensive: As experienced during the Great Patriotic War 1941-1945,** Moscow, Voenizdat, 1988. 456 pp. Tirazh 10000. Footnotes with some archival material; maps.

Signals Troops

1093. Kisliakov P.D. Voiska sviazi Sovetskoi Armii. Kratkii ocherk **Signals Troops of the Soviet Army. A brief study,** Moscow, 1955. 213 pp. Photographs.

1094. Balaev N.I. *et al*, Voennye sviazisty v dni voiny i mira **Military signallers in war and peace,** Moscow, Voenizdat, 1968. 320 pp. Tirazh 35000. Fifty years' history of the Signals Troops. Illustrations, footnotes with archival material, tables, photographs.

1095. Peresypkin I T., Marshal of Signals Troops, ...A v boiu eshche vazhnei **...And in combat it is even more important,** Moscow, Sovetskaia Rossiia, 1970. 253 pp. Tirazh 50000. Appendix of photographs from his personal archives.

1096. Peresypkin I.T., Marshal of Signals Troops, Sviazisty v gody Velikoi Otechestvennoi **Signallers in the Great Patriotic (War),** Moscow, Sviaz', 1972. 248 pp. Tirazh 35000. Photographs, short bibliography. Based on reminiscences of veteran signallers.

1097. Peresypkin I.T., Marshal of Signals Troops, Sviaz' v Velikoi Otechestvennoi voine **Signals in the Great Patriotic War,** Moscow, Nauka, 1973. 283 pp. Tirazh 25000. Photographs, maps, illustrations, footnotes with archival material.

1098. Zaistev V.P. *et al*, Voennye sviazisty v boiakh za rodinu **Military signallers in the battles for the Fatherland,** Moscow, Voenizdat, 1984. 256 pp. Tirazh 40000. Footnotes with archival material, photographs, illustrations, appendixes.

Radio-electronic Combat REC/EW

1099. Vakin S.A., Shustov L.N., Osnovy radioprotivodeistviia i radiotechnicheskoi razvedki **Fundamentals of electronic counter measures (ECM) and radio technical reconnaissance,** Moscow, Sovetskoe Radio, 1968. 445 pp. Tirazh 12000. Bibliography, math, diagrams.

1100. Maksimov M.V. Zashchita ot radiopomekh **Protection against radio-jamming,** Moscow, Sov. Radio, 1976. 496 pp. Tirazh 30000. Math, diagrams, index, bibliography of 214 entries.

1101. Palii A.I. Radioelektronnaia bor'ba. (Sredstva i sposoby podavleniia i zashchity radioelektronnykh sistem) **Radio-electronic combat. (Means and methods of suppression and defence of radio-electronic systems)**, Moscow, Voenizdat, 1981. 320 pp. Tirazh 20000. Diagrams, tables, illustrations. First published in 1963; revised in 1974.

Airborne Assault Troops VDV

1102. Sofronov G.P. Lt. General, Vozdushnye desanty vo vtoroi mirovoi voine. Kratkii voenno-istoricheskii ocherk, **Airborne assaults in the Second World War. Brief military-historical study**, Moscow, Voenizdat, 1962. 143 pp. Tirazh 7000. For military readers. Maps, tables.

1103. Lisov I.I. Desantniki (vozdushnye desanty). **Airborne assault troops (airborne assaults)**, Moscow, Voenizdat, 1968. 320 pp. Tirazh 25000. Footnotes, tables, photographs, maps.

1104. Lisov I.I., Lt. General, et al Vozdushno-desantnaia podgotovka, **Airborne-assault training**, Moscow, Voenizdat, 1977. 223 pp. Tirazh 20000. For personnel of Airborne Assault Troops, also DOSAAF organizations. Hundred and four illustrations, short bibliography.

1105. Ivonin V.I. Krylataia gvardiia: Sbornik (Kniga o proslavlennykh gvardeitsakh-desantnikakh) **Winged Guard: Collection (Book about famous airborne Guards)**, Moscow, DOSAAF SSSR, 1978. pp. 135. Tirazh 100000. Rare archival photographs.

1106. Margelov V.F., General, et al, Sovetskie vozdushno-desantnye: Voenno-istoricheskii ocherk **Soviet Airborne Assault Troops: Military-historical study**, Moscow, Voenizdat, 1980. 311 pp. Tirazh 40000. Footnotes with archival material, photographs, appendix. 2nd edn. Voenizdat, 1986. 400 pp. Tirazh 30000.

Engineers

1107. Andreev V.P. et al, Inzhenernye voiska Sovetskoi Armii v vazhneishikh operatsiiakh Velikoi Otechestvennoi voiny **Engineer troops of the Soviet Army in the most important operations during the Great Patriotic War**, Moscow, Voenizdat, 1958. 310 pp. Collection of essays with illustrations.

1108. Varenyshev B.V., Dubinin K.N., Mudragei I.P., et al, Voenno-inzhenernaia podgotovka: Uchebnoe posobie **Military field engineering training: Training manual** Moscow, Voenizdat, 1982. 232 pp. Tirazh 35000. For Ground Forces reserve officers, higher military schools. Illustrations, tables.

1109. Kolibernov E.S., Kornev V.I., Soskov A.A., Inzhenernoe obespechenie boia **Engineer combat support,** Moscow, Voenizdat, 1984. 287 pp. Tirazh 25000. For Ground Forces officers, students. Ten appendixes, tables, illustrations, footnotes with some archival material. 2nd edn. 1988. 333 pp. Tirazh 15000.

1110. Aganov S.Kh., Marshal of Engineer Troops, Ed. Inzhenernye voiska Sovetskoi Armii 1918-1945 **Engineer Troops of the Soviet Army 1918-1945**, Moscow, Voenizdat, 1985. 488 pp. Tirazh 17000. For army officers and generals. Photographs, illustrations, tables, footnotes with archival material.

1111. Shamurov V.K. Inzhenernoe obespechenie boia v osobykh usloviiakh **Engineer support of combat under special conditions**, Moscow, Voenizdat, 1985. 240 pp. Tirazh 20000. A handbook for officers of Ground Forces, students in higher military schools. Illustrations, tables.

1112. Kolibernov E.S. *et al*, Spravochnik ofitsera inzhenernykh voisk **Handbook for engineer officers**, Moscow, Voenizdat, 1989. 432 pp. Tirazh 27000. For engineer troops officers and specialists. Illustrations, tables, 16 appendixes, index.

Air Defence Troops/PVO

1113. Bubnov G.P. Avtomatizatsiia v PVO **Automation in Air Defence**, Moscow, Voenizdat, 1963. 96 pp. Tirazh 10000. For wide circle of officers engineers and technicians. Illustrations, diagrams, short bibliography.

1114. Morozov P.V. Bor'ba s vozdushno-kosmicheskimi tseliami **Combat against aerospace targets**, Moscow, Voenizdat, 1967. 144 pp. Tirazh 10000. Photographs, illustrations, tables, short bibliography.

1115. Batitskii PF. Marshal, Ed. Voiska protivo-vozdushnoi oborony strany. Istoricheskii ocherk **The country's Air Defence troops. Historical study**, Moscow, Voenizdat, 1968. 439 pp. Tirazh 50000. Five appendixes, photographs, illustrations, footnotes with archival material.

1116. Bezymiannyi V.M., Lavrent'ev V.I., Slivin I.P., Shaturnyi A.N. Na strazhe neba stolitsy. Kratkii ocherk istorii ordena Lenina Moskovskogo okruga protivovozdushnoi oborony **Guarding the skies of the capital. Brief study of the history of Order of Lenin Moscow's air defence district**, Moscow, Voenizdat, 1968. 392 pp. Tirazh 25000. Two appendixes, photographs, illustrations.

1117. Romanov A.N., Frolov G.A., Osnovy avtomatizatsii sistemy upravleniia (Postroenie avtomatizirovannykh sistem upravleniia PVO) **Principles in automation systems control (Formation of automated systems of Air Defence [PVO])**, Moscow, Voenizdat, 1971. 248 pp. Tirazh 9300. For engineers of automated control systems in the PVO. Math, bibliography, diagrams, illustrations, tables.

1118. Surikov B.T. Raketnye sredstva bor'by s nizkoletiashchimi tseliami **Missiles to combat low-flying targets**, Moscow, Voenizdat, 1973. 204 pp. Tirazh 10000. Four appendixes, illustrations, diagrams, bibliography.

1119. Konstantinov A.U. Ed., Bakinskii okrug protivovozdushnoi oborony. Istoricheskii ocherk 1920-1974 gg. **Baku Air Defence District. Historical study 1920-**

1974, Baku, Azerbaidzhanskoe Gosudarstvennoe Izdatel'stvo, 1974. 364 pp. Tirazh 14000. Photographs, 3 appendixes, footnotes with some archival material.

1120. Golovanov N.Ia. Zhitomirskoe Krasnoznamennoe imeni Leninskogo Komsomola. Istoriia Zhitomirskogo vysshego komandnogo Krasnoznamennogo uchilishcha radioelektroniki protivovozdushnoi oborony imeni Leninskogo Komsomola **Zhitomir Red Banner in the name of Lenin Komsomol Higher Command School Radio-electronic Air Defence**, Moscow, Voenizdat 1977. 232 pp. Tirazh 30000. Photographs, footnotes with archival material.

1121. Andersen Iu.A., Drozhzhin A.I., Lozik P.M., Protivovozdushnaia oborona sukhoputnykh voisk **Air Defence of Ground Forces**, Moscow, Voenizdat, 1979. 304 pp. Tirazh 23000. For officers, students. Illustrations, short bibliography.

1122. Neupokoev F.K. Strel'ba zenitnymi raketami **Firing surface to air missiles**, Moscow, Voenizdat, 1980. 294 pp. Tirazh 12500. For specialists in combat application of surface to air missiles. Nine appendixes, math, diagrams, illustrations, tables, bibliography.

1123. Romanov A.N. Trenazhery dlia podgotovki operatorov RLS s pomoshch'iu EVM **Simulators for training radar operators with help of computers**, Moscow, Voenizdat, 1980. 128 pp. Tirazh 6000. Diagrams, bibliography, math, tables.

1124. Komarov N.Ia. *et al*, Voiska PVO strany v Velikoi Otechestvennoi voine 1941-1945: Kratkaia khronika. **Air Defence troops of the country during the Great Patriotic War 1941-1945: A short chronicle**, Moscow, Voenizdat, 1981. 375 pp. Tirazh 40000.

1125. Poliakov G.P. *et al*, Ordena Lenina Moskovskii okrug PVO (Istoriia ordena Lenina Moskovskogo okruga protivovozdushnoi oborony) **Order of Lenin Moscow Air Defence District (History of the Order of Lenin Moscow Air Defence District)**, Moscow, Voenizdat, 1981. 319 pp. Tirazh 50000. Footnotes with some archival material, photographs, illustrations, tables.

1126. Druzhinin V.V., Kontorov D.S., Konfliktnaia radiolokatsiia **Conflict theory and systems engineering and radar operations**, Moscow, Radio i Sviaz, 1982. 124 pp. Tirazh 4000. For scientists and engineers. Appendix, bibliography, subject index, tables, math, illustrations.

1127. Volzhin A.N., Sizov Iu.G., Bor'ba s samonavodiashchimisia raketami **Combat with homing missiles**, Moscow, Voenizdat, 1983. 144 pp. Tirazh 15000. For army and navy officers. Uses foreign publications. Illustrations, tables, graphs, bibliography.

1128. Leonov S.A. Radiolokatsionnye sredstva protivovozdushnoi oborony **Radar equipment in air defence**, Moscow, Voenizdat, 1988. 180 pp. Tirazh 18000. For engineers and students in PVO schools. Appendix, bibliography, illustrations, tables.

1129. Demidov V.P., Kutyev N.Sh., Upravlenie zenitnymi raketami 2nd edn. **Control of surface to air missiles (SAMs)**, Moscow, Voenizdat, 1989. 336pp. Tirazh 14000. For officers, lecturers. Subject index, bibliography, diagrams, math, tables.

1130. Neupokoev F.K. Protivovozdushnyi boi **Air Defence combat**, Moscow, Voenizdat, 1989. 262 pp. Tirazh 15000. For commanders of units and subunits of PVO. Tables, math, illustrations, subject index, bibliography.

Air Force

1131. Berezin P.F. Ed., Voenno-vozdushnye sily v sovremennoi voine (po inostrannym vzgliadam) **Air forces in modern war (according to foreign views)**, Moscow, Voenizdat, 1957. 239 pp. Extract from USAF AFM 1-2 'Basic Doctrine' plus 13 articles by American and West European aviation specialists. For army and navy generals, admirals and officers.

1132. Krasovskii S.A. *et al*, Aviatsiia i kosmonavtika SSSR **Aviation and cosmonautics of the USSR**, Moscow, Voenizdat, 1968. 599 pp. Tirazh 25000. Photographs, footnotes with archival material, tables, illustrations, 3 appendixes.

1133. Buzunov V.K. Aerodrom - boevaia pozitsiia aviatsii aerodromno-tekhnicheskoe obespechenie aviatsii **Aerodrome - combat position of aviation aerodrome-technical support of aviation**, Moscow, Voenizdat, 1969. 126 pp. Photographs, illustrations, short bibliography.

1134. Shavrov V.B. Istoriia konstruktsii samoletov v SSSR do 1938 goda (Materialy k istorii samoletostroeniia) **The history of aircraft construction in the USSR up to 1938 (Material regarding the history of aircraft construction)**, Moscow. Mashinostroenie, 1969. 606 pp. Tirazh 5800. Photographs, illustrations, footnotes with archival material, bibliography, tables, index of subjects, names. 2nd edn. 1978; 3rd edn. 1986, 752 pp. Tirazh 40000.

1135. Kobzarev A.A. Ed., Sovetskaia aviatsionnaia tekhnika **Soviet aviation technology**, Moscow, Mashinostroenie, 1970. 175 pp. Tirazh 6500. Good quality black and white and colour photographs.

1136. Sotnikov I.M., Brusentsev N.A., Aviatsiia protiv podvodnykh lodok **Aviation against submarines**, Moscow, Voenizdat, 1970. 206 pp. Tirazh 7000. For personnel of armies and Fleets. Illustrations, photographs, maps, 2 appendixes, tables, bibliography.

1137. Durov V.R. Boevoe primenenie i boevaia effektivnost' istrebitelei-perekhvatchikov (zadachi s resheniiami) **Combat application and combat effectiveness of fighter-interceptors (problems with solutions)**, Moscow, Voenizdat, 1972. 280 pp. Tirazh 8000. For Air Force, Air Defence specialists and students. Math, tables, 2 appendixes, bibliography.

1138. Mikhailin I.I., Major General, Ed., Spravochnik spetsialista tyla aviatsii **Handbook of air force rear-services specialist**, Moscow, Voenizdat, 1972. 503 pp. Tirazh 10000. Bibliography.

1139. Tsykin A.D. Ot "Il'i Muromtsa" do raketonostsa. Kratkii ocherk istorii dal'nei aviatsii **From "Ilya Muromets" to the missile carrier. Short essay on the history of Long Range Aviation**, Moscow, Voenizdat 1975. 251 pp. Tirazh 40000. Photographs, footnotes with archival material.

1140. Kopylov I.S., Lazukin A.N., Raikin G.L., Orenburgskoe letnoe. Ocherki istorii Orenburgskogo vysshego voennogo aviatsionnogo Krasnoznamennogo uchilishcha letchikov imeni I.S. Polbina **The Orenburg Flying (School). Essays in the history of the Orenburg Higher Military Red Banner Aviation School for pilots in the name of I.S. Polbin**, Moscow, Voenizdat, 1976. 268 pp. Tirazh 40000. For students entering aviation schools. Photographs, footnotes.

1141. Timokhovich I.V. Operativnoe iskusstvo Sovetskikh VVS v Velikoi Otechestvennoi voine **Operational art of the Soviet Air Force during the Great Patriotic War**, Moscow, Voenizdat, 1976. 343 pp. Tirazh 18000. Footnotes with archival material, illustrations.

1142. Tishchenko M.N., Nekrasov A.V., Radin A.S., Vertolety. Vybor parametrov pri proektirovanii **Helicopters. Selection of design parameters**, Moscow, Mashinostroenie, 1976. 366 pp. Tirazh 5500. For engineers and scientists. Math, illustrations, photographs, tables, bibliography.

1143. Kozhevnikov M.N. The command and staff of the Soviet Air Force in the Great Patriotic War 1941-1945 **Komandovanie i shtab VVS Sovetskoi Armii v Velikoi Otechestvennoi voine 1941-1945 gg.**, Translated and published under the auspices of the United States Air Force. Russian original published in Moscow by Nauka, 1977. 288 pp. Tirazh 70000. Photographs, tables, footnotes with archival material, appendix of Air Force leadership in the war, index of names.

1144. Pakilev G.N. Truzheniki neba **Toilers of the sky**, Moscow, Voenizdat, 1978. 208 pp. Tirazh 20000. Deals with Air Transport. Photographs, footnotes.

1145. Akimov A.I., Berestov L.M., Mikheev R.A., Letnye ispitaniia vertoletov **Helicopter flight testing**, Moscow, Mashinostroenie, 1980. 399 pp. Tirazh 2700. For engineers. Math, tables, bibliography.

1146. Obraztsov I.F. Ed., Razvitie aviatsionnoi nauki i tekhniki v SSSR. Istoriko-tekhnicheskie ocherki **The development of aviation science and technology in the USSR. Historical-technical studies**, Moscow, Nauka, 1980. 496 pp. Tirazh 18000. Tables, illustration, photographs, index of names, bibliography.

1147. Izakson A.M. Sovetskoe vertoletostroenie **Soviet helicopter construction**, 2nd edn. Moscow, Mashinostroenie, 1981. 295 pp. Tirazh 14600. For engineers, technical and scientific workers. Illustrations, photographs, 3 appendixes, index of names, of helicopters.

1148. Iakovlev A.S. <u>Sovetskie samolety</u> **Soviet aircraft**, Moscow, Nauka, 1982. 407 pp. Tirazh 25000. Photographs, tables, illustrations, index of subjects, names.

1149. Kravchenko I.V. <u>Letchiku o meteorologii</u> **Meteorology for pilots**, 4th edn. Moscow, Voenizdat, 1982. 255 pp. Tirazh 20000. For flying and technical personnel. Illustrations, maps, photographs.

1150. Ponomarev B.A. <u>Nastoiashchee i budushchee aviatsionnykh dvigatelei</u> **The present and the future of aero engines**, Moscow, Voenizdat, 1982. 240 pp. Tirazh 10000. For Air Force engineers and technical personnel. Illustrations, index of engines, bibliography.

1151. Sidorin V.M. Ed., <u>Lazery v aviatsii</u> **Lasers in aviation,** Moscow, Voenizdat, 1982. 160 pp. Tirazh 13000. For specialist in aviation lazers. Illustrations, math, tables, index of subjects.

1152. Zimin G.V. <u>Taktika v boevykh primerakh</u> <u>Istrebitel'naia aviatsionnaia diviziia</u> **Tactics in combat examples. Fighter Interceptor Aviation Division**, Moscow, Voenizdat, 1982. 175 pp. Tirazh 14000. Illustrations, maps, appendixes.

1153. Babich V.K. <u>Istrebiteli meniaiut taktiku</u> **Fighters change tactics**, Moscow, Voenizdat, 1983. For Air Force commanders, pilots, engineers. Illustrations, footnotes.

1154. Komarov A.A., *et al*, <u>Radiolokatsionnye stantsii vozdushnoi razvedki</u> **On-board radar for aerial reconnaissance**, Moscow, Voenizdat, 1983. 152 pp. Tirazh 18000. Photographs, tables, illustrations, math, short bibliography.

1155. Tsikhosh E. <u>Sverkhzukovye samolety</u> **Supersonic aircraft**, (Translation from Polish) Moscow, Mir, 1983. 424 pp. Tirazh 43000. For aircraft designers/builders. Photographs, illustrations, tables.

1156. Korobeinikov V.A. *et al*, <u>Ikh pozvalo nebo: Voenno-istoricheskii ocherk Boris-oglebskogo vysshego voennogo aviatsionnogo ordena Lenina, Krasnoznamennogo uchilishcha letchikov imeni V.P. Chkalova</u> **They were called by the sky: Military historical study of the Borisoglebsk higher military aviation school for pilots, of the Order of Lenin and the Red banner, in the name of V.P. Chkalov**, Moscow, Voenizdat, 1984. 216 pp. Tirazh 30000. Photographs, footnotes with some archival material.

1157. Pavlenko V.F., D'iachenko A.A., Zhulev V.I., Kolpakov B.K., Nazarov A.P., Tikhonravov V.A., <u>Boevaia aviatsionnaia tekhnika: Letatel'nye apparaty, silovye ustanovki i ikh ekspluatatsiia</u> **Combat aviation technology: aircraft, power plants and their use (exploitation)**, Moscow, Voenizdat, 1984. 320 pp. Tirazh 23000. For Air Force engineers, pilots. Illustrations, photographs, bibliography.

1158. Ponomarev A.N., Lt. General, <u>Aviatsiia nastoiashchego i budushchego</u> **Aviation of the present and the future**, Moscow, Voenizdat, 1984. 256 pp. Tirazh 50000. For aviation specialists. Illustrations, photographs, short bibliography.

1159. Skomorokhov N.M., Air Marshal, Ed., Voenno-vozdushnaia akademiia imeni Iu.A. Gagarina **The Gagarin Air Force Academy**, Moscow, Voenizdat, 1984. 238 pp. Tirazh 35000. Photographs, footnotes, appendix.

1160. Kozhevnikov M.N. Komandovanie i shtab VVS Sovetskoi Armii v Velikoi Otechestvennoi voine 1941-1945 2nd edn. **Command and Staff of the Soviet Army Air Force during the Great Patriotic War 1941-1945**, Moscow, Nauka, 1985. 288 pp. Photographs, tables, footnotes with archival material, 2 appendixes.

1161. Maslenikov Iu.I. Taktika v boevykh primerakh: Eskadril'ia-ekipazh **Tactics in combat examples: The squadron-the crew**, Moscow, Voenizdat, 1985. 88 pp. Tirazh 12000. Illustrations, footnotes.

1162. Skomorokhov N.M., Air Marshal, Chernetskii V.N., Taktika v boevykh primerakh: Aviatsionnyi polk **Tactics in combat examples: Aviation regiment,** Moscow, Voenizdat, 1985. 175 pp. Tirazh 14000. Illustrations, tables, bibliography.

1163. Korchemnyi P.A. Psikhologiia letnogo obucheniia **Psychology of flying training**, Moscow, Voenizdat, 1986. 136 pp. Tirazh 15000. For flying instructors, lecturers and students. Illustrations, tables, footnotes.

1164. Shumikhin V.S. Sovetskaia voennaia aviatsia 1917-1941 **Soviet military aviation 1917-1941**, Moscow, Nauka, 1986. 286 pp. Tirazh 16000. Tables, footnotes with archival material, index of names.

1165. Timokhovich I.V. V nebe voiny 1941-1945 **In the sky of war 1941-1945**, Moscow, Voenizdat, 1986. 332 pp. Tirazh 30000. Second edn. of 1976 book with a changed title. Photographs, footnotes with archival material.

1166. Gladkov D.I. Boevaia aviatsionnaia tekhnika: Aviatsionnoe vooruzhenie **Combat aircraft technology: Aircraft armament,** Moscow, Voenizdat, 1987. 280 pp. Tirazh 24000. For Air Force pilots, engineers, technical staff. Math, illustrations, short bibliography.

1167. Krasnov A.B. Bar'ery vozdushnoi razvedki **Barriers of air reconnaissance**, Moscow, Voenizdat, 1987. 176 pp. Tirazh 15000. For Air Force flight and command personnel. Illustrations, footnotes, photographs.

1168. Shavrov V.B. Istoriia konstruktsii samoletov v SSSR 1938- 1950 (Materialy k istorii samoletostroeniia) **The history of aircraft construction in the USSR 1938-1950 (Material regarding the history of aircraft construction)**, 2nd edn. Moscow, Mashinostroenie, 1988. 568 pp. Tirazh 20000. Tables, photographs, illustrations, footnotes, appendix, bibliography, index of subjects, names.

1169. Dobrolenskii Iu.P. Ed., Boevaia aviatsionnaia tekhnika: Aviatsionnoe oborudovanie **Combat aircraft technology: Aviation equipment**, Moscow, Voenizdat, 1989. 248 pp. Tirazh 19000. For aviation specialists. Illustrations, tables, math.

1170. Ponomarev A.N. Sovetskie aviatsionnye konstruktory Soviet aircraft constructors, 3rd edn. Moscow, Voenizdat, 1990. For aircraft specialists. Photographs.

1171. Sidorin V.M. Ed., Boevaia aviatsionnaia tekhnika: Radioelektronnoe oborudovanie Combat aircraft technology: Electronic equipment, Moscow, Voenizdat, 1990. 288 pp. Tirazh 18000. For pilots, navigators, engineers. Illustrations, math, subject index, short bibliography.

1172. Krasnov A.B. Sekrety neotrazimykh atak Secrets of irresistible attacks, Moscow, Voenizdat, 1991. 271 pp. Tirazh 6000. Tactics of new generation fighters, technology, tactical C3. Schematic diagrams.

1173. Volodko A.M., Verkhozin M.P., Gorshkov V.A., Vertolety: Spravochnik po aerodinamike, dinamike poleta, konstruktsii, oborudovaniiu i tekhnicheskoi ekspluatatsii Helicopters: Manual regarding aerodynamics, dynamics of flight, construction, equipment and technical use, Moscow, Voenizdat, 1992. 557 pp. Tirazh 10000. For technical and flying personnel. Illustrations, tables, appendix, subject index.

Navy

1174. V'iunenko N.P., Mordvinov R.N., Voennye flotilii v Velikoi Otechestvennoi voine Military flotillas in the Great Patriotic War, Moscow, Voenizdat, 1957. 272pp. Maps, photographs, footnotes.

1175. Prostakov A.L. Protivolodochnaia oborona torgovykh sudov (Po opytu inostrannikh flotov) Anti-submarine defence of merchant ships (In the experience of foreign fleets), Moscow, Voenizdat, 1960. 172 pp. For wide circle of officers and general readers; tables, maps, illustrations, photographs.

1176. Eremeev L.M., Shergin A.P., Podvodnye lodki inostrannykh flotov vo vtoroi mirovoi voine Operativno-statisticheskie materiialy po opytu vtoroi mirovoi voiny Foreign fleets' submarines in the Second World War Operational and statistical data from the Second World War, Moscow, Voenizdat, 1962. Tirazh 5000. For officers, admirals, navy generals, academies. Tables of missions, periods of missions, losses, cause of losses for operations of all non-Soviet submarines, footnotes, bibliography.

1177. Lifshits A.L. Kibernetika v voenno-morskom flote Cybernetics in the navy, Moscow, Voenizdat, 1964. 259 pp. Tirazh 4500. For navy officers, other officers, lecturers and students in Navy establishments; tables, illustrations, bibliography.

1178. Kozlov I.A., Shlomin V.S. Severnyi Flot The Northern Fleet, Moscow, Voenizdat, 1966. 296 pp. Tirazh 15000. Chronology of the most important events in the opening up of the Artic Ocean and the history of the Northern Fleet, photographs, footnotes with archival material, maps, tables. 2nd edn. Krasnoznamennyi Severnyi flot The Red Banner Northern Fleet, published 1977. Third edition published 1983.

1179. Belli V.A., Penzin K.V., <u>Boevye deistviia v Atlantike i na Sredizemnom more 1939-1945 gg.</u> **Combat actions in the Atlantic and the Mediterranean Sea 1939-1945,** Moscow, Voenizdat, 1967. 478 pp. Tirazh 5000. For officers, generals and admirals; 6 appendixes, bibliography, index of the most important actions and events at sea 1939-1945, illustrations.

1180. Bogolepov V.P., Rear Admiral, Ed., <u>Blokada i kontrblokada, Bor'ba na okeansko-morskikh soobshcheniiakh vo vtoroi mirovoi voine</u> **Blockade and counter blockade, The struggle on oceanic and sea lines of communication in the Second World War,** Moscow, Nauka, 1967. 768 pp. Tirazh 6500. Sixty-five appendixes, 10 page bibliography, index of subjects, names, maps, tables, footnotes. Written by 6 naval specialists.

1181. Nikolaev V., Romanovski V., <u>Morskie sapery</u> **The sea sappers,** Moscow, Voenizdat, 1967. 152 pp. Tirazh 25000. Photographs, tables, few footnotes.

1182. Suzdalev N.I. <u>Podvodnye lodki protiv podvodnykh lodok</u> **Submarines against submarines,** Moscow, Voenizdat, 1968. 164 pp. Tirazh 10500. For Army and Fleet personnel; illustrations, tables, photographs, bibliography.

1183. Zakharov S.E., Zakharov M.N., Bagrov V.N., Kotukhov M.P. <u>Tikhookeanskii flot</u> **Pacific Fleet,** Moscow, Voenizdat, 1968. 287 pp. Tirazh 35000. Photographs, maps, index of names, bibliography, chronology of the most important events, index of vessels.

1184. Rall' V.Iu. *et al*, <u>Trenazhery i imitatory VMF.</u> **Naval trainers and simulators,** Moscow, Voenizdat, 1969. 212 pp. Bibliography Soviet, non-Soviet sources.

1185. Smukul A.O., Fedurin A.S. <u>Suda obespecheniia VMF</u> **Fleet support ships,** Moscow, Voenizdat, 1969. 232 pp. Tirazh 3500. Study of US Navy support ships. For Soviet naval officers, shipbuilders and students of naval schools. Tables, illustrations, photographs, bibliography.

1186. Shablikov N.I., Rear Admiral, Ed., <u>"Okean". Manevry Voenno-Morskogo Flota SSSR, provedennye v aprele-mae 1970 goda</u> **"Ocean". Manoeuvres of the naval fleet of the USSR, performed in April-May 1970,** Moscow, Voenizdat, 1970. 208 pp. Tirazh 20000. Photographs.

1187. Gordeev N.P. <u>Maskirovka v boevykh deistviiakh flota</u> **Camouflage in combat actions of the fleet,** Moscow, Voenizdat, 1971. 159 pp. Tirazh 4000. Useful for navy personnel and other branches of armed forces. Maps, footnotes, photographs.

1188. Achkasov V.I., Pavlovich N.B. <u>Sovetskoe voenno-morskoe iskusstvo v Velikoi Otechestvennoi voine</u> **Soviet naval art in the Great Patriotic War,** Moscow, Voenizdat, 1973. 404 pp. Tirazh 15000. For navy officers, generals and admirals, students attending navy schools or military academies. Footnotes with some archival material.

1189. Prasolov S.N., Amitin M.B. Ustroistvo podvodnykh lodok **Submarine construction**, Moscow, Voenizdat 1973. 312 pp. Tirazh 16000. For sailors, petty officers, warrant officers; 119 illustrations, 33 items of bibliography.

1190. Skugarev V.D., Kudin L.V. Setevoe planirovanie na flote **Network planning in the fleet**, Moscow, Voenizdat, 1973. 248 pp. Tirazh 5000. For naval officers. Twenty four tables, 56 illustrations, 45 items of bibliography.

1191. Zakharov S.E., Bagrov V.N, Bevz S.S., Zakharov M.N., Kotukhov M.P. Krasnoznamennyi Tikhookeanskii Flot 2nd edition, **The Red Banner Pacific Fleet**, Moscow, Voenizdat, 1973. 320 pp. Tirazh 35000. Recomended literature, chronology of events in the Pacific Fleet and Amur Flotilla, index of names, vessels, units. 3rd edition published 1983.

1192. Sytin A.V. Ed., Neobitaemye podvodnye apparaty **Unmanned under water instruments**, Moscow, Voenizdat, 1975. 160 pp. Tirazh 14500. For navy officers and specialists of under water technology; illustrations, tables, photographs.

1193. Bagrov V.N., Sungorkin N.F. Krasnoznamennaia Amurskaia flotiliia 2nd edition. **The Red Banner Amur Flotilla**,   Moscow, Voenizdat, 1976. 198 pp. Photographs, footnotes, maps.

1194. Gel'fond, G.M., Zharov A.F., Strelov A.B., Khrenov V.A., Tam za Nevoi moria i okeany, Istoria Vysshego voenno-morskogo ordena Lenina, Krasnoznamennogo, ordena Ushakova uchilishcha imeni M.V. Frunze **There beyond Neva, seas and oceans, History of the Higher naval Order of Lenin, Order of Ushakov, Red Banner Academy in the name of M.V. Frunze**, Moscow, Voenizdat, 1976. 363 pp. Tirazh 40000. Photographs, footnotes with archival material, appendix.

1195. Gorshkov S.G. Admiral of the Fleet, Morskaia moshch' gosudarstva **The Sea Power of the State**,   Moscow, Voenizdat, 1976. 464 pp. Tirazh 60000. For military reader; Footnotes, tables, maps. 2nd edition published 1979. English edition published by Pergamon Press, Oxford, New York, 1979. 290 pp. Index. ISBN 0 08 021944 6.

1196. Suzdal' V.G. Teoriia igr dlia flota **Theory of games as applied to a fleet**, Moscow, Voenizdat, 1976. 320 pp. Tirazh 10000. For specialists; tables, illustrations, bibliography.

1197. Bronevitskii G.A., Zuev Iu.P., Stoliarenko A.M., Osnovy voenno-morskoi psikhologii **The basics of naval psychology**, Moscow, Voenizdat, 1977. 339 pp. Tirazh 30000. For navy officers, students, Party activists. Bibliography.

1198. Potapov I.N. Nauchno-tekhnicheskii progress i flot **Scientific-technical progress and the fleet**, Moscow, Voenizdat, 1977. 160 pp. Tirazh 18000. For Soviet Army and Navy officers. Footnotes, tables.

1199. Rodionov B.I. Protivolodochnye sily i sredstva flotov **Fleet anti-submarine forces and equipment**, Moscow, Voenizdat, 1977. 136 pp. Tirazh 18000. For

Navy and Air Force personnel, academy students. Short bibliography, tables, illustrations, photographs.

1200. Vaneev G.I. Chernomortsy v Velikoi Otechestvennoi voine **Black Sea Fleet forces in the Great Patriotic War**, Moscow, Voenizdat, 1978. 384 pp. Tirazh 50000. Footnotes with some archival material, maps photographs.

1201. Basov A.V. Flot v Velikoi otechestvennoi voine 1941 - 1945 Opyt operativno-strategicheskogo primeneniia **The Fleet in the Great Patriotic War 1941-1945. Experience of operational-strategic application**, Moscow, Nauka, 1980. 304 pp. Tirazh 22700. Colour maps, tables, footnotes with archival material, appendix of 29 operational documents.

1202. Khor'kov G.I. Sovetskie nadvodnye korabli v Velikoi Otechestvennoi voine **Soviet surface ships in the Great Patriotic War**, Moscow, Voenizdat, 1981. 272 pp. Tirazh 20000. For navy officers and students of naval schools; 6 appendixes, recommended literature, illustrations.

1203. Makovskii A.A., Radchenko B.M., Kaspiiskaia Krasnoznmenaia **Caspian Red Banner (Flotilla)**, 2nd edition, Moscow, Voenizdat 1982. 176 pp. Tirazh 35000. Photographs with archival material, chronology of the most significant events, command composition of the Caspian Flotilla.

1204. Ryss Iu.L. Komandir korablia **Ship's commander**, Moscow Voenizdat, 1982. 270 pp. Tirazh 19000. For officers and students of higher military and naval schools. Footnotes.

1205. Dmitriev A.N., Zaferman M.L., Neretin V.I. Podvodnye razvedchiki Rybopoiskovyi podvodnyi flot **Underwater scouts Fish searching underwater fleet**, Leningrad, Sudostroenie, 1984. 168 pp. Tirazh 2300. Photographs and illustrations of Soviet mini submarines; short bibliography.

1206. Isakov I.S. Admiral of the Soviet Fleet of the Soviet Union Izbrannye trudy Okeanologiia, geografiia i voennaia istoriia **Selected works Oceanography, geography and military history**, Moscow, Nauka, 1984. 584 pp. Tirazh 18200. Twelve tables, 10 illustrations, 200 items of bibliography, index of vessels, names, places, appendix.

1207. Pirumov V.S., Chervinskii R.A. Radioelektronika v voine na more **Radioelectronics in the war at sea**, Moscow, Voenizdat 1987. 176 pp. Tirazh 10000. For navy officers and students; illustrations, footnotes.

1208. Rodionov B.I., Novichkov N.N. Krylatye rakety v morskom boiu **Cruise missiles in naval combat**, Moscow, Voenizdat, 1987. 216 pp. Tirazh 10000. Tables, illustrations. Material from foreign press.

1209. Berezhnoi S.S. Korabli i suda VMF SSSR 1928-1945, spravochnik **Ships and vessels of the Soviet Navy 1928-1945, reference book**, Moscow, Voenizdat, 1988. 712 pp. Tirazh 25000. Types, pennant numbers, displacement, armament, deployment. Index of vessel names. Photographs.

1210. Khiiainen L.P. Razvitie zarubezhnykh podvodnykh lodok i ikh taktiki **The development of foreign submarines and their tactics**, Moscow, Voenizdat, 1988. 240 pp. Tirazh 35000. 2nd edition; 1st edition published 1979. For Navy personnel; tables, footnotes, short bibliography.

1211. V'iunenko N.P., Makeev B.N., Skugarev V.D. Voenno-morskoi flot: rol', perspektivy razvitiia, ispol'zovanie **The Fleet: its role, expected development and utilization**, Moscow, Voenizdat, 1988. 227 pp. Tirazh 25000. Under the general editorship of Admiral of the Fleet SU S.G. Gorshkov. For naval personnel. An exposition of the role of naval forces in armed conflict and perspectives of future naval developments. Tables and bibliography.

1212. Khvoshch V.A. Taktika podvodnikh lodok **Submarine tactics**, Moscow, Voenizdat, 1989. 264 pp. Tirazh 30000. Illustrations, tables, short bibliography.

1213. Kondratovich A.A., Piianzov G.G., Protivominnoe oruzhie **Counter-mine weapons**, Moscow, Voenizdat, 1989. 88 pp. Tirazh 10000. Illustrations, tables.

1214. Belavin N.I. Avianesushchie korabli **Air-capable ships**, Moscow, Patriot, 1990. 216 pp. Tirazh 30000. Tables, illustrations.

1215. Dmitriev V.I. Sovetskoe podvodnoe korablestroenie **Soviet submarine construction**, Moscow, Voenizdat, 1990. 288 pp. Tirazh 35000. Eight appendixes, footnotes with archival material, photographs, tables, graphs.

1216. Muru N.P. Osnovy nepotopliaemosti korablia **The basics of ship unsinkability**, Moscow, Voenizdat, 1990, 2nd edition. pp. 224. Tirazh 15000. For naval officers and students; photographs, illustrations, footnotes, bibliography.

1217. Stupnikov N.A. Dvazhdy Krasnoznamennyi Baltiiski flot **Twice Red Banner Baltic Fleet**, Moscow, Voenizdat, 1990. 344 pp. Tirazh 35000. 3rd edition. Chronology of the most important dates of the Baltic Fleet, index of names, photographs.

1218. Ivashkin G.A. Ed., Flagmany **Flag officers**, Moscow, Voenizdat, 1991. 283 pp. Tirazh 65000. Footnotes with archival material, illustrations.

Rear Services

1219. Vysotskii V.K. Professor, Lt. General, *et al* Tyl Sovetskoi Armii **Soviet Army Rear Services**, Moscow, Voenizdat, 1968. 320 pp. Tirazh 20000. Photographs, footnotes with archival material.

1220. Mikhal'chuk A.K. Voennoe uchilishche imeni A.V. Khruleva **Military school in the name of A.V. Khrulev**, Moscow, Voenizdat, 1971. 264 pp. Tirazh 11500. Photographs, footnotes with some archival material.

1221. Klemin A.S. Eshelon za eshelonom **Echelon after echelon**, Moscow, Voeniz-dat, 1981. 248 pp. Tirazh 30000. Deals with railway troops. Photographs, foot-notes with some archival material.

1222. Golushko I.M., Lt. General, Varlamov N.V., Osnovy modelirovaniia i avtoma-tizatsii upravleniia tylom **Basics of modeling and automation of the manage-ment of the Rear Services,** Moscow, Voenizdat, 1982. 237 pp. Tirazh 9000. For Rear Services officers and specialists in automated command and control. Illustrations, tables, math, bibliography.

1223. Kosovich S.S., Filimonov A.M., Sovetskie zheleznodorozhnye: Voenno-istori-cheskii ocherk **Soviet Railway Troops: Military-historical study,** Moscow, Voenizdat, 1984. 310 pp. Tirazh 30000. Photographs, footnotes with archival material.

1224. Golushko I.M. Lt. General, Ed., Voiskovoe i korabel'noe khoziaistvo. Spravochnik **Troop and ship management. A handbook,** Moscow, Voenizdat, 1987. 293 pp. Tirazh 40000. For generals, admirals, officers and non-commis-sioned officers. Tables, illustrations, subject index.

1225. Rodin V.N. Ed., Razvitie Tyla Sovetskikh Vooruzhennykh Sil (1918-1988) **The development of the Rear Services of the Soviet Armed Forces,** Moscow. Voenizdat, 1989. 311 pp. Tirazh 45000. For officers. Footnotes with archival material.

Military Medical Services

1226. Kuvshinski D.D., Georgievski A.S., Ocherki istorii Sovetskoi voennoi meditsiny **Essays in the history of the Soviet military medicine,** Leningrad, Izdatel'stvo Meditsina, 1968. 528 pp. Tirazh 5400. Photographs, footnotes with archival material, illustrations, extensive bibliography, diary of events.

1227. Ivanov F.I. Reaktivnye psikhozy v voennoe vremia **Reactive psychosis in war time,** Leningrad, Meditsina, 1970. 168 pp. Tirazh 4500. Thirty-six tables, bibli-ography.

1228. Smirnov E.I. Voina i voennaia meditsina. 1939-1945 gody. **War and military medicine,** Moscow, Meditsina, 1979. 528 pp. Tirazh 11000. Fifty-eight tables, illustrations, footnotes with archival material, photographs.

1229. Burnazian A.I. Bor'ba za zhizn' ranenykh i bol'nykh Kalininskom - Pervom Pribaltiiskom fronte (1941-1945 gg.) **Fight for the survival of the wounded and sick on the Kalinin - First Baltic Front (1941-1945),** Moscow, Meditsina, 1982. 304 pp. Tirazh 900. Thirty-eight tables, footnotes with archival material, illustrations, photographs.

1230. Krylov N.L. Major-General in the Medical Service, Editor. Glavnyi voennyi gospital' **The Main Military Hospital,** Moscow, Voenizdat, 1985. 240 pp. Ti-razh 20000. Photographs, tables, footnotes with some archival material.

1231. Aleksanian I.V., Knopov M.Sh., Rukovoditeli meditsinskoi sluzhby frontov i flotov v Velikoi Otechestvennoi voine 1941-1945 gg. **Leaders of the medical service of fronts and fleets during the Great Patriotic War 1941-1945,** Moscow, Meditsina, 1992. 288 pp. Tirazh 1291. Photographs and footnotes with archival material.

MILITARY DISTRICTS

1232. Mal'tsev E.E., Lt.-General *et al* Ed., Boevoi put' voisk Turkestanskogo voennogo okruga **Combat route of the Turkestan Military District troops,** Moscow, Voenizdat, 1959. pp 307. Photographs, maps, footnotes with some archival material, end notes.

1233. Mishchenko A.F., Major-General, *et al*, V plameni i slave. Ocherki istorii Sibirskogo voennogo okruga In the blaze and glory. **Studies in the history of the Siberian Military District,** Novosibirsk, Zapadno-Sibirskoe Knizhnoe Izdatel'stvo, 1969. 432 pp. Tirazh 25000. Photographs, coloured maps.

1234. Egorevskii A.A., Col. General, *et al*, Istoriia Ural'skogo voennogo okruga **The history of the Urals Military District,** Moscow, Voenizdat, 1970. 352 pp. Tirazh 11500. Photographs, maps, footnotes with archival material, index of commanders of the Urals MD.

1235. Ivanovskii E.F., General, Ordena Lenina Moskovskii voennyi okrug **Order of Lenin Moscow Military District,** Moscow, Voenizdat 1971. 572 pp. Tirazh 43000. Photographs, 12 coloured maps, footnotes with archival material, biographical index of commanders of the District, chronological index of important events.

1236. Bedniagin A.I. *et al*, Kievskii Krasnoznamennyi. Istoriia Krasnoznamennogo Kievskogo voennogo okruga 1919-1972 **Kiev Red Banner District. The history of the Red Banner Kiev Military District,** Moscow, Voenizdat, 1974. 432 pp. Tirazh 40000. Photographs, coloured maps.

1237. Gribkov A.I. *et al*, Istoriia ordena Lenina Leningradskogo voennogo okruga **The history of the Order of Lenin Leningrad Military District,** Moscow, Voenizdat, 1974. 613 pp. Tirazh 53000. Photographs, coloured maps, 5 appendixes including brief biographical index, index of events.

1238. Voloshin I.M. *et al*, Odesskii Krasnoznamennyi **Odessa Red Banner Military District,** Kishinev, Izdatel'stvo "Kartia Moldovenskaia", 1975. 343 pp. Tirazh 12000. Photographs, footnotes with archival material, supplement of 13 coloured maps, list of commanders, index of names.

1239. Budakovskii P.D., Lt. General *et al*, Krasnoznamennyi Turkestanskii **The Red Banner Turkestan Military District,** Moscow, Voenizdat 1976. 438 pp. Tirazh 40000. Coloured maps, photographs, footnotes with archival material, appendix of events, biographical sketches of commanders.

1240. Salmanov G.I., General, Ed., Ordena Lenina Zabaikal'skii Istoriia ordena Lenina Zabaikal'skogo voennogo okruga **Order of Lenin Trans-Baikal Military District The history of the Order of Lenin TransBaikal Military District**, Moscow, Voenizdat, 1980. 374 pp. Tirazh 75000. Photographs, appendix, footnotes with archival material, coloured map.

1241. Belikov V.A. *et al*, Krasnoznamennyi Prikarpatskii **The Red Banner Carpathian Military District**, 2nd edn, Moscow, Voenizdat, 1982. 285 pp. Tirazh 39000. Photographs, footnotes with archival material, coloured maps.

1242. Ivanovskii E.F., General, Ed., Krasnoznamennyi Beloruskii voennyi okrug **Red Banner Belorussian Military District**, 2nd edn. Moscow, Voenizdat, 1983. 406 pp. Tirazh 65000. Photographs, footnotes with archival material. 1st. edn. Belarus' 1973.

1243. Tiagunov M.A. *et al*, Krasnoznamennyi Uralskii. Istoriia Krasnoznammenogo Ural'skogo voennogo okruga **The Red Banner Urals Military District. The history of the Red Banner Urals Military District**, Moscow, Voenizdat, 1983. 285 pp. Tirazh 35000. Photographs, footnotes with some archival material, appendix of biographical details of commanders.

1244. Gromov G.A. *et al*, Krasnoznamennyi Privolzhskii: Istoriia voisk Krasnoznamennogo Privolzhskogo voennogo okruga **Red Banner Volga (Military District): History of the troops of the Red Banner Volga Military District**, Moscow, Voenizdat, 1984. 392 pp. Tirazh 39000. Photographs, footnotes with archival material. First edition published by Kuibyshevskoe knizhnoe izdatel'stvo, 1975.

1245. Lushchev P.G., General, Repin I.P., Lt. General, Ed., Ordena Lenina Moskovskii voennyi okrug **Order of Lenin Moscow Military District**, Moscow, Moskovskii Rabochii 1985. 3rd edn. 621 pp. Tirazh 70000. Photographs, maps, footnotes with some archival material, updated biographical details of command staff, chronology of important events.

1246. Tret'iak I.M., General, *et al*, Krasnoznamennyi Dal'nevostochnyi. Istoriia Krasnoznamennogo Dal'nevostochnogo okruga **The Red Banner Far Eastern Military District. The history of the Red Banner Far Eastern District**, 3rd edition, Moscow, Voenizdat, 1985. 348 pp. Tirazh 50000. Photographs, footnotes with archival material, maps, chronology of important events.

1247. Shustko L.S. Ed., Krasnoznamennyi Severo-Kavkazskii, **The Red Banner North-Caucasus Military District**, Moscow, Voenizdat 1990. 380 pp. Tirazh 10000. Based on documents. Photographs, footnotes with archival material.

NATO AND WTO (Warsaw Pact)

NATO

1248. Andrukhov I.I. *et al*, Vozdushnodesantnye voiska NATO **NATO Airborne Troops**, Moscow, Voenizdat, 1970. 238 pp. Tirazh 16000. Tables, photographs.

1249. Nelin Iu.G. Atom i NATO **The Atom and NATO**, Moscow, Voenizdat, 1970. 132 pp. Tirazh 24000. Tables, illustrations, footnotes.

1250. Shevchenko A.M., Lt. General, Ed., Armii stran NATO. Voenno-politicheskii ocherk **NATO armies. Military-political study**, Moscow, Voenizdat, 1974. 285 pp. Tirazh 36000.

1251. Glazunov N.K. Bundesver i NATO. Istoriia sozdaniia i razvitiia vooruzhennykh sil Federativnoi Respubliki Germanii (1955-1978) **The Bundeswehr and NATO. History and creation of the armed forces of the Federal Republic of Germany**, Moscow, Voenizdat, 1979. 272 pp. Tirazh 30000. Endnotes, bibliography.

1252. Maslennikov P.E. *et al*, Vooruzhennye sily kapitalisticheskikh gosudarstv **Armed forces of the capitalist countries**, Moscow, Voenizdat, 1979. 2nd ed. 511 pp. Tirazh 50000. Photographs, tables, illustrations.

1253. Glazunov N.K., Maslennikov P.E., Sukhoputnye voiska kapitalisticheskikh gosudarstv (uchastnikov Severoatlanticheskogo soiuza) **Ground Forces of the capitalist countries (members of NATO)**, Moscow, Voenizdat, 1980. 2nd edn. 416 pp. Tirazh 90000. Footnotes, tables, bibliography.

1254. Golokolenko I.I., Nikitin N.S., Podrazdeleniia inostrannykh armiii **Subunits of foreign armies**, Moscow, Voenizdat, 1980. 3rd edn. 320 pp. Tirazh 35000. Photographs, illustrations, tables, short bibliography.

1255. Gromov A.V. *et al*, Vooruzhenie i tekhnika: Spravochnik **Arms and equipment: Handbook**, Moscow, Voenizdat, 1982. 352 pp. Tirazh 50000. For officers. Western countries ground, airborne, naval forces. Photographs, statistics.

1256. Khalosha B.M. Voenno-politicheskie soiuzy imperializma. Osnovnye osobennosti i tendentsii razvitiia v 70-kh - nachale 80-kh godov **Imperialist military-political unions. Basic characteristics and tendencies of developments in the 70s and the beginning of the 80s**, Moscow, Nauka, 1982. 336 pp. Tirazh 4100. Footnotes, bibliography.

1257. Glazunov N.K., Nikitin N.S., Operatsiia i boi **Operations and combat**, Moscow, Voenizdat, 1983. 320 pp. Tirazh 24000. For generals and officers. Illustrations, tables, footnotes.

1258. Volkogonov D. **Psikhologicheskaia voina**, The psychological war Moscow, Voenizdat, 1983. 288 pp. Tirazh 60000. Footnotes. English translation: Progress, 1986. 240 pp. Tirazh 11085. Footnotes.

1259. Grishin S.V., Tsapenko N.N., Soedineniia i chasti v boiu **Formations and units in battle**, Moscow, Voenizdat, 1985. 279 pp. Tirazh 37000. Illustrations, tables.

1260. Nikitin N.S, Podrazdeleniia v boiu **Subunits in combat**, Moscow, Voenizdat, 1985. 208 pp. Tirazh 39000. Ground forces of USA, Germany and Great Britain. Illustrations.

1261. Zhilin P.A. *et al* Ed., Gosudarstva NATO i voennye konflikty. Voenno-istoricheski ocherk **NATO governments and military conflicts. Military-historical study**, Moscow, Nauka, 1987. 312 pp. Tirazh 5700. Endnotes.

1262. Shishaeva A.V. Voenno-promyshlennye kompleksy v Zapadnoi Evrope **Military-industrial complex in the Western Europe**, Moscow, Mezhdunarodnye otnosheniia, 1988. 176 pp. Tirazh 8500. Tables, endnotes.

WTO (Warsaw Pact): Warsaw Treaty Organisation

1263. Antosiak A.V. *et al*, Zarozhdenie narodnykh armii stran-uchastnits Varshavskogo dogovora 1941-1949 gg **The birth of the peoples armies - member-countries of the Warsaw Pact 1941-1949**, Moscow, Nauka, 1975. 392 pp. Tirazh 5100. Footnotes with archival material, photographs, tables, maps.

1264. Iakubovskii I.I. Marshal, Ed., Boevoe sodruzhestvo bratskikh narodov i armii **Combat co-operation of the fraternal peoples and armies**, Moscow, Voenizdat, 1975. 295 pp. Tirazh 50000. Photographs, footnotes, tables.

1265. Zhilin P.A. Lt. General, Iadziaka E., Ed., Bratstvo po oruzhiiu Braterstwo broni **Brotherhood in arms**, Moscow, Voenizdat, 1975. 383 pp. Tirazh 30000. Joint Soviet-Polish authorship. Footnotes, photographs.

1266. Vladimirov S., Teplov L, Varshavskii Dogovor i NATO: dva kursa, dve politiki **Warsaw Pact: two directions, two policies**, Moscow, Mezhdunarodnye otnosheniia, 1979. 296 pp. Tirazh 22000. Footnotes.

1267. Mal'tsev V.F. Organizatsiia Varshavskogo Dogovora. Dokumenty i materialy 1955-1980 **Organisation of the Warsaw Pact. Documents and materials 1955-1980**, Moscow, Politizdat, 1980. 296 pp. Tirazh 20000.

1268. Zhilin P.A. Lt. General, Ed., Stroitel'stvo armii Evropeiskikh stran sotsialisticheskogo sodruzhestva 1949-1980 **The building of the armies of the European countries of the socialist community 1949-1980**, Moscow, Nauka, 1984. 312 pp. Tirazh 7700. Endnotes, photographs, bibliography, index of names.

1269. Zhilin P.A. Lt. General, Prokhazki Z. Ed., Na vechnye vremena; Na vecné casy **For ever and ever**, Moscow, Voenizdat, 1985. 2nd edn. 358 pp. Tirazh 10000. Soviet-Czech combat collaboration. Photographs, footnotes with archival material, maps.

1270. Mal'tsev V.F. Organizatsiia Varshavskogo Dogovora 1955-1985: Dokumenty i materialy **Warsaw Pact Organisation 1955-1985: Documents and materials**, Moscow, Politizdat, 1986. 422 pp.

1271. Orlik I.I. Ed., Vneshnaia politika stran Varshavskogo Dogovora (Pervaia polovina 80-ikh godov) **Foreign policy of the Warsaw Pact countries (First half of the eighties)**, Moscow, Nauka, 1986. 320 pp. Tirazh 2000. Endnotes.

1272. Babin A.I. *et al*, Boevoe sodruzhestvo, rozhdennoe Velikim Oktiabrem: O sovetsko-vengerskom boevom sodruzhestve *A Nagy Oktoberi forradalomban született fegyverbaratsag* **Combat co-operation born of the Great October: About Soviet-Hungarian combat co-operation**, Moscow, Voenizdat, 1987. Joint Soviet Hungarian authorship. Footnotes with archival material, photographs, maps.

1273. Semin V.V. *et al*, Ed., Voenno-politicheskoe sotrudnichestvo sotsialisticheskikh stran **Military-political co-operation of the socialist countries**, Moscow, Nauka, 1988. 320 pp. Tirazh 2100. Endnotes with some archival material.

ARMAMENT AND DISARMAMENT

1274. Maryganov I. T. Peredovoi kharakter sovetskoi voennoi nauki **Advanced character of Soviet military science**, Moscow, Voenizdat, 1953. 151 pp.

1275. Lagovskii A.N. Strategiia i ekonomika **Strategy and economics**, Moscow, Voenizdat, 1957. 200 pp.

1276. Vasilenko V.A., Ed., Sovremennaia imperialisticheskaia voennaia ideologiia **Contemporary imperialist military ideology**, Moscow, Voenizdat, 1958. 496 pp.

1277. Rybkin E.I. Voina i politika **War and politics**, Moscow, Voenizdat, 1959. 144 pp. Footnotes.

1278. Kozlov S.N. *et al*, O sovetskoi voennoi nauke **Soviet military science**, 2nd. edn. Moscow, Voenizdat, 1964. 405 pp. Tirazh 15000. For officers. Discusses significance of nuclear weapons. Footnotes.

1279. Sokolovskii V.D., Marshal, Voennaia strategiia **Military strategy**, Moscow, Voenizdat, 1962. 458 pp. Tirazh 20000. Footnotes, tables. 2nd edn. 1963. 504 pp. Tirazh 40000. English translation: Soviet Military Strategy, Santa Monica, RAND Corporation, 1963.

1280. Tiushkevich S.A. Neobkhodimost' i sluchainost' v voine **Determinism and chance in war**, Moscow, Voenizdat, 1962. 136 pp. Tirazh 11500. For officers. Footnotes.

1281. Popov M.V. Sushchnost' zakonov vooruzhennoi bor'by **The essence of law in armed conflict**, Moscow, Voenizdat, 1964. 134 pp. Tirazh 7000. For officers, generals and admirals. Discusses philosophical problems. Footnotes.

1282. Derevianko P.M., Ed., Problemy revoliutsii v voennom dele. Sbornik statei **Problems of revolution in military affairs. Collection of articles**, Moscow, Voenizdat, 1965. 195 pp. Tirazh 16000. Senior Soviet officers as contributors. Footnotes.

1283. Akhmatshin M.A. *et al*, Zashchita naseleniia v usloviiakh primeneniia iadrenogo, khimicheskogoi bakteriologicheskogo oruzhiia **Protection of population under the conditions of nuclear, chemical and bacteriological warfare**, Kiev, Zdorov'ia, 1969. 474 pp. Tirazh 80000. Illustrations, tables, bibliography, 6 appendixes.

1284. Gromozdov G.G., Ed., Bakteriologicheskoe oruzhie i zashchita ot nego **Bacteriological weapons and protection from them**, Moscow, Voenizdat, 1971. 2nd edn. 207 pp. Tirazh 100000. Illustrations, tables.

1285. Ivanov A., Naumenko I, Pavlov M., Raketno-iadrenoe oruzhie i ego porazhaiushchee deistvie **Nuclear weapons and their destructive effect**, Moscow, Voenizdat, 1971. 224 pp. Tirazh 60000. Illustrations, tables, math.

1286. Akimov N.I., Il'in V.G. Grazhdanskaia oborona na ob''ektakh sel'skokhozaistvennogo proizvodstva **Civil defence of farms**, Moscow, Kolos, 1973. 432 pp. Tirazh 250000. Text book. Tables, illustrations.

1287. Mil'shtein V.M. Voenno-promyshlennyi kompleks i vneshnaia politika SShA **The military-industrial complex and American foreign policy**, Moscow, Mezh. otnosh., 1975. 240 pp. Tirazh 10000. Endnotes, tables.

1288. Vorontsov G.F. Voennye koalitsii i koalitsionnye voiny **Military coalitions and coalition wars**, Moscow, Voenizdat, 1976. 334 pp. Tirazh 24000. Footnotes, charts, tables.

1289. Bogdanov R.G. *et al*, Ed., SShA: Voenno-strategicheskie kontseptsii **USA: Military-strategic concepts**, Moscow, Nauka, 1980. 304 pp. Tirazh 4550. Footnotes.

1290. Zhilin P.A., Lt. General, Briul' R., Major General, Ed., Voenno-blokovaia politika imperializma. Istoriia i sovremenost' **Military-bloc politics of imperialism. History and the present**, Moscow, Voenizdat, 1980. 383 pp. Tirazh 39000. Footnotes, tables, charts.

1291. Kokoshin A.A. SShA: za fasadom global'noi politiki (Vnutrennie faktory formirovaniia vneshnei politiki amerikanskogo imperializma na poroge 80-kh godov) **USA: behind the facade of global politics (Internal factors influencing the foreign policy of American imperialism on the threshold of the eighties)**, Moscow, Politizdat, 1981. 368 pp. Tirazh 50000. Endnotes, footnotes, tables.

1292. Faramazyan R. Disarmament and the economy **Razoruzhenie i ekonomika**, Moscow, Progress Publishers, 1981. 172 pp. Footnotes, tables. Russian edn. Mysl', 1978.

1293. Nikonov A.D., Ed., Problemy voennoi razriadki **Problems of military detente**, Moscow, Nauka, 1981. 380 pp. Tirazh 4500. Footnotes, short bibliography.

1294. Otkuda iskhodit ugroza miru **Whence the threat to peace**, Moscow, Voenizdat, 1982. 95 pp. Tirazh 100000. Coloured photographs, maps, illustrations. English edn. 1984. Published as a rejoinder to the US publication, Soviet Military Power, Washington, D.C., 1st edn. September 1981.

1295. Shavrov I.E., General, Ed., Lokal'nye voiny: istoriia i sovremenost' **Local wars: History and the present**, Moscow, Voenizdat, 1981. 304 pp. Tirazh 30000. Coloured maps, footnotes tables, 3 appendixes.

1296. Rzheshevskii O.A. Ed., Vnezapnost' v operatsiiakh vooruzhennykh sil SShA **Surprise in the operations of the armed forces of the USA**, Moscow, Voenizdat, 1982. 328 pp. Tirazh 20000. Footnotes, maps.

1297. Barabanov M.V., Ed., Disastrous Effects of Nuclear War (Socio-Economic Aspects), Moscow, Nauka, 1985. 63 pp. Endnotes. Illustrations. Translation from Russian of **Gubitel'nye posledstviia iadrenoi voiny (sotsial'no-ekonomicheskie aspekty)**. Series 'International peace and disarmament'.

1298. Dvinina L.I., Ed., "Zvezdnye voiny". Illiuzii i opasnosti **Star wars. Illusions and dangers**, Moscow, Voenizdat, 1985. 56 pp. Tirazh 17400. Material from western publications. Coloured illustrations.

1299. Emelyanov V. Risk of accidental Nuclear War, Moscow, Nauka, 1985. 63 pp. Endnotes. Translation from Russian of **O vozmozhnosti "sluchainoi" iadrenoi voinny**. Series 'International peace and disarmament'.

1300. Ogarkov N.V., Marshal, Istoriia uchit bditel'nosti **History teaches us vigilance**, Moscow, Voenizdat, 1985. 96 pp. Tirazh 30000. Footnotes.

1301. Velikhov E.P., Ed., The night after...Scientists' warning. Climatic and biological consequences of a nuclear war **Iadernaia noch...Klimaticheskie i biologicheskie posledstviia iadernoi voiny. Uchennye preduprezhdaiut**, Moscow, Mir, 1985. 165 pp. Tirazh 11470. Chapter endnotes, illustrations, photographs.

1302. Velikhov E.P., Sagdeev R., Kokoshin A., Ed., Weaponry in space: the dilemma of security, Moscow, Mir, 1986. 147 pp. Endnotes, diagrams, math, tables.

1303. Velikhov E.P., Ed., Klimaticheskie i biologicheskie posledstviia iadernoi voiny **Climatic and biological consequences of nuclear war**, Moscow, Nauka, 1987. 286 pp. Tirazh 12000. Chapter endnotes, illustrations, documents, 6 appendixes.

1304. Karakchiev N.I. Voennaia toksikologiia i zashchita ot iadrenogo i khimicheskogo oruzhiia: Ucheb. posobie dlia med. in-tov **Military toxicology and protection from nuclear and chemical weapons: Text book for medical internists**, 4th edn. Tashkent, Meditsina, 1988. 368 pp. Tirazh 30000. Illustrations, tables, bibliography, subject index.

1305. Kireev A.P. Kto oplatit "zvezdnye voiny"? Ekonomicheskie aspekty imperialisticheskikh planov militarizatsii kosmosa **Who will pay for the "star wars"? Economic aspects of the imperialist plans for militarising space**, Moscow, Mezhdunarodnye otnosheniia, 1989. 264 pp. Tirazh 10000. Endnotes, tables, illustrations.

1306. Kokoshin A.A. V poiskakh vykhoda. Voenno-politicheskie aspekty mezhdunarodnoi bezopasnosti **In search of solution. Military-political aspects of international security**, Moscow, Politizdat, 1989. 271 pp. Tirazh 40000. Footnotes.

1307. Osipov G.A. Mezdunarodno-pravovye problemy kontrolia za ogranicheniem vooruzhenii i razoruzheniem **International-legal problems regarding the control of arms limitation and disarmament**, Moscow, Nauka, 1989. 144 pp. Tirazh 1000. Offset. Footnotes.

1308. Primakov E.M. Ed., Razoruzhenie i bezopasnost'. 1988-1989: Ezhegodnik **Disarmament and security. 1988-1989: Year book**, Moscow, Novosti, 1989. 736 pp. Tirazh 3000. Footnotes, illustrations, tables, 4 appendixes.

1309. Wardak G.D. The Voroshilov lectures. Materials from the Soviet General Staff Academy Vol. I Issues of Soviet Military Strategy Washington, National Defense University Press, 1989. 411 pp. Vol. II 1990, 222 pp. Both: appendix, glossary, index.

1310. Zhurkin V., Karaganov S., Kortunov A., Razumnaia dostatochnost' i novoe politicheskoe myshlenie **Reasonable sufficiency and new political thinking**, Moscow, Nauka, 1989. 70 pp. Tirazh 1580. Endnotes.

THE ARMY AND
THE PARTY

1311. Geronimus A. Partiia i Krasnaia Armiia. Istoricheskii ocherk **The Party and the Red Army. Historical study**, Moscow-Leningrad, Gosizdat. Otdel voen. lit. 1928. 196 pp.

1312. Blumental F. Ed., Partiino-politicheskaia rabota v Krasnoi Armii. Sistematicheskii ukazatel' literatury za 1918-1928 **Party-political work in the Red Army. Systematic guide to publication for the years 1918-1928**, Moscow, Leningrad, Voenno-politicheskaia Akademiia Tolmacheva, 1929. 126 pp.

1313. Tsvetkov R.V. Major-General, Britvin N.I. Ed., Partiino-politicheskaia rabota v Sovetskoi Armii i Voenno-Morskom flote **Party-political work in the Soviet Army and Navy**, Moscow, Voenizdat, 1960. 286 pp. Footnotes.

1314. Znamenskaia L.D. et al., Partiino-politichesakaia rabota v Krasnoi Armii (aprel' 1918-fevral' 1919). Dokumenty **Party-political work in the Red Army (April 1918-February 1919). Documents**, Moscow, Voenizdat, 1961. 360 pp. Tirazh 9000. Based on archives. Statistics, endnotes, list of sources.

1315. Krainiukov K.V. et al., Partiino-politicheskaia rabota v Sovetskikh Vooruzhennykh Silakh v gody Velikoi Otechestvennoi voiny 1941-1945. Kratkii istoricheskii obzor **Party-political work in the Soviet Armed Forces during the Great Patriotic War 1941-1945. Short historical review**, Moscow, Voenizdat, 1963. 527 pp. Tirazh 13000. For commanders and Party workers. Footnotes with archival material, photographs. 2nd edn 1968.

1316. Petrov Iu.P. Partiinoe stroitel'stvo v Sovetskoi Armii i Flote. Deiatel'nost' KPSS po sozdaniiu i ukrepleniiu politorganov, partiinykh i komsomol'skikh organizatsii v vooruzhennykh silakh (1918-1961 gg.) **Party structure in the Soviet Army and Navy. Communist Party's activity in creation and strengthening of political organs, Party and Komsomol organisations in the Armed Forces (1918-1961)**, Moscow, Voenizdat, 1964. 512 pp. Tirazh 12000. Footnotes, mainly archival.

1317. V'iunova N.M. *et al*, Partiino-politicheskaia rabota v Krasnoi Armii (mart 1919-1920 gg.) Dokumenty **Party-political work in the Red Army (March 1919-1920) Documents**, Moscow, Voenizdat, 1964. 536 pp. Tirazh 4500. Archival material. Endnotes, list of sources.

1318. Komkov G.D. Ideino-politicheskaia rabota KPSS v 1941-1945 gg. **Ideological-political work of the Communist Party during 1941-1945**, Moscow, Nauka, 1965. 440 pp. Tirazh 6000. Footnotes with archival material, bibliography.

1319. Petrov Iu.P. Stroitel'stvo politorganov, partiinykh i komsomol'skikh organizatsii armii i flota (1918-1968) **Founding and structure of the political organs, Party and Komsomol organisations in Army and Navy (1918-1968)**, Moscow, Voenizdat, 1968. 544 pp. Tirazh 18000. For commanders and Party-political workers. Footnotes with archival material, photographs, index of names.

1320. Chernenko K.U., Savinkin N.I., KPSS o Vooruzhennyikh Silakh Sovetskogo Soiuza. Dokumenty 1917-1968 **Communist party on Soviet Armed Forces. Documents 1917-1968**, Moscow, Voenizdat, 1969. 472 pp. Tirazh 100000.

1321. Chmykhov V.G. *et al*, Partiinyi komitet polka (korablia) **Party committee of the regiment (ship)**, Moscow, Voenizdat, 1969. 164 pp. Tirazh 20000. For Party activists.

1322. Zhelatov A.S. Soldat i voina. Problemy moral'no-politicheskoi i psikhologicheskoi podgotovki sovetskikh voinov **The soldier and the war. Problems of morale-political psychological preparation of Soviet troops**, Moscow, Voenizdat, 1971. 318 pp. Tirazh 43000. Footnotes.

1323. Badmaev B.Ts. Ed., Vazhnyi faktor boegotovnosti **The important factor for battle readiness**, Moscow, Voenizdat, 1972. 216 pp. Tirazh 25000. Collection of essays. For political workers. Footnotes.

1324. Korobeinikov M.P. Sovremennyi boi i problemy psikhologii **Contemporary war and problems of psychology**, Moscow, Voenizdat, 1972. 240 pp. Tirazh 38000. Footnotes, tables.

1325. Mareev I.S. *et al*, Partiino-politicheskaia rabota v Sovetskoi Armii i Flote. Uchebnoe posobie dlia vysshykh komandnykh i inzhenernykh voennykh uchilishch **Party-political work in the Soviet Army and Fleet. Text book for officers' and engineers' military schools**, Moscow, Voenizdat, 1972. 400 pp. Tirazh 65000. Footnotes.

1326. Mednikov I.S. *et al*, Partiinaia rabota v Sovetskikh Vooruzhennykh Silakh. Posobie dlia partiinogo aktiva, slushatelei vechernikh partiinykh shkol i vechernikh universitetov marksizma-leninizma **Party work in the Soviet Armed Forces. Handbook for the Party activists, students of party evening schools and night universities of Marxism-Leninism**, Moscow, Voenizdat, 1972. 304 pp. Tirazh 50000. Footnotes.

1327. Sobolev M.G., Lt. General, *et al*, Ed., Partiino-politicheskaia rabota v Sovetskikh Vooruzhennykh Silakh. Uchebnoe posobie dlia vysshikh voenno-politicheskikh uchilishch **Party-political work in the Soviet Armed Forces. Textbook for higher military-political schools**, Moscow, Voenizdat, 1974. 623 pp. Tirazh 100000. Footnotes, charts, illustrations.

1328. Sobolev M.G. Pervichnaia partorganizatsiia v voinskom kollektive **Primary Party organisation in a military collective**, Moscow, Voenizdat, 1975. 286 pp. Tirazh 40000. Footnotes.

1329. Yepishev A.A. General, Some aspects of Party-political work in the Soviet Armed Forces **Nekotorye voprosy partiino-politicheskoi raboty v Sovetskikh Vooruzhennykh Silakh**, Moscow, Progress publishers, 1975. 278 pp. English translation. Footnotes, photographs.

1330. Suvenirov O.F. Kommunisticheskaia Partiia - organizator politicheskogo vospitaniia Krasnoi Armii i Flota 1921-1928 **Communist Party - organiser of the political education in the Red Army and Navy**, Moscow, Nauka, 1976. 292 pp. Tirazh 4450. Footnotes with some archival material, bibliography.

1331. Sobolev M.G. Lt. General, Partiinaia organizatsiia v voinskom kollektive **Party organisation in a military collective**, Moscow, Voenizdat, 1977. 349 pp. Tirazh 35000. Footnotes.

1332. Soshnev V.G. Praktika partiinoi raboty v armii i flote **Party work practice in army and navy**, Moscow, Voenizdat, 1977. 334 pp. Tirazh 50000. Footnotes.

1333. Karpenko P.I. Ed., Partiino-politicheskaia rabota v Sovetskikh Vooruzhennykh Silakh. Uchebnoe posobie dlia studentov grazhdanskikh vuzov **Party-political work in the Soviet Armed Forces. Textbook for students of Higher Education Institutes**, 2nd edn. Moscow, Voenizdat, 1978. 294 pp. Tirazh 100000. Footnotes.

1334. Komarov A.V. *et al*, Spravochnik politrabotnika **Political worker's handbook**, 2nd edn. Moscow, Voenizdat, 1978. 304 pp. Tirazh 100000.

1335. Smorigo N.I. Major General, Ed., Ideologicheskaia rabota v chasti: soderzhanie, organizatsiia, metodika **Ideological work in a unit: content, organisation, methodology**, Moscow, Voenizdat, 1978. 190 pp. Tirazh 50000. Footnotes.

1336. Kolychev V.G. Partiino-politicheskaia rabota v Krasnoi Armii v gody grazhdanskoi voiny 1918-1920 **Party-political work in the Red Army during the Civil War 1918-1920**, Moscow, Nauka, 1979. 408 pp. Tirazh 2750. Footnotes with archival material, index of names.

1337. Sorokin A.I. Partiino-politicheskaia rabota v Sovetskikh Vooruzhennyikh Silakh. Uchebnik dlia slushatelei voennykh akademii **Party-political work in the Soviet Armed Forces. Textbook for students of military academies**, Moscow, Voenizdat, 1979. 416 pp. Tirazh 50000. Also for officers and generals. Footnotes.

1338. Ustimenko V.A. Voennye voprosy v dokumentakh KPSS i Sovetskogo gosudarstva. Annotirovannyi bibliograficheskii ukazatel' **Military questions in Party and Soviet state documents. Annotated bibliographical index**, Moscow, Voenizdat, 1979. 461 pp. Tirazh 18000. For officers, generals, admirals. Includes documents from 1917-1979. Chronological index of documents.

1339. Mareev I.S. Propagandisty armii i flota (Metodika i opyt raboty) **Propagandists in the army and the navy (Methodology and experience of the work)**, Moscow, Voenizdat, 1980. 208 pp. Tirazh 30000. Footnotes.

1340. Rudenko N.N. Slovo pravdy v bor'be s fashizmom. Propagandistskaia deiatel'-nost' politorganov Krasnoi Armii sredi voisk protivnika na territorii SSSR 1941-1944 **The word of truth in the fight with Fascism. Propaganda work of the political organs of the Red Army amongst the enemy troops on the USSR territory**, Kiev, Naukova dumka, 1980. 192 pp. Tirazh 800. Endnotes, bibliography.

1341. Kariaeva T.F., et al, Partiino-politicheskaia rabota v Krasnoi Armii. Dokumenty. 1921-1929 gg. **Party-political work in the Red Army. Documents 1921-1929**, Moscow, Voenizdat, 1981. 576 pp. Tirazh 14000. Based on archives. For officers generals, admirals. Endnotes, appendix, list of documents not included in the volume.

1342. Bublik L.A. et al, Partiino-politicheskaia rabota v Sovetskoi Armii i Voenno-morskom Flote **Party-political work in the Soviet Army and Navy**, Moscow, Voenizdat, 1982. 256 pp. Tirazh 100000. (Biblioteka ofitsera). For officers. Footnotes.

1343. Podkopaev P.S. Ideologicheskaia rabota KPSS v Sovetskom Voenno-Morskom Flote v gody Velikoi Otechestvennoi voiny **Ideological work of KPSS in the Soviet Navy during the Great Patriotic war**, Leningrad, Izdatel'stvo Leningradskogo universiteta, 1983. 136 pp. Tirazh 841. Footnotes with archival material.

1344. Yepishev A.A., General, Ed., Ideologicheskaia rabota v Vooruzhennykh Silakh SSSR. Istoriko-teoreticheskii ocherk **Ideological work in the USSR Armed Forces. Historical-theoretical study**, Moscow, Voenizdat, 1983. 344 pp. Tirazh 40000. For officers, military academies. Footnotes with archival material.

1345. Isakov P.F., Major General, et al., Politorgany Sovetskikh Vooruzhennykh Sil: Istoriko-teoreticheskii ocherk **Political organs in the Soviet Armed Forces: Historical-theoretical study**, Moscow, Voenizdat, 1984. 400 pp. Tirazh 30000. Footnotes with archival material, appendix.

1346. Kariaeva T.F. Vsearmeiskie soveshchaniia politrabotnikov 1918-1940 (resuliutsii) **All-army conferences of the political workers 1918-1940 (resolutions)**, Moscow, Nauka, 1984. 282 pp. Tirazh 2100.

1347. Sobolev M.G., Col. General, Ed., <u>Partiino-politicheskaia rabota v Sovetskoi Armii i Flote. Uchebnoe posobie dlia vysshikh voennykh uchilishch</u> **Party-political work in the Soviet army and Navy, Text book for higher military schools**, 2nd edn., Moscow, Voenizdat, 1984. 286 pp. Tirazh 75000. Footnotes.

1348. Aleshin V.A. *et al.*, <u>Komsomol'skaia rabota v Sovetskoi Armii i Flote</u> **Work of the Komsomol in the Soviet Army and Navy**, Moscow, Voenizdat, 1985. 287 pp. Tirazh 60000. Footnotes, appendix.

1349. Kariaeva T.F. *et al.*, <u>Partiino-politicheskaia rabota v Krasnoi Armii: Dokumenty. Iiul' 1929 g. - mai 1941 g.</u> **Party-political work in the Red Army: Documents. July 1929-May 1941**, Moscow, Voenizdat, 1985. Based on archives. For officers, generals, admirals, as a handbook. Endnotes, list of documents not included in the volume.

1350. Kisilev A.D. *et al.*, <u>Ideologicheskaia rabota KPSS v deistvuiushchei armii 1941-1945 gg.</u> **Ideological work of the CPSU in the field army 1941-1945**, Moscow, Voenizdat, 1985. 270 pp. Tirazh 19000. For officers. Footnotes with archival material.

OVERVIEW

1351. Voroshilov K.E., Marshal, <u>Oborona SSSR</u> **Defence of the USSR**, Moscow, Voennyi Vestnik, 1927. 188 pp.

1352. Rodionov F.G., Ed. <u>Raboche-Krest'ianskaia Krasnaia Armiia</u> **Workers'-Peasants' Red Army**, Moscow, Izogiz, 1934. 104 pp. Rare photographic album.

1353. Kadishev A.B. <u>Istoriia sovetskogo voennogo iskusstva 1917-1940</u> **History of Soviet military art 1917-1940**, 2nd edn., Moscow, Frunze Academy, 1949. 370 pp. Illustrations, maps, bibliography.

1354. Ivlev A.A. <u>Sovetskoe voennoe iskusstvo (Strategiia, operativnoe iskusstvo, taktika). Bibliograficheskii ukazatel' literatury za 1945-1950 gg.</u> **Soviet military art (Strategy, operational art, tactics). Bibliographical guide to 1945-1950 literature**, Moscow, Frunze Academy, 1953. Pt. I 352 pp. Pt. II 350 pp. Index of names, bibliography.

1355. <u>Voenno-istoricheskaia i operativno-takticheskaia literatura za 1951 god bibliograficheskii ukazatel'</u> **Military-historical and operational-tactical literature for 1951 bibliographical index**, Moscow, Frunze Academy, 1953. 243 pp. Index of names, bibliography.

1356. Pobezhimov I.F. <u>Ustroistvo Sovetskoi Armii. Kratkii istoricheskii ocherk</u> **Formation of the Soviet Army. Short historical study**, Moscow, Voenizdat, 1954. 144 pp. Footnotes.

1357. <u>Voennaia literatura za 1957 god</u> **Military literature for 1957**, Moscow, Frunze Academy, 1958. 411 pp. Index of names, bibliography.

1358. Korablev Iu.I., Loginov M.I., Ed., <u>KPSS i stroitel'stvo Vooruzhennykh Sil SSSR (1918-June 1941)</u> **The CPSU and the formation of the Armed Forces of the USSR (1918-1941)**, Moscow, Voenizdat, 1959. 452 pp. Footnotes with archival material.

1359. Portiankin I.A. Ed., Sovetskaia voennaia pechat'. (Istoricheskii ocherk) **The Soviet military press. (Historical study)**, Moscow, Voenizdat, 1960. 418 pp. Footnotes with archival material.

1360. Vorob'ev V.F., Lt. General, Ed., Boevoi put' Sovetskikh Vooruzhennykh Sil **Combat road of the Soviet Armed Forces**, Moscow, Voenizdat, 1960. 572 pp. Footnotes with archival material, photographs, maps, map supplement.

1361. Kadishev A.B. et al Voprosy strategii i operativnogo iskusstva v Sovetskikh voennykh trudakh (1917-1940) **Strategy and operational art in Soviet military works**, Moscow, Voenizdat, 1965. 768 pp. Tirazh 6500. Collection of articles. Foreword by Marshal M.V. Zakharov. Authors' list includes Tukhachevskii, Isserson, Frunze, Shaposhnikov, Svechin, Uborevich, Vatsetis. Tables, tactical diagrams, bibliographical essay, endnotes, footnotes.

1362. Kiriaev N.M. et al Ed., KPSS i stroitel'stvo Sovetskikh Vooruzhennykh Sil 1917-1964 **The CPSU and the formation of the Soviet Armed Forces 1917-1964**, Moscow, Voenizdat, 1965. 472 pp. Tirazh 12000. Footnotes with archival material, photographs.

1363. Ivanov V.D. 50 let Sovetskikh Vooruzhennykh Sil. Fotodokumenty **50 years of the Soviet Armed Forces. Documentary photographs**, Moscow, Voenizdat, 1967. No page numbers. Tirazh 50000.

1364. Zakharov M.V., Marshal, Ed., 50 let Vooruzhennykh Sil SSSR **50 years of the USSR Armed Services**, Moscow, Voenizdat, 1968. 583 pp. Tirazh 100000. Coloured maps, photographs, footnotes, chronology.

1365. Kadishev A.B. et al Voprosy taktiki v Sovetskikh voennykh trudakh (1917-1940 gg.) **Tactics in Soviet military writings (1917-1940)**, Moscow, Voenizdat, 1970. 520 pp. Tirazh 8000. Collection of articles. Authors' list includes I.P. Uborevich, A.I. Verkhovskii, G.S. Isserson, M.N. Tukhachevskii, B.M. Shaposhnikov, D.M. Karbyshev. Tactical diagrams, endnotes, bibliographical essay, illustrations.

1366. Sorkin N.S. V nachale puti (zapiski instruktora mongol'skoi armii) **At the beginning of the road, (memoirs of the instructor to the Mongolian Army)**, Moscow, Nauka, 1970. 126 pp. Tirazh 6000. Period 1923-1931. Photographs, footnotes.

1367. Kamerer Iu.Iu., Kharkevich A.E., Avariinye raboty na kommunal'nykh setiakh v ochage iadernogo porazheniia **Rescue/repair work on community networks (power, gas, water, transport) at the centre of a nuclear burst**, Moscow, Izd. lit. stroitel'stvu. 1972. 3rd edn. 301 pp. Bibliography, 3 technical appendixes.

1368. Kostenko I.K., Demin S.I., Sovetskie samolety **Soviet aircraft**, Moscow, Izd. DOSAF, 1973. 118 pp. Tirazh 55000. For aircraft modellers. Drawings, photographs.

1369. Kolesnikov G.A., Rozhkov A.M., Ordena i medali SSSR **Orders and medals of the USSR**, Moscow, Voenizdat, 1974. 264 pp. Tirazh 65000. Coloured plates.

1370. Zhilin P.A., Lt. General, Ed., Ocherki sovetskoi voennoi istoriografii **Studies of Soviet military historiography**, Moscow, Voenizdat, 1974. 415 pp. Tirazh 14000. Extensive footnotes, illustrations, photographs, index of basic historiographic works.

1371. Pokryshkin A.I., Air Marshal, Krasnoznamennoe oboronoe Kniga o DOSAAF **Red Banner Defence   A Book about DOSAAF**, Moscow, Izdatel'stvo DOSAAF, 1975. 2nd edn. 366 pp. Tirazh 100000. (Dobrovol'noe obshchestvo sodeistviia armii , aviatsii i flota) Photographs.

1372. Shkadov I.N. Army General, Ed., Voprosy obucheniia i vospitaniia v voenno-uchebnykh zavedeniiakh **Training and education in military-education establishments**, Moscow, Voenizdat, 1976. 523 pp. Tirazh 20000. Footnotes, tables, illustrations.

1373. Gashchuk A.P., Major General, Ed., Turistskie bazy Ministerstva oborony SS-SR. Spravochnik **Tourist centres of the Ministry of Defence of the USSR. Handbook**, Moscow, Voenizdat, 1977. 174 pp. Tirazh 50000. Maps, photographs.

1374. Mikhailov M.I. Ed., TsDSA imeni M.V. Frunze **The Central Soviet Army Club named after M.V. Frunze**, Moscow, Voenizdat, 1978. 190 pp. Tirazh 40000. Photographs, footnotes, appendix.

1375. Tiushkevich S.A. et al, Sovetskie Vooruzhennye Sily. Istoriia stroitel'stva **Soviet Armed Forces. The history of their formation**, Moscow, Voenizdat, 1978. 516 pp. Tirazh 50000. For officers and generals. Footnotes with archival material, photographs, tables.

1376. Ovcharenko I.M., Lt. General, et al, Voennaia akademiia imeni M.V. Frunze. Istoriia voennoi ordenov Lenina i Oktiabr'skoi revolutsii, Krasnoznamennoi, ordena Suvorova akademii **Military Academy M.V. Frunze. The history of the military Order of Lenin and the October Revolution, Red Banner, Order of Suvorov Academy**, Moscow, Voenizdat, 1980. 280 pp. Tirazh 50000. Footnotes with archival material, photographs, main events chronology.

1377. Mal'tsev E.E., Army General, Ed., Akademiia imeni V.I. Lenina. Istoricheskii ocherk o voenno-politicheskoi ordenov Lenina i Oktiabr'skoi revolutsii, Krasnoznamennoi akademii imeni V.I. Lenina **V.I. Lenin Academy. Historical study of the military-political Order of Lenin and the October revolution, Red Banner Academy V.I.Lenin**, Moscow, Voenizdat, 1980. 2nd edn. 318 pp. Tirazh 35000. Footnotes with archival material, photographs, appendix.

1378. Dragunskii D.A. et al, Polevaia akademiia:Istoriia Visshikh ofitserskikh ordenov Lenina i Oktiabr'skoi Revolutsii, Krasnoznamennykh kursov "Vystrel" imeni Marshala Sovetskogo Soiuza B.M. Shaposhnikova **Field academy: The history of the Order of Lenin and October Revolution, Red Banner Higher Officers**

Courses "Vystrel" named for Marshal Shaposhnikov, Moscow, Voenizdat, 1982. 290 pp. Tirazh 35000. Footnotes with some archival material, photographs.

1379. Epishev A.A., Army General, Ed., KPSS i voennoe stroitel'stvo **Communist Party and military organisation**, Moscow, Voenizdat, 1982. 311 pp. Tirazh 50000. For officers. Footnotes with archival material.

1380. Lobanov M.M., Lt. General, Razvitie sovetskoi radiolokatsionnoi tekhniki **Development of Soviet radar technology**, Moscow, Voenizdat, 1982. 239 pp. Tirazh 22000. Footnotes with archival material, photographs of Soviet equipment, technical data, tables, short bibliography.

1381. Tabunov N.D., Bokarev V.A., Ed., Marksistsko-leninskaia filosofiia i metodologicheskie problemy voennoi teorii i praktiki: Uchebnoe posobie **Marxist-Leninist philosophy and methodological problems of military theory and practice: Educational handbook**, Moscow, Voenizdat, 1982. 406 pp. Tirazh 39000. Footnotes.

1382. Zhuk, A.B. Revolvery i pistolety **Revolvers and pistols**, Moscow, Voenizdat, 1983. 303 pp. Tirazh 50000. Text, multi-national production types, 105 pages weapon illustrations. Index, appendixes. 2nd edn. 1990. 431 pp. Tirazh 150000. Also Vintovki i avtomaty **Rifles and machine carbines**, Moscow, Voenizdat, 1987, 222 pp. Tirazh 150000. Text, illustrations, bibliography, index.

1383. Artamonov D.N et al, Geroi Sovetskogo Soiuza **Heroes of the Soviet Union**, Moscow, Voenizdat, 1984. 288 pp. Tirazh 70000. Footnotes, tables.

1384. Shumakova A.V., Aleeva R.G., Plakaty Velikoi Otechestvennoi. Fotoal'bum **Posters of the Great Patriotic. Photo-album**, Moscow, Planeta, 1985. 197 pp. Tirazh 15000. Mostly coloured photographs.

1385. Serykh V.D. Voinskie ritualy **Military ceremonials**, Moscow, Voenizdat, 1986. 2nd edn. 255 pp. Tirazh 65000. Coloured photographs, diagrams, short bibliography, footnotes.

1386. Bobylev P.N. et al, Sovetskie Vooruzhennye Sily. Voprosy i otvety. Stranitsy istorii **Soviet Armed Forces. Questions and answers. Pages of history**, Moscow, Politizdat, 1987. 414 pp. Tirazh 250000.

1387. Popov N.G., Lt. General, Ed., Akademiia General'nogo shtaba: Istoriia Voennoi ordenov Lenina i Suvorova I stepeni akademii General'nogo shtaba Vooruzhennykh Sil SSSR imeni K.E Voroshilova **General Staff Academy: History of the Military Academy of the General Staff of the Soviet Armed Forces, Order of Lenin and Suvorov I class, named for K.E. Voroshilov**, Moscow, Voenizdat, 1987. 246 pp. Tirazh 25000. Footnotes with archival material, photographs, 5 appendixes.

1388. Volkogonov D.A., General, Ed., <u>Sovetskaia Armiia</u> **The Soviet Army**, Moscow, Planeta, 1987. 232 pp. Tirazh 36000. Album of mostly coloured photographs.

1389. Zakharov M.L., <u>L'goty uchastnikam Velikoi Otechestvennoi voiny</u> **Privileges for the participants of the Great Patriotic war**, Moscow, Iuridicheskaia literatura, 1987. 2nd edn. 96 pp. Tirazh 50000. Handbook of entitlements for veterans and families.

1390. Iazov D.T., Army General, <u>Verny otchizne</u> **Faithful to the Fatherland**, Moscow, Voenizdat, 1988. 352 pp. Tirazh 150000. Maps, photographs, footnotes with some archival material.

1391. Reznichenko V.G. *et al*, <u>Voennaia akademiia imeni M.V. Frunze. Istoriia voennoi ordenov Lenina i Oktiabr'skoi Revoliutsii, Krasnoznamennoi, ordena Suvorova akademii</u> **Frunze Military Academy. History of the Order of Lenin and the October Revolution, Red Banner, Order of Suvorov, Military Academy**, Moscow, Voenizdat, 1988. 3rd edn. 294 pp. Tirazh 20000. Footnotes with archival material, photographs.

1392. Pikov N.I. *et al*, <u>Voina v Afganistane</u> **War in Afghanistan**, Moscow, Voenizdat, 1991. 367 pp. Tirazh 35000. Endnotes, photographs, appendix.

1393. D'iakov Iu.L., Bushueva T.S., <u>Fashistskii mech kovalsia v SSSR: Krasnaia Armiia i Reikhsver. Tainoe sotrudnichestvo. 1922-1933. Neizvestnye dokumenty</u> **The Fascist sword was forged in the USSR: The Red Army and the Reichswehr. Secret collaboration. 1922-1933. Unknown documents**, Moscow, Sovetskaia Rossiia, 1992. 384 pp. Tirazh 100000. Index of names, photographs.

1394. Sverdlov F.D. <u>V stroiu otvazhnykh. Ocherki o evreiakh- Geroiakh Sovetskogo Soiuza</u> **In the ranks of the brave. Studies about Jews - Heroes of the Soviet Union**, Moscow, Kniga i Biznes, 1992. 304 pp. Tirazh 3000. Photographs.

1395. Yakupov N. <u>Tragediia polkovodets. Posviashchaetsia komandiram Krasnoi Armii mertvam stalinskogo terrora. Iakir, Uborevich, Bliukher Tukhachevskii,</u> **The tragedy of the commanders. In memory of those commanders who died in Stalin's terror. Iakir, Uborevich, Bliukher, Tukhachevskii**, Moscow, Mysl', 1992. 349 pp.

1396. Gromov B.V. Col. General, <u>Ogranichennyi kontingent</u> **Limited contingent**, Moscow, Progress/Kul'tura, 1994. 352 pp. Tirazh 100000. Commander 40th Army in Afghanistan, documentary material on origins of Soviet intervention.

VSEVOBUCH/DOSAAF

1397. Dobrovol'noe obshchestvo sodeistviia armii, aviatsii i flota (Voluntary Society for Collaboration with the Army, Air Force and Navy). Successor to **Osoaviakhim**, Obshchestvo Druzei oborony i aviatsionno-khimicheskogo stroitel'stva (Society of Friends of Defence and Aviation-Chemical Construction)

1398. Otchet o Pervom S''ezde po vseobshchemu voennomu obucheniiu. (Sostavlen po stenogrammam zasedanii) 1918 g. **Report on the First Congress of the Universal Military Training (Compiled according to the stenographic report of the sessions)**, Moscow, Izd. Tsentr. Otdela Vsevobuch. 179 pp. Six appendixes.

1399. Pokryshkin A.I., Marshal, Ed., Krasnoznamennoe oboronnoe. Kniga o DOSAAF, o voznikovenii i razvitii obshchestva, ego voenno-patrioticheskoi deiatel'nosti, ego vklade v ukreplenie oboronogo mogushchestva strany **The Red Banner defence. Book about the DOSAAF, its birth and development as a society, its military-patriotic actions, its contribution to the stregthening of defence capability of the country**, Moscow, Izd. DOSAAF, 1975. 366 pp. Tirazh 100000. Photographs.

1400. Kolybel'nikov V.F., Kvitnitskii A.A., Annotirovannyi katalog literatury izdatel'stva DOSAAF SSSR (1945-1977 gg.) **Annotated catalogue of literature published by DOSAAF USSR (1945-1977)**, Moscow, DOSAAF, 1979. 278 pp. Tirazh 5000. Index of names, publications.

"BREAKTHROUGH BOOKS," 1944–1994

1401. White D. Fedotoff <u>The Growth of the Red Army</u>, Princeton, N.J.: Princeton University Press, 1944. 486 pp. Endnotes, index.

1402. <u>Handbook on USSR Military Forces. Technical manual. TM 30-430</u> Nov. 1945. Washington, D.C.: War Department, 1946.

1403. Garthoff R.L. <u>Soviet Military Doctrine</u>, Glencoe, Ill.: The Free Press. Published as <u>How Russia Makes War</u>, London: Allen and Unwin, 1954. 587 pp. Index names, subject, bibliography. See also: <u>Soviet Strategy in the Nuclear Age</u>, New York: Praeger, 1962. 301 pp. Endnotes, bibliography, index names, subjects.

1404. Erickson J. <u>The Soviet High Command 1918-1941</u>, London: Macmillan, 1962. 889 pp. Endnotes, bibliography, biographical index, index, 4 appendixes. Reprinted Boulder, London: Westview Press, 1984.

1405. Goure L. <u>The Siege of Leningrad</u>, Stanford, Calif.: Stanford University Press, 1962. 363 pp. Endnotes, bibliography, index, maps, photographs.

1406. Kolkowicz R. <u>The Soviet Military and the Communist Party</u>, Princeton, N.J.: Princeton University Press, 1967. 429 pp. Footnotes, bibliography, appendixes, index.

1407. Herrick R.W. <u>Soviet Naval Strategy. Fifty Years of Theory and Practice</u>, Annapolis, Md: United States Naval Institute, 1968. 198 pp. Footnotes, bibliography, index.

1408. Odom W.E. <u>The Soviet Volunteers: Modernization and Bureaucracy in a Public Mass Organization</u>, Princeton, N.J.: Princeton University Press, 1973. 360 pp. Footnotes, index names, subjects, bibliography.

1409. Goldhammer H. <u>The Soviet Soldier. Soviet Military Management at the Troop Level</u>, New York: Crane, Russak & Company Inc., London: Leo Cooper Ltd., 1975. 352 pp. Footnotes, index.

1410. Hardesty V. Red Phoenix. The Rise of Soviet Air Power, 1941-1945, Washington, D.C.: Smithsonian Institution Press, 1982. 288 pp. Photographs, endnotes, bibliography, index, maps.

1411. Wildman A.K. The End of the Russian Imperial Army. Vol. I The Old Army and the Soldiers' Revolt (March-April 1917), Princeton, N.J.: Princeton University Press, 1980. 402 pp. Vol. II The Road to Soviet Power and Peace, 1987. 443 pp. Footnotes, photographs, index. Vol. II, bibliography.

1412. Conner A.Z., Poirier R.G., Red Army Order of Battle in the Great Patriotic War, Novato, Calif.: Presidio, 1985. 408 pp.

1413. Hagen M. von, Soldiers in the Proletarian Dictatorship. The Red Army and the Soviet Socialist State, 1917-1930, Ithaca, N.Y.: Cornell University Press, 1990. 369 pp.

1414. Glantz D.M. Soviet Military Operational Art. In Pursuit of Deep Battle, London: Frank Cass, 1991. 295 pp. Endnotes, illustrations, tables, index.

1415. Holloway D. Stalin and the Bomb. The Soviet Union and the Atomic Energy 1939-56, New Haven and London: Yale University Press, 1994. 464 pp. Photographs, endnotes, biographical notes, index.

NAME INDEX

SUBJECT INDEX

About the Compilers

JOHN ERICKSON is Professor Emeritus and Director of Defense Studies at the University of Edinburgh. He is the author of *The Soviet High Command, 1918–1941*.

LJUBICA ERICKSON has worked with John Erickson for many years, researching, editing, and translating Russian materials on Russian and Soviet military history.